LÉANN NA TRÍONÓ
TRINITY IRISH STU]
No. 1

GW00541142

UNITY IN DIVERSITY

STUDIES IN IRISH AND SCOTTISH GAELIC LANGUAGE, LITERATURE AND HISTORY

edited by

**Cathal G. Ó Háinle
and
Donald E. Meek**

Published by

The School of Irish, Trinity College, Dublin

2004

ISBN 0-9546882-0-1
ISSN 1649-4725

Acknowledgements:
Cover: Elaine Cullen
Technical assistance: Caoimhe Ní Bhraonáin
Financial support: The Centre for Irish and Scottish Studies, Trinity College, Dublin

Printed by
THE LEINSTER LEADER, NAAS

CONTENTS

Introduction   1

The Scottish tradition of Fian ballads in the middle ages   9
    DONALD E. MEEK

On satire and the poet's circuit   25
    LIAM BREATNACH

The Norse element in Scottish place-names   37
    RICHARD A. V. COX

Gaelic military history and the later brehon law commentaries   51
    KATHARINE SIMMS

The Gaelic of Islay, a North Channel dialect?   69
    JAMES GRANT

The bardic poet as teacher, student and critic: 97
a context for the Grammatical Tracts
    DAMIAN MCMANUS

The novel frustrated: 125
developments in 17th- to 19th-century fiction in Irish
    CATHAL G. Ó HÁINLE

Andrew Sall (1624-82):   153
textual editor and facilitator
of the Irish translation of the Old Testament
    TERENCE P. MCCAUGHEY

Religion, riot and romance: 173
Scottish Gaelic perceptions of Ireland in the 19th century
    DONALD E. MEEK

INTRODUCTION

Ireland and Gaelic Scotland are often considered by scholars to have constituted a 'single culture-province'. This perception, which was given formal expression by Professor Kenneth Jackson, is broadly sustainable, but it is no less evident that areas of considerable divergence have existed across the centuries. It is well known that both countries share the Gaelic language, of which the vernacular forms of Irish and Scottish Gaelic are the modern representatives. The relationship of Scottish Gaelic and Irish to one another is the subject of keen debate, and the Jacksonian model, positing the existence of 'Common Gaelic', from which both the vernacular languages evolved from the thirteenth century, is currently being challenged. Whatever the starting point of their divergence, Irish and Scottish Gaelic are now so different from one another that a speaker of either language requires to undertake some form of induction course in, or period of exposure to, the other language in order to gain sufficient confidence to communicate in it. This, however, does not mean that the two languages do not share many features, both dialectal and lexical, which reflect an earlier common core, and also an enduring capacity to preserve common elements. A contributor to this volume suggests that Scottish Gaelic and Irish should be treated as major dialects of the one language. What is true of these languages (or dialects) is equally true of their literatures and institutions. Scotland and Ireland maintained a common tradition of bardic verse in the Middle Ages (1200-1600), and its practitioners on both sides of the North Channel travelled from one country to the other in pursuit of training and patronage. After 1600, however, the formal bardic institutions of both regions collapsed, and vernacular verse composed in Irish and Scottish Gaelic began to assume regional complexions determined by the social needs and capabilities of each country. The loss of shared paradigms and templates encouraged the emergence of demotic and individualistic forms of verse. Similarly, in the case of Gaelic prose, Ireland and Scotland shared many of the tales of the Middle Ages, but after 1600 their own regional needs and identities were stamped to an increasing degree on the brands of prose which found their way to the printing presses.

In 1567 Gaelic Scotland led the way in producing the first printed Gaelic book, which neatly encapsulates the shared – and yet very different – experiences of both countries. This epoch-making volume was a translation of the principal directory of the Reformed Church, *The Book of Common Order*. The work was undertaken by John Carswell, the

Superintendent of the Reformed Church in Argyll, who enjoyed the patronage of the Fifth Earl of Argyll and lived in renaissance grandeur in Carnasserie Castle, overlooking Kilmartin Glen. It is particularly striking that, in introducing the tenets of the Reformed Church to the Gaelic people, Carswell harnessed the classical language of the poets, with which he was thoroughly familiar, as well as some of the key conventions employed by these poets. In this way, the classical Gaelic language shared by both countries became the vehicle of Protestant expression in Gaelic Scotland. Carswell intended that his book should be used by the Gaels of both countries, but his vision of a single culture-province which embraced Protestantism was to be thwarted by the course of events. Gaelic Scotland gradually lost most of its medieval Catholicism, and the greater part of the Highlands and Islands absorbed Protestant beliefs, sometimes under duress. Ireland, on the other hand, remained predominantly Roman Catholic. This important divergence helped to determine language use and literary development, but it also changed perceptions on both sides of the water. As perceptions changed, so also did the relationship between the two countries. It is undeniable that, whatever Gaelic continuum there may have been from Cape Wrath to Cape Clear before 1500, it was weakened substantially by the arrival and progressive extension of the Reformation in Scotland. Yet, despite such fissures and fractures, Ireland and Gaelic Scotland have never completely lost sight of their common linguistic and cultural heritage. For those with hearts and minds to appreciate it, there remains to this day, however tenuously, an underlying thread of unity which connects the ambiguities and contentions inherent in diversity. It is this unity in diversity which the present volume seeks to illumine. Its existence generates a tension with which Gaels in both countries have had to live for many centuries.

The diversity of Ireland and Gaelic Scotland undoubtedly predates the Reformation, and religious change (or lack of it) cannot be held solely responsible for the separation of the two countries. This is an all-too-common misconception. There was plenty of room for variety within a common culture. In the opening chapter of this book, Donald Meek surveys the corpus of Fenian lays contained in the Book of the Dean of Lismore, compiled in Scotland between 1512 and 1542. As he demonstrates, the evidence suggests that by the first half of the sixteenth century Gaelic Scotland was diverging from Ireland in its corpus of such verse, and that it had developed a particular taste in Fenian lays which appears to be different from that of Ireland. The Book of the Dean of Lismore, which contains verse by both Irish and Scottish authors, reflects the reality of a shared cultural inheritance, whose distinctively Irish dimensions were by no means hidden from the Dean of Lismore and his fellow scribes, who hailed from Perthshire. Meek argues tentatively that the change may have been precipitated by the demise of the Lordship of the Isles, which was forfeited in 1493, and which probably acted as a cultural bridgehead between the two countries. Loss of common institutions led to loss of shared traditions.

The Fenian lays are well distributed in both Scotland and Ireland, but this is not true of all parts of Gaelic culture. It is possible to view different aspects of the shared Gaelic culture of both countries more effectively in one country than in the other. Much depends on how, and especially where, the evidence has been preserved. Thus, although the practitioners of bardic verse operated in both countries and verse by Irish poets is well preserved in Gaelic Scotland, as the Book of the Dean of Lismore clearly demonstrates, the evidence for the training and formation of these practitioners, the rules by which they composed their verse, and the manner in which they and their verse was to be received by their subjects, are much more fully illustrated in sources found in Ireland. Liam Breatnach is therefore able to provide an analysis of the manner in which satire was used as a means of enforcing claims in medieval Ireland and of the arrangements made for, and the formalities to be observed by, a visiting poet, whether the purpose of his visit was for satire or praise. It seems highly likely that similar conventions were observed in Gaelic Scotland, where blistering satire is well attested (as, for example, in the satirical elegy on Ailéin mac Ruairí, deceased chief of Clanranald, in the Book of the Dean of Lismore).

From Irish sources Damian MacManus likewise assembles a very valuable body of material which illumines the 'formation' of Gaelic poets, their attendance at bardic schools and their desire to conform to the best practices of their masters, the professors of poetry in the bardic schools. It was no easy challenge. The tradition that bardic poets composed best when in a darkened room, which is corroborated by the Irish poets themselves, is also attested in Gaelic Scotland. Martin Martin, a Skyeman writing in the seventeenth century, provides some details of bardic schools, and he notes that trainee poets composed their verses in the dark with a stone on their stomachs.

Poets were not alone in crossing the North Channel, and in providing some degree of cultural cohesion between the two countries. Soldiers also played their part. Gaelic Scotland offered a rich source of military reinforcements for Ireland. The Lordship of the Isles, which had interests in the Glens of Antrim, was important in this respect. Of particular significance, however, in the creation of *gallóglaigh* in Ireland were the MacSweeney family, domiciled at an early stage in Fánad, but originating in Knapdale, Argyll, from which they were ousted apparently by the middle of the thirteenth century. Katharine Simms duly notes the link between Gaelic institutions in Scotland and those in Ireland, but she examines primarily aspects of the later (eleventh- to sixteenth-century) passages of commentary on the Old Irish law tracts which deal specifically with military service. She concentrates particularly on the different types of 'hostings' which might be required by lords from their people, and the obligations which were placed on their vassal chiefs. The conditions which had to be satisfied by those participating in the hostings are discussed. In Gaelic Scotland, where hostings were governed by similar concepts of overlordship, it is likely that further research will uncover close correspondences.

Whereas the evidence for bardic schools and the conditions of military hostings is better preserved in Ireland than in Scotland, studies of the Gaelic language in its different forms can harness a particularly rich body of material from both sides of the North Channel. Much of this material is readily accessible in recent published surveys. James Grant's paper, based on a close study of the Gaelic dialect of Islay, provides a very interesting overview of the relationship of that dialect to those of what he calls the 'Greater Gaidhealtachd', embracing Ireland and Scotland. Grant identifies eleven features of the dialect of Islay which might be regarded as 'unnatural' or 'hypercorrect' by the speakers of majority dialects in present-day Gaelic Scotland. He shows convincingly how these features are also found in different parts of Ireland, and of special interest is his contention that Islay and neighbouring islands formed a 'transitional zone' between the dialects of Ireland on the one hand, and those of Scotland on the other. Indeed, Grant goes so far as to say that 'for the purposes of Gaelic dialectology it would seem helpful to set aside the labels "Scottish" and "Irish" and consider the place which the Gaelic dialect of Islay occupies in the wider context of the continuum of dialects of Gaelic which at one time existed, unbroken by the intrusion of English or Scots, between Cape Wrath in Scotland and Cape Clear in Ireland.' As Grant demonstrates, the Gaelic language remains the most potent indicator of the shared culture of both countries.

Grant draws attention to a powerful early medieval intrusion that helped to shape the destinies of both Ireland and Gaelic Scotland – the arrival of the Norse. His view that the anti-Norse actions of Somhairle mac Gille Bhrìghde and his dismissal of the Norse from Argyll helped to delimit one particular dialectal feature is interesting. More frequently it is the contribution of the Norse themselves to the formation of the Gaelic dialects of Scotland that attracts the attention of scholars. Their contribution to the creation of the Scottish onomasticon is no less significant. Richard Cox locates potential Norse models for syntactically unusual forms of place-names within the Gaelic area. He concludes that the place-names of the west side of Lewis which consist of 'a generic followed by a specific element' represent 'relatively late Norse names with generic-initial structures similar to those found in the Faroes, in the Northen Isles and in Caithness'. This is an important reminder that Ireland and Gaelic Scotland did not share their cultural characteristics solely with one another. They were part of a much wider Atlantic province which connected with the North Sea regions, and with Scandinavia.

In certain fields, such as the development of place-names, there exists a high degree of regional variation and distinctiveness, whether we are dealing with individual parts of Scotland or Ireland, or with the relationship between both countries. In literature, particularly after 1600, we will seldom find precise correspondences in the material produced in the two regions, but we can find parallels in its development (or lack thereof). Even where the details of the case may differ significantly, we can often ask similar sets of questions, and provide similar answers. Cathal Ó Háinle's examination of why the novel was so slow to emerge in Irish is a good example of such parallelism, as it will find a ready echo in Gaelic Scotland. There too the emergence of the novel was 'frustrated' by such factors as lack of access to the printing presses (usually situated in towns), the antipathy of institutions such as the Church to 'mendacity', and the absence of an extensive reading public. In Gaelic Scotland, as in Ireland, there was no absence of potential authors, but from 1750 their skills were largely diverted into translating Puritan texts for the spiritual edification – and certainly not the entertainment – of literate Gaels, of whom there were relatively few prior to 1810. When an indigenously created literature began to appear in Scotland in the first half of the nineteenth century, thanks to the efforts of the Rev. Dr Norman MacLeod, its purpose was predominantly didactic, and its target readership were those who had become literate in Gaelic schools (established from 1811) which used the Gaelic Bible as their main text. Novels did not emerge in Scottish Gaelic until the early twentieth century, and only in the last quarter of the century did they do so in any appreciable number.

The Gaelic Bible was of immense importance as a key text in Ireland and Gaelic Scotland. If Gaelic Scotland produced the first printed Gaelic book, Ireland produced the first Gaelic texts of the New and Old Testaments, the former (completed by Uilliam Ó Domhnaill) in 1602/3 and the latter (undertaken by Uilliam Bedell) in 1685. These Gaelic Testaments were of great significance to Gaelic Scotland also, as copies surplus to requirements in Ireland were dispatched to Scotland after 1688, where they were regularly chained to the pulpits of churches in the Gaelic-speaking areas. From 1690 Gaelic Scotland had its own version of these Testaments, brought together as a single pocket Bible by the Rev. Robert Kirk of Balquidder and Aberfoyle. Kirk's Bible, which adopted Roman font and dispensed with the *corra-litir* of the Gaelic script and with scribal abbreviations of the earlier (Irish) texts, became the standard Gaelic Bible in Scotland until 1767, when the first Scottish Gaelic New Testament was published. It was followed by the Scottish Gaelic Old Testament, completed in 1801. Although the language of the Scottish Gaelic Testaments was ostensibly Scottish Gaelic, the texts showed the clear influence of the Classical tradition represented by the volumes of Ó Domhnaill and Bedell, and in this respect the Gaelic Bibles of Scotland and Ireland were the last major works of literature to harness and to represent the Classical Gaelic tradition developed by the medieval poets and literati of both countries. Meanwhile in the seventeenth century Irish scholars such as Tadhg Ó Cianáin, Aodh Mac Aingil, Flaithrí Ó Maolchonaire, Giolla Brighde Ó Heódhasa, Mícheál Ó Cléirigh and Séathrún Céitinn had turned their attention to writing works of contemporary and historical commentary, linguistic scholarship and Counter-reformation apologetics. Trained in the bardic schools and/or associated with the traditional learned families, their use of prose rather than verse as their medium afforded some of them the opportunity to develop Classical Irish in interesting ways. Their work was published, either in print in the case of religious writing or in manuscript in the case of historical works, and survived to provide an illuminating guide to subsequent writers of Irish prose, so that as late as the end of the nineteenth century and the beginning of the twentieth some Irish language revivalists urged, quite unrealistically, that contemporary writers should adopt the language of the seventeenth-century prose writers as their model. Classical Gaelic thus long outlived the terminus of c. 1600 normally ascribed to the Classical Gaelic period. In fact, the influence of Classical Gaelic remains embedded in Protestant religious texts in Gaelic Scotland to the present day. Scottish Gaelic religious texts, and particularly the Scottish Gaelic Bible, preserve a linguistic hybridity which has been of great importance in maintaining familiarity with the Classical Gaelic tradition.

It is therefore singularly appropriate that the present volume should contain Terence McCaughey's study of one of the key scholars who worked on Uilliam Bedell's translation of the Old Testament, namely Dr Andrew Sall. As 'textual editor and facilitator' of the translation, Sall – a former Jesuit priest – encountered prejudices and opposition which were deeply felt in a predominantly Roman Catholic context and put his own life in danger. Such tensions did not exist to the same degree in Gaelic Scotland, but in their broader outline they were not, however, entirely unknown. Even within Protestantism, a desire to 'wear out' (i.e. eliminate) Gaelic unquestionably delayed the project to translate the Bible into Scottish Gaelic, and the translation was something of a last resort. McCaughey's chapter provides a window into the life and work of Andrew Sall, and serves as a model for much-needed future studies of the main literary figures of the 'biblical enlightenment' shared by Ireland and Gaelic Scotland.

The history of the Gaelic Bibles demonstrates that, despite their very different religious histories, Ireland and Gaelic Scotland had much to unite them in a common purpose, where that purpose was recognised. Increasingly, however, the areas of possible co-operation became fragmented, and joint endeavour was, as a result, much harder to expedite successfully. By the end of the nineteenth century, Ireland was seen in contradictory ways by Scottish Gaels who wished to interact with it. This is the theme of Donald Meek's concluding paper, in which Gaelic cultural connexionalism, which still occupied a prominent place in the minds of poets like William Livingston, is seen to be in conflict with political aspirations, religious difference, and external and non-Gaelic stereotyping of the Irish in Scotland. It would be no less fascinating to know what the Irish Gaels thought of Scottish Gaels in the same period.

The genesis of this collection of essays lies in the establishment in 1994 of the Irish-Scottish Academic Initiative as a partnership between the Departments and Schools of Celtic, English and History at Aberdeen and Strathclyde Universities and Trinity College, Dublin, the objective of which has been to promote academic research and teaching in the history, languages and literature of Ireland and Scotland. In 1997-8 under the aegis of the Initiative, the School of Irish and Celtic Languages at Trinity College, Dublin, and the Department of Celtic at Aberdeen University organised a series of seminars which involved members of staff of each institution travelling to the other to lecture to staff and students of the sister department and of other departments. On each occasion a formal response was made to the lecture and a general discussion of the topic followed. Seven of the essays of this collection are based on the lectures that were delivered: Donald E. Meek's essay on 'The Scottish tradition of Fian ballads', and those by Liam Breatnach, Richard A.V. Cox, Katharine Simms, James Grant, Damian McManus and Cathal G. Ó Háinle. Terence P. McCaughey's lecture 'The Gaelic Bible in Ireland' became part of another publication by him, and has been replaced here by an essay on a related topic, 'Andrew Sall (1624-82): textual editor and facilitator of the Irish translation of the Old Testament'. Subsequent to the conclusion of the ISAI series of lectures, Donald Meek visited Dublin again in 2001 to deliver a lecture in a series at Trinity College which was funded by the Conference of University Rectors in Ireland, and when it was suggested to him that the lecture 'Religion, riot and romance: Scottish Gaelic perceptions of Ireland in the nineteenth century' would complement those of the ISAI series, he agreed to submit it for publication in this collection.

The various chapters in this book should be regarded as a potent indicator that Ireland and Gaelic Scotland continue to share their common Gaelic culture even in the early twenty-first century. On this occasion, however, they do so within the scholarly domain of reflection, analysis and argument. Unquestionably, the individual chapters represent one side of the conversation – sometimes the Scottish side, sometimes the Irish side. It is therefore to be hoped that scholars in their respective countries will take up the challenge of further enquiry and response. Much remains to be done. The book will have succeeded if it stimulates its readers to examine afresh the unity and diversitiy of culture at the heart of the relationship between Gaelic Ireland and Gaelic Scotland.

THE SCOTTISH TRADITION OF FIAN BALLADS
IN THE MIDDLE AGES

Donald E. Meek

One of the working principles of scholars who, across the years, have examined the Gaelic cultures of Scotland and Ireland, particularly the cultures of the Middle Ages, is that Ireland and Scotland constituted 'a single culture-province'.[1] Such scholars have pointed to several features common to the cultures of both countries. First and foremost there is the language which the two countries shared, namely Gaelic, and especially the form of language used by the medieval *literati*, namely Classical Gaelic. It is now dangerous to use the term 'Common Gaelic', thus named and identified by the late Professor Kenneth Jackson, or even 'Classical Common Gaelic', since the concept of 'Common Gaelic', if blindly applied, can give too many hostages to linguistic fortune. At present, the hostages of the last half-century are being reassessed for parole and release into a less constricted linguistic environment.[2] Even so, we can retain the concept of an upper-register linguistic bridge across which the Gaelic *literati* of both countries travelled regularly to and from Ireland and Gaelic Scotland. Classical Gaelic acted as a standard linguistic medium, a *lingua franca*, for the learned classes, while the vernacular languages, or dialects of an ancestral vernacular language, went their separate ways, and may have been doing so for considerably longer than the hitherto standard (Jacksonian) definition of 'Common Gaelic' would allow.[3] Classical Gaelic was supra-dialectal; it stood apart from the vernacular dialects, but it was not entirely free from their influence. Gradually the boundaries crumbled. From at least the mid-sixteenth century, the classical language began to be eroded significantly by these dialects, as the wider classical inheritance waned. Certainly by the eighteenth century, a modified and distinctively Scottish form of Classical Gaelic had emerged, and can be observed most clearly in Protestant religious texts.[4] The ministers and schoolmasters of the Protestant movement in

---

[1] Jackson, Kenneth, '"Common Gaelic": the evolution of the Goedelic languages', Sir John Rhys Memorial Lecture, *Proceedings of the British Academy* 37 (1951), 77.

[2] Jackson, '"Common Gaelic"'; for a reassessment, see Ó Buachalla, Breandán, '"Common Gaelic" revisited', in Ó Baoill, Colm & Nancy R. McGuire (eds.). *Rannsachadh na Gàidhlig 2000*, Aberdeen 2002, 1-12.

[3] Ó Buachalla, '"Common Gaelic" revisited', 9.

[4] Thomson, Robert L., 'The emergence of Scottish Gaelic', in Aitken, Adam J., Matthew P. MacDiarmid & Derick S. Thomson (eds), *Bards and makars: Scottish language and literature: medieval and Renaissance*, Glasgow 1977, 127-135, examines its theme and assesses the evidence of Scottish religious texts on the Jacksonian model. It could be argued that 'emergence' is, in this case, no more than the visible appearance of Scottish Gaelic features in written (and printed) texts, reflecting the erosion of the classical language by the

the Scottish Highlands and Islands became the custodians of the literary dialect and its standards, rather than the poets, historians and craftsmen of the catholic Middle Ages. These ministers and schoolmasters also collected and edited much popular Gaelic literature, doubtless with good and bad results.[5]

Those who argue for the common inheritance have also paid due attention to the similarities in the institutions found in the two countries. It is generally accepted that the learned orders tend to correspond on both sides of the North Channel, as do the broader features of the traditions which they sustained, whether in art, poetry, law or ecclesiastical institutions.[6] The great tradition of bardic poetry has perhaps been used as the most obvious example of the shared tradition. It is regularly presented as a tradition emanating from Ireland along with the Scottish Gaels themselves, but this latter assumption too is currently under challenge.[7] While developing in Scotland along lines which acknowledged the Irish dimension, the bardic verse tradition had its own capacity for adaptation and change. Nevertheless, reciprocal visits by poets to and from their respective countries were normal, and it is likely that Scottish poets trained at Irish bardic schools and vice versa. Looking at the prose tradition, one finds similar evidence of a body of *scéalaíocht* which includes tales which were current in both countries.[8] A common core of historical and religious writing can also be perceived, *mutatis mutandis*, and, whatever caveats may emerge from further detailed study, the case for the wider shared inheritance remains, and will remain, a strong one.[9]

As with the tales, so also with that great body of material known in Ireland as *an Fhiannaíocht*, containing tales and poems about Fionn mac Cumhaill and the various *fiana* under his command (at least in theory, if not in practice).[10] In

---

vernacular. This says nothing about the emergence (in the sense of 'creation') of Scottish Gaelic as such. For the creation of a post-classical Protestant form of upper-register Gaelic, see Meek, Donald E., 'Language and style in the Scottish Gaelic Bible (1767-1807)', *Scottish language* 9 (winter 1990), 1-16.

[5] Meek, Donald E., 'The pulpit and the pen: clergy, orality and print in the Scottish Gaelic world', in Fox, Adam & Daniel Woolf (eds), *The spoken word*, Manchester (forthcoming).

[6] Thomson, Derick S., 'The Gaelic learned orders and literati in medieval Scotland' in Nicolaisen, W.F.H. (ed), *Proceedings of the third international congress of Celtic Studies*, Edinburgh 23-29 July 1967, Edinburgh 1968, 57-78.

[7] Dumville, David N., 'Ireland and North Britain in the earlier Middle Ages: contexts for *Miniugad Senchasa fher nAlban*', in Ó Baoill and McGuire, *Rannsachadh na Gàidhlig 2000*, 185-211.

[8] Bruford, Alan, *Gaelic folk-tales and medieval romances*, Dublin 1969.

[9] This is evident in, for example, Carswell's *Foirm na n-urrnuidheadh* (1567) and the MacMhuirich Histories (seventeenth century), which can be compared with *Desiderius* and Keating respectively on the Irish side.

[10] Almqvist, Bo, Séamas Ó Catháin & Pádraig Ó Héalaí (eds), *The heroic process: form, function and fantasy in folk epic*, Dublin 1987; Ó Fiannachta, Pádraig (ed), *An fhiannaíocht*, *Léachtaí Cholm Cille* 26 (1995).

this essay attention will be given to the poems or ballads of the *fiana*, and to aspects of the Scottish dimension of this highly productive medieval genre. While accepting here too, in broad terms, the background of a 'common core' for Ireland and Gaelic Scotland, we need to be aware nevertheless of regional variation and distinctiveness. Indeed, I intend to demonstrate that, alongside the 'common core', a noticeable degree of 'Scottishness' existed within the ballad corpus by the early sixteenth century. I shall also attempt to deal, in a preliminary way, with some of the possible causes of the emergence of a distinctively Scottish dimension. The title of my essay is therefore meant to be slightly provocative, but I would hope that it will be seen that it is a title which is worth sustaining. I shall argue that, as far as the Fian ballads are concerned, there is a significant body of evidence which shows a shared inheritance, but that there is also some evidence that by 1550 a degree of distinctiveness existed on the Scottish side, in language, text-type and what might be termed 'genre preference'. Indeed, I shall go as far as to claim that the shape of significant parts of the post-1700 Scottish Gaelic ballad tradition had been formed by the first half of the sixteenth century.

The Book of the Dean of Lismore

Over the last twenty years or so, I have been studying the Fian ballads and related ballad verse in the Scottish manuscript known as the Book of the Dean of Lismore. This remarkable manuscript was compiled in the first half of the sixteenth century (1512-42) chiefly by James MacGregor, titular Dean of Lismore, and his brother Duncan.[11] It was probably compiled not at Lismore, a small island close to Oban, Argyllshire, but at Fortingall in Perthshire. As is well known, one of the least endearing features of this manuscript is that its scribes departed from what we would regard as the 'normal' Gaelic orthography of the Middle Ages, shared by Ireland and Scotland, and employed a spelling-system based on that of Middle and Early Modern Scots, the language of the Scottish Lowlands. This means that anyone who wants access to the manuscript has to engage in a form of code-breaking. To the scribes of the manuscript itself, however, this was quite probably an entirely normal spelling system. Elsewhere I have argued that it was an accepted form of written Gaelic, somewhat akin to the system one can see in Manx.[12] In this respect, one could not hope to find a more thoroughly Scottish manuscript. At

---

[11] Meek, Donald E., 'The Scots-Gaelic scribes of late medieval Perthshire: an overview of the orthography and contents of the Book of the Dean of Lismore', in McClure J.D. & M.R.G. Spiller (eds), *Bryght lanternis: essays on the language and literature of medieval and Renaissance Scotland*, Aberdeen 1989, 387-404.

[12] Meek, 'The Scots-Gaelic scribes'; see also Meek, Domhnall E., 'Gàidhlig is Gaylick anns na meadhon aoisean', in Gillies, William (ed), *Alba agus a' Ghàidhlig: Gaelic and Scotland*, Edinburgh 1989, 131-45.

the same time, this is a thoroughly Gaelic manuscript, since its contents cover the whole range of Gaelic poetry from the classical Middle Ages, while paying considerable attention to Ireland. The eastern orientation of its spelling system is complemented by the remarkably western interest of the collectors. Fortingall was, it would seem, a pivotal place, poised between two cultures, Gaelic and Scots, but capable of integrating both.[13]

The Book of the Dean of Lismore is a very important indication of the value which Scottish scribes set by the heroic ballad texts. Alongside bardic poems, courtly love poems and other specimens of syllabic verse, it contains 27 Gaelic ballads, and some fragments. The majority of these are Fian ballads; there are two Ulster ballads, and one ballad relating the death of a Connacht hero associated with Ulster, and popularly known as 'Laoidh Fhraoich' ('The lay of Fraoch').[14]

The Book of the Dean predates by a century the major Irish collection, *Duanaire Finn*. Devoted entirely to Finn ballads, the *Duanaire* was compiled at Louvain and Ostend in Belgium in 1626-27, and contains 69 ballad texts. Its contents belong to the north of Ireland, and appear to represent texts taken to Ostend by Franciscans fleeing from persecution in Ireland. The manuscript consists of prose (a version of *Acallamh na senórach*) and verse (the *fian* ballads). The prose was written by Niall Gruama Ó Catháin, and the verse was transcribed, apparently from a series of smaller manuscript compilations, by Aodh Ó Dochartaigh. The scribes' patron was Captain Somhairle Mac Domhnaill, whose roots lay in the Glens of Antrim and were thus entwined in the wider Clan Donald empire in Ireland and Scotland.[15] Given the northern Irish provenance of the *Duanaire* and the Scottish background of its patron, one might expect his collection of ballads to share some texts with Scotland, and specifically with the Book of the Dean of Lismore.

The onomastic legacy
Before discussing the Scottish dimension of the ballad texts, it is important to acknowledge the palpably Irish perspectives of the corpus in the Book of the Dean of Lismore. At the very least, a basic and sustained toponymic interest in Ireland is evident in certain ballads in this source. We need not, however, assume that the place-names which anchor the stories of narrative ballads in particular areas indicate a passion for Ireland on the part of the scribes, since place-names of this kind were no more than iconic markers, portable and

---

[13] Meek, 'The Scots-Gaelic scribes'.
[14] Meek, Donald E., '*Táin bó Fraích* and other "Fráech" texts: a study in thematic relationships, Part I', *Cambridge medieval Celtic Studies* 7 (Summer 1984), 1-37.
[15] Ó hUiginn, Ruairí, '*Duanaire Finn*', in Ó Fiannachta, *An fhiannaíocht*, 147-68. The standard edition is Mac Néill, Eoin & Gerard Murphy (eds), *Duanaire Finn*, 3 vols, London and Dublin 1908-53.

transferable within the tradition.[16] Nevertheless, the Irish place-names in the Book of the Dean are crystal clear and accessible, uncorrupted by transmission and indicating that the scribes had a very decent working knowledge of salient Irish sites. For example, one of the ballads shared by *Duanaire Finn* and the Book of the Dean begins, 'Is fada anocht i nOil Finn' ('Time passes tediously in Elphin tonight'). Oisín here laments his plight, hauling stones, and sadly deprived of the delights of the old days of the *fiana*. 'Oil Finn' is likely to be Elphin in Co. Roscommon. The range of place-names in the Book of the Dean ballads reaches to the south and west of Ireland:[17] another poem, again found in both collections, recounts the greatest hunt of the Fian, 'Sealg Sliabh na mBan bhFionn', which is located at Slievenamon in Co. Tipperary. A remarkable piece, unique to the Book of the Dean, which recounts the Fian's encounter with Dogheads and Catheads, and the raising of their banners to defeat the enemy, preserves place-names as far south as Co. Kilkenny.[18] In such poems, there is often an element of quest, which involves an expedition or an adventure of some kind with appropriate sign-posting.

The most impressive of such place-name sequences, in the context of a quest, is found in a ballad generally known as 'Caoilte and the Creatures', in which Caoilte, the swiftest runner among the Fian, runs round Ireland in order to catch a pair of all wild animals as a ransom to free Fionn, who is being held captive in Tara by Cormac mac Airt. The locations of the animals are given in the ballad, and when we plot them on a map, we see that they are distributed round the centre of Ireland.[19] The scribes expended a great deal of energy on this ballad, evidently gathering and comparing variant versions of the text. Nothing could better indicate their interest in Ireland than the time so evidently devoted to writing out, and emending, this potentially very tedious catalogue with no relevance to the toponomy of Scotland. It is a sign of the common inheritance of ballad texts that *Duanaire Finn* contains an attenuated version of 'Caoilte and the Creatures', but it is particularly striking that the Book of the Dean should contain such an extensive text in such fine condition.[20]

The scribes of the Book of the Dean and of *Duanaire Finn* represent what is perhaps the high point of meticulous recording of the Finn ballad texts within the medieval tradition. Although Ireland and Scotland both produced major collections of the ballads at the end of the Middle Ages, one of the key

---

[16] Meek, Donald E., 'Place-names and literature: evidence from the Gaelic ballads', in Taylor, Simon (ed), *The uses of place-names*, Edinburgh 1998, 147-68.

[17] The spread of place-names in the ballads is consistent with the evidence of bardic verse in the manuscript, which shows an interest in the west and south (rather than the north) of Ireland; see Meek, 'The Scots-Gaelic scribes'.

[18] Meek, Donald E., 'The banners of the Fian in Gaelic ballad tradition', *Cambridge medieval Celtic Studies* 11 (summer 1986), 29-69.

[19] Meek, 'Place-names and literature', 158, 160-61.

[20] It appears to be the longest of the surviving versions.

differences between the two countries is that Ireland preserved the medieval classical tradition of manuscript copying much longer than Scotland did. In Ireland, the ballad texts were prime beneficiaries of scribal devotion in the eighteenth and nineteenth centuries, and a whole stream of small manuscripts of ballads was produced by such scribes as the Ó Longáin family of Co. Cork.[21] After 1600, the Scottish tradition tended to be sustained primarily by oral transmission, with occasional interventions from the residual classical tradition within Scotland. The main written collections in Scotland were made from the early eighteenth century onwards, but particularly after 1760, when the Ossianic Controversy got into its stride.[22] As we have already noted, ministers and schoolmasters were key figures in making the collections.

Turning now to the selections of texts in our medieval anthologies, we can perhaps appreciate the complementarity of the tradition, rather than its identity, in Ireland and Scotland, if we consider (a) selections of texts, and (b) preferences in themes. We will proceed by comparing the content of the Book of the Dean of Lismore with that of *Duanaire Finn* and then with that of other, later, Irish collections.

The Book of the Dean and *Duanaire Finn*

I have already suggested that the apparently northern interest of *Duanaire Finn* might lead us to expect a close correspondence between its selection of ballads and that in the Book of the Dean. In fact, the Book of the Dean has surprisingly little in common with *Duanaire Finn* – only some four ballads or so out of a total of some 95 are found in both manuscripts. It is most interesting that these two collections, whose *corpora* are relatively close to one another in terms of the 'northern' affiliations of the scribes, should show such marked divergence. What is happening may have little to do with time and place, but much more to do with the sources being used by the scribes. It would seem to me that the scribe of *Duanaire Finn* was tapping a very much older, and much more conservative, tradition of ballads than the scribes of the Book of the Dean of Lismore. Indeed, a considerable number of the poems in *Duanaire Finn* are unique to that manuscript.[23] It is, however, evident that the material in the *Duanaire* becomes more modern as one progresses through it, until by Poem LVII, 'A Oisín as fada do shúan', we reach the kind of selection attested in the later Irish poem-books.

---

[21] For the Ó Longáin family, see Ní Úrdail, Meidhbhín, *The scribe in eighteenth- and nineteenth-century Ireland*, Münster 2000. This important volume does not, however, refer at all to the many manuscripts of *fian-laoithe* which were compiled by this major family of scribes.

[22] Samples of these can be accessed most easily in Campbell, J.F. (ed.), *Leabhar na Fèinne*, London 1872.

[23] A detailed assessment of the sample in *Duanaire Finn*, showing its correspondences with later collections, is long overdue. In the meantime, see Ó hUiginn, '*Duanaire Finn*'.

It is therefore of great interest to observe that three of the four poems common to *Duanaire Finn* and the Book of the Dean of Lismore occur towards the end of the *Duanaire*, while all four occur at the beginning of the collection in the Book of the Dean. These three poems are items LV, LVIII and LXV in *Duanaire Finn*, corresponding to IV, V and VII in the Book of the Dean.[24] The poem which lies out of sequence, as number VII in *Duanaire Finn*, is the ballad on 'Caoilte and the Creatures', Poem IX in the Book of the Dean. There may be a hint here that the first nine poems in the Book of the Dean belong to an earlier phase of ballad composition than those beginning with Poem X, but what is 'earlier' in terms of the sequence of the Book of the Dean is 'later' in terms of *Duanaire Finn*. Thus, though the Book of the Dean as a compilation is older than *Duanaire Finn*, its ballad sample as a whole appears to be more recent. The opening section of the Book of the Dean (as we now have it) may also be tapping a different source of material from the rest of the collection, since it is noticeable that it contains only one text (Poem V) found subsequently in Scotland, and also the highest proportion of poems peculiar to itself, namely four complete items.

From Poem X onwards, the Book of the Dean corresponds much more closely with later Scottish and Irish tradition, though not at all with the *Duanaire*. The corresponding Irish items are found in the little poem-books, or *duanairí*, of the eighteenth and nineteenth centuries. Poems X and XI in the Book of the Dean are part of the contention between Oisín and Pádraig. A more modern complexion appears in *Duanaire Finn* too from Poem LVII, which is also part of the Oisín-Pádraig debate. If this is more than a coincidence, it may suggest that in both Ireland and Scotland there was some awareness within the scribal tradition of a watershed between 'older' and 'newer' texts, and that the 'newer' texts were generally found in conjunction with, or introduced by, a section of verse from the Oisín-Pádraig debate. If we lay the later Irish poem-books alongside the Book of the Dean, we discover that, in total, no fewer than fourteen complete texts and part of a text in the Dean's anthology are found in the later Irish collections.[25]

Despite this significant element of correspondence, the Book of the Dean also contains evidence to suggest that Scotland was preserving, if not actually creating, ballad texts which do not appear to have been known in Ireland. This is apparent in the number of poems which are peculiar to the manuscript. Two of these, Poems II and III, actually contain linguistic features, fixed by metre, which tend to suggest that they were composed in Scotland, at a time when the Scottish vernacular was already interacting with the standard Classical

---

[24] The numbering follows that in Meek, Donald E., 'The corpus of heroic verse in the Book of the Dean of Lismore', unpublished Ph.D. thesis, University of Glasgow 1982.

[25] See Summary Diagram on p. 16.

THE FREQUENCY OF BDL ITEMS IN LATER IRISH AND SCOTTISH SOURCES

A Summary Diagram

 Occasional   Fairly common   Very common

BDL	DF	Later Irish Mss	Later Scottish trad.
I: "Atá fán tulaigh so…"		Very common	
II: "A Gharaidh, triallmaid…"			
III: "Do-chonna mé teaghlach"			
IV: "Is fada a-nocht…"	LV	Occasional	
V: Slievenamon	LVIII	Occasional	Occasional
VI: Cath Fionntrágha			
VII: The Magic Cloak	LXV	Very common	
VIII: "Anbhfann a-nocht…"			
IX: Caoilte and the Creatures	VII		
X: "Truagh liom Tulach…"		Fairly common	Occasional
XI: "Innis dúinn, a Phádraig"			Occasional
XII: "Ard aigne Ghuill…"		Fairly common	Fairly common
XIII: The Death of Diarmaid			Very common
XIV: "Cumhain liom		Occasional	Occasional
XV: "Binn guth duine…"			Occasional
XVI: "Naoinear a chuadhmar…" Banner qq.		Occasional	Very common
XVII: "Fleadh mhór…"			
XVIII: "An so chunnaic…"			Occasional
XIX: Na Cinn		Fairly common	Occasional
XX: Eas Ruaidh		Very common	
XXI: "Innis dūinne…"		Fairly common	Occasional
XXII: "Mór a-nocht…"		Very common	Occasional
XXIII: The Death of Conlaoch		Fairly common	
XXIV: "Do mhillis mise…"			?
XXV: "Lá dhā rabhmar…"			Occasional
XXVI: "Sé lá gus an dé…"		Occasional	
XXVII The Death of Fraoch			Very common

language to produce a distinctively Scottish style of Early Modern Gaelic.[26] I have looked at textual developments elsewhere, but here it is useful to bear in mind the clear evidence for the emergence of Scottish text-types found in the Book of the Dean. We can see this demonstrated effectively in the ballad on 'Sealg Sliabh na mBan bhFionn', which I mentioned earlier. A quatrain found only in Scotland is tacked on to the version in the Book of the Dean.[27]

The Book of the Dean also includes two major Gaelic ballads which both have identifiable links with Ireland, but which, for some reason, are not to be found in surviving Irish tradition. I refer, of course, to 'Laoidh Fhraoich' ('The lay of Fraoch'), which has firm onomastic connections with Co. Roscommon, and also 'Laoidh Dhiarmaid' ('The lay of Diarmaid'). I have suggested elsewhere, somewhat boldly, that the latter may have been composed in Gaelic Scotland,[28] and, to keep the balance right, I have credited Co. Roscommon with 'Laoidh Fhraoich'.[29] However, I would add – provocatively – that there is no reason why 'Laoidh Fhraoich' should not have been composed in Scotland too. Given the movement between Ireland and Scotland in the Middle Ages, it is not at all impossible that a peripatetic Scotsman with a knowledge of Roscommon was responsible for this poem! Be these contentious matters as they may, both ballads were extremely popular in Scotland; in fact, I suspect that 'The Lay of Diarmaid' was one of the most popular ballads of all time in Scottish tradition.

Elegy and loss
The presence of the Diarmaid and Fraoch ballads in the Book of the Dean of Lismore is instructive in another way. It points to a very dominant note within the collection – a note which is by no means as dominant in any of the later Irish collections. That dominant note is elegiac. In fact, the book contains the four main elegies of Gaelic ballad tradition – those on the deaths of Fraoch, Diarmaid, Oscar and Conlaoch. In addition to these, there are a further five poems which are retrospective and elegiac in their substance, looking back to the great, golden age of warriors, lamenting their passing, and enumerating their graves. The first ballad in the Book of the Dean sets what is, in effect, the keynote of the collection, by identifying the graves of the best warriors of the *fiana*. The loss of the warrior era is further lamented in two poems put in the

---

[26] These features will be discussed in my forthcoming (and now almost completed) edition of the Gaelic ballads in the Book of the Dean of Lismore.
[27] Meek, Donald E., 'Development and degeneration in Gaelic ballad texts', in Almqvist *et al.*, *Fiannaíocht*, 153-55.
[28] Meek, Donald E., 'The death of Diarmaid in Scottish and Irish tradition', *Celtica* 21 (1990), 335-61.
[29] Meek, '*Táin bó Fraích*'.

mouth of the aged Oisín. At least 11 out of the 27 poems in the Book of the Dean are thus elegiac.[30]

It might be said, fairly, that the mood of the Finn Cycle as a whole is elegiac, and that we should not be surprised by the prominence of this note in the Book of the Dean. However, I would have to say that the mood of *Duanaire Finn* is not at all as melancholic. Indeed, the predominant interest of the *Duanaire* appears to lie in encounters with exotic enemies or strangers, as may befit the worldview of a soldier of fortune like Somhairle Mac Domhnaill. Its interest in elegiac verse is slight – and there is no other Irish collection which contains the proportion of elegies found in the Book of the Dean of Lismore. The standard elegiac poem in the later Irish poem-books is that relating the death of Oscar at the battle of Gabhair, and forming part of a large medley of texts called 'Tuarasgabháil chatha Gabhra'.[31] In Scotland, by contrast, all four elegies are common in popular tradition, and are reproduced in the earliest printed selection of Gaelic ballads, namely that of John Gillies of Perth, published in 1786.[32]

Why is it that the Scottish tradition, in the late Middle Ages, should show such a marked interest in elegiac themes? Perhaps we should rephrase this and ask, instead, what caused the Scottish tradition to move into elegiac mode. Having let that question lie in my mind over many years, I feel that I can edge my way towards an answer. The Book of the Dean of Lismore has both profoundly western and profoundly eastern connections. Its eastern links are marked by its provenance (probably Fortingall), and by its MacGregor scribes, who were vassals of the Clan Campbell. The Campbell-MacGregor axis is of paramount importance in the compilation of the book. Yet, part of the selection of verse in the book looks westwards, and, however much we concede (quite rightly) to the Campbells, it is hard to deny that the book owes a fair proportion of its Gaelic material to the influence of the Gaelic cultural province of the Lordship of the Isles.[33] The Book of the Dean was, in fact, compiled within fifty years of the forfeiture of the Lordship in 1493. It contains bardic verse which is thoroughly elegiac, lamenting the demise of the last Lords of the Isles, and including a very moving poem by Giolla Coluim mac an Ollaimh, inspired directly by the forfeiture, which begins: 'Ní h-éibhneas gan Chlann Domhnaill' ('There is no joy without Clan Donald').[34] The decline and eventual loss of the Lordship appear to have generated a mood of retrospection, a kind of cultural

---

[30] Cf. Meek, Donald E., 'The Gaelic ballads of Scotland: creativity and adaptation', in Gaskill, Howard (ed), *Ossian revisited*, Edinburgh 1991, 35-39.

[31] Poem XXII in the Book of the Dean of Lismore.

[32] *A collection of ancient and modern Gaelic poems and songs*, Perth 1786, 24-29, 107-12, 284-87, 313-21.

[33] Meek, 'The Scots-Gaelic scribes'.

[34] Watson, William J. (ed), *Scottish verse from the Book of the Dean of Lismore*, Edinburgh 1937, 90-95.

depression and sense of hopelessness, particularly among those closest to the Lords and their patronage. It is remarkable that scribes who lived in Fortingall, Perthshire, should have been so keenly aware of the passing of the old order in the west. The scribes' Lismore connection may have been more significant than we have hitherto supposed. James MacGregor was a pluralist cleric, typical of his time, and, although we may doubt if he attended diligently to his benefice in Lismore, he may have visited the island and become very familiar with the west coast and its islands. Certainly, Lismore with its cathedral church of the Diocese of the Isles, and its presumably close contacts with the Lordship, would have provided an ideal window through which to view the changing world from an island-based perspective.

The Book of the Dean itself may be, in part at least, an attempt to gather some of the surviving poetic gems from the Lordship. If so, the high proportion of elegiac ballads in the Book, may, like the elegy for the Lordship by Giolla Coluim, reflect the mood of the time. The keynote is the death of the heroes, and in terms of Scottish Gaelic history, it may be that the forfeiture of the Lordship had a significance not unlike that of the Flight of the Earls in 1607.[35] Oisín, spending night after night dragging boulders and crying out, 'Is fada anocht i nOil Finn' ('Time passes tediously in Elphin tonight') – in a ballad which (as we have seen) is found in both the Book of the Dean and *Duanaire Finn* – may have represented the feelings of the late medieval Scottish Gaelic and Irish poet, if only in fairly general terms. As the Lordship fell apart, and as similar changes occurred in Gaelic Ireland, the bygone world of the high Middle Ages might well have appeared much brighter than the contemporary scene. Distance, then as now, may have lent enchantment to the view. Romantic retrospection of this kind was no new thing within the Finn tradition, nor was it unknown in Ireland, but the social and political circumstances of the day may have encouraged a greater emphasis on it in the Book of the Dean than in *Duanaire Finn*. It is very significant that later Scottish tradition gave considerable prestige to the four warrior elegies in the Book of the Dean, and that it regarded them as very special compositions. Ireland, on the other hand, if we go by the sample in *Duanaire Finn*, had developed a greater interest in adventure and expedition, and it is evident too that verse which related the genealogies and pedigrees of heroes and their weapons had much more appeal to the scribe of *Duanaire Finn* than to the scribes of the Book of the Dean.

The point I am making here is simply this: a major cultural dynamo like the Lordship of the Isles, when in full working order, had the power to shape the literary output of the Gaelic world under its sway. Similarly, the 'phasing out' or 'decommissioning' of a cultural dynamo of this kind had the capacity to

---

[35] The creation of *Duanaire Finn* in Ostend was one of the indirect consequences of the Flight of the Earls, but there is no evidence that the selection of its material, or the ethos of that material, was influenced by contemporary political circumstances.

impart a certain shape to literary output by curtailing creativity or by putting a heavier emphasis on particular themes at a critical point in historical development. Perhaps too its demise removed a bridging mechanism which might have allowed texts to travel more easily between Scotland and Ireland. As a consequence, some texts may have become 'stuck' on one side or other of the North Channel, and an element of cultural 'freezing' may have occurred. Indeed, I would go as far as to say that the thematic complexion of the modern ballad corpus in Gaelic Scotland may owe much to the loss of the Lordship, which evidently stimulated an elegiac mood within the Gaelic sector under its sway. Around the same time as the Lordship collapsed, the compilers of the Book of the Dean of Lismore appear to have caught what seems to have been one of the last, if not *the* last, of the major creative surges of Gaelic ballad composition, though we must note that this surge appears largely to have bypassed the scribe of *Duanaire Finn*. Both Gaelic Scotland and Ireland were heirs of this last 'fling', so to speak, but preserved it with different emphases. In Scotland, elegiac narrative ballads seem to have been particularly highly prized, with less emphasis on non-elegiac ballads of warrior adventure than is found in Ireland.

Contending with Patrick

It needs, however, to be said with equal strength that the Book of the Dean of Lismore also contains certain items which fit much better with the subsequent profile of Irish, rather than Scottish, ballad tradition. This is demonstrated effectively by the two ballads, numbers X and XI, in the Book of the Dean, in which Oisín engages in a spirited and acrimonious contention with Pádraig, first attacking the arrival of the clerics on the Hill of the *Fiana*, and then questioning the saint about the *fiana*'s suitability to gain access to the heavenly city. The first of these poems is not attested in later Scottish tradition, while the second is found only in an attenuated form.[36] There was relatively little interest in the Oisín v. Pádraig debate in later Scottish tradition. I suspect that, in Scotland, Patrick gradually came to have much less relevance than he had in Ireland, and that his status was seriously eroded by the consequences of the Reformation and the subsequent evangelical movements in the Highlands. We can thus conclude that the Book of the Dean reflects an emerging Scottish taste in elegy, but a pre-Reformation 'Patrician' taste in theology.

What is particularly interesting, in terms of the shape of the collection in the Book of the Dean, is that the poems of debate between Pádraig and Oisín occur at the beginning of what seems to be the second phase or 'flow' of ballad texts in the manuscript. This second 'flow' is, as we have already noted, much closer to the later traditions of both Ireland and Scotland. As we have also seen, there is a convention within the later Irish poem-books that they begin with a quarrel

---

[36] Campbell, *Leabhar na Fèinne*.

between Pádraig and Oisín, usually represented by the ballad, 'A Oisín, as fada do shuan'. In Ireland, however, the debate between Oisín and Pádraig became a major set piece which developed into the *Acallamh* between the two figures (studied in depth by Professor Pádraig Ó Fiannachta).[37] The presence of two anti-Pádraig poems in the Book of the Dean reflects the growing prominence of this genre. In later Irish tradition they are usually found as part of the omnibus of poems on the Battle of Gabhair known as 'Tuarasgabháil chatha Gabhra'. The central item in the poetic omnibus, that narrating Oscar's death, forms Poem XXII in the Book of the Dean, and this hints again at a wider Scottish-Irish consensus on textual preference.

The oddities of the Dean

In certain other respects, the Book of the Dean is rather odd in the context of all the later collections. It seems to show little interest in some major themes which emerged in the later traditions of Scotland and Ireland. This can be illustrated by the theme of Viking invasion, which appears to have been considerably more popular in post-medieval Gaelic Scotland than in Ireland, but is nevertheless only barely represented in the Book of the Dean of Lismore. The ballads on Viking topics commonly portray the *fiana* as the defenders of the sovereignty of Ireland.[38] In the Book of the Dean, there is only one Viking ballad (Poem VI) worthy of the name, and it describes the great battle which took place at Fionntrágha, namely Ventry, in Co. Kerry. The Book of the Dean is unique in preserving this ballad, but the location of the narrative demonstrates, once again, the importance of the Irish dimension of the tradition in providing focal points for the narrative and in stimulating creativity.

The story of the battle of Ventry was, of course, well known in a prose tale, and versions of this tale were very popular in Scotland in the eighteenth century.[39] The Book of the Dean is thus consistent with the Scottish interest in this tale. However, it is remarkable that the Dean and his fellow scribes have recorded so few ballads which feature the Vikings. This could be ascribed to the land-locked nature of eastern Perthshire, which was hardly calculated to encourage an interest in sea-going invaders, but against this we must set the western interests of the Book as a whole. *Duanaire Finn*, by contrast, contains six overtly Viking ballads, and later Scottish tradition has a very high proportion of such poems (with versions of three of the *Duanaire* ballads).[40]

---

[37] Ó Fiannachta, Pádraig, 'The development of the debate between Pádraig and Oisín', in Almqvist *et al.*, *The heroic process*, 183-205.

[38] Christiansen, Reidar Th., *The Vikings and the Viking wars in Irish and Gaelic tradition*, Oslo 1931.

[39] A version was transcribed by the 18th-century poet, Alexander MacDonald.

[40] Christiansen, *The Vikings*, 90-131. A reassessment of the Viking ballads which would place them in their original literary and social contexts is long overdue.

Indeed, it would seem that Scotland was very creative in this area, and there is a good case for believing that it manufactured a few Viking ballads of its own, among them 'Duan a' Mhuileartaich' ('The lay of the Muileartach'), featuring a sea-going virago who is defeated by the Fian.[41]

Perhaps we should see the growth of the Viking theme and its popularity in Gaelic Scotland, and also in Ireland, as a development which reached its peak later than the Book of the Dean of Lismore. Reading the Viking ballads in *Duanaire Finn*, I am struck by how modern certain texts (notably 'The lay of Airrghean the Great') appear to be in terms of their language, and there is just a possibility that the texts which became dominant after 1600 are a late reflex of the earlier concern with mythological strangers or invaders within the tradition – a concern well reflected in the Book of the Dean itself, as in 'The magic cloak' (Poem VII) and 'Eas Ruaidh' (Poem XX). Both involve a female visitor from the Otherworld, who challenges the Fian warriors. Why, one wonders, did the Viking theme become so important in both countries, but so specially important in Scotland? Perhaps it was particularly well suited to the Hebrides, but it may also have been peculiarly geared to the consequences of the loss of the Lordship of the Isles, and the arrival of new overlords who displaced the earlier kings of the isles.[42] Invasion by successive adventurers was the fate of Ireland, but it was also the fate of Gaelic Scotland, and, in the context of the Fian ballads, the people of both areas may have been able to come to terms with the settlers by invoking the spirit, if not the success, of Fionn mac Cumhaill and his followers. The triumphalist note of these ballads acted as a counterbalance to the elegiac tendency within the Scottish tradition.

Conclusion

Enough has been said to show that, by the end of the Middle Ages, Gaelic Scotland had much in common with Gaelic Ireland in its range of ballad texts. The sample in the Book of the Dean also shares common ground with the post-1700 Irish collections, though it has curiously little in common with *Duanaire Finn*. Nevertheless, it is evident that distinctive emphases had developed within Scotland's Gaelic ballad tradition as we observe it in the period 1500-50 in the Book of the Dean of Lismore, and that some of these emphases survived long after 1600. In particular, we noted the recent complexion (in medieval terms) of most of the Dean's texts, and also the concern with elegy in the selection, which is an enduring feature of the Scottish tradition. This emphasis, I suggested, may have been created to some extent by the social and political changes taking place in Gaelic Scotland, notably the loss of the Lordship of the

---

[41] Christiansen, *The Vikings*, 215-31.

[42] The relationship of the *fian-laoithe* and the *fiannaíocht* to different political and military groups and particular families in the Gaelic west (e.g. the MacSweens of Knapdale and Fánad) is worthy of much further examination.

Isles. This, in turn, may have aided the preservation in Scotland of ballads which were regarded as the last markers of a once-great heroic age, but which were lost or discarded in Irish tradition. The lays of Diarmaid and Fraoch are in this category, and it may be that, in Ireland, they may have been displaced by prose versions of the same stories which differed from the ballad texts in significant points of detail.[43] We must, of course, bear in mind constantly that we do not have a complete ballad sample from either country, and that both countries endured social and political upheavals in the nineteenth century which may have destroyed a substantial proportion of the *corpus*.

Scotland evidently developed its own text-types, and probably had its own poets, capable of composing ballads, since at least a couple of poems in the Book of the Dean are possibly of Scottish origin, and one text has an additional quatrain found only in later Scottish versions. After the Book of the Dean was compiled, the degree of distinctiveness within the Scottish tradition would have increased. Loss of scribal contact with Ireland was doubtless one factor in stimulating further divergence, and religious developments were probably another. The Scottish tradition was influenced, it would seem, by the spirit of the Reformation, leading to the demotion of Patrick as a major clerical figure, and it is highly likely that certain ballads (e.g. 'The magic cloak') were suppressed as they were considered 'risky' by clerical collectors or by their informants, who might have had scruples about telling them to the minister'. At some point in the late Middle Ages, the Viking theme assumed great prominence in Scotland, as it did in Ireland, and there is some evidence of Scottish creativity in this field. Nevertheless, such creativity did not lead to any major disjunction between Ireland and Scotland. As happened throughout the Middle Ages, it took place within the context of the Gaelic cultural heritage of both countries, whose unity and diversity we celebrate and study in this volume.[44]

---

[43] See further Meek, '*Táin bó Fraích*', and Meek, 'The death of Diarmaid'.

[44] I am grateful to Dr Nancy R. McGuire for producing the final version of the Summary Diagram.

ON SATIRE AND THE POET'S CIRCUIT

Liam Breatnach

In the glossary appended to his edition of *Críth Gablach*, D.A. Binchy (1941, 69) describes *áer.* 'satire' as 'the formidable weapon with which members of the poetic orders (*grád filed*) enforced claims either on their own behalf or on behalf of other persons' who employed them', noting the distinction in that text between justified satirising of a person who has committed an offence and satirising without lawful ground, and suggesting that in the latter case *áer* 'may possibly be used in the wider sense of "defamation", "slander".' This paper will begin by looking at satire as a means of enforcement by a poet both within and outside his own territory, and go on to examine what Early Irish texts have to tell us about the arrangements made for, and the formalities to be observed by, a visiting poet, whether the purpose of his visit be for satire or praise.[1]

Where satire may justifiably be resorted to, a number of formalities must be observed, all with the purpose of giving ample warning to the offender and providing him with the opportunity of avoiding being satirised by settling the matter at issue. These include the composition of a *trefocal*, which consists of a mixture of praise and blame (including a statement of the offence) and which serves as a warning; for details see Meroney (1953), which includes (96-112) an edition of an Old Irish example of such a composition, and Breatnach (1987, 138 9; 1988, 17-19). Its mixed nature is noted in the frequently found image of the three colours of poetry, e.g., *Att ē trī datha na hēc[se] sin .i. find *7 dub *7 brecc. Find ūa moltar, dub ūa n-āerthar, brecc ūa fōcarar* 'Those are the three colours of poetry, i.e. white and black and speckled. White by which one praises, black by which one satirises, speckled by which one gives notice' (Calder, 1917, 264, lines 5244-6); for further examples see Breatnach (1981, 79). The three 'words' or 'utterances' of *trefocal* are naming the offence, naming the offender, and praise. According to the Middle Irish commentary edited and translated in Meroney (1953, 122-30)[2] the *trefocal* must be metrically perfect, which could explain this term being applied to the two texts on metrical and stylistic faults edited in Calder (1917, 148-64 and 258-69).[3] *Trefocal* can also be used of the procedure as à whole, as in the following brocard with commentary in Middle Irish:

> *Foer cāna filed .i. a fōirithin frīa gell bīata in filed gur acinta(?)* {read *gura cinter*} *a cuairt dō; nó dano in fili echtarcrīchi, a bīathad don rīg in airet bes ag dēnam a trefocail .i. rē na dechmaide apaid *7 na dechmaide trefocail *7 na dechmaide suidighe gell.*
>
> 'Provision of a poet's tribute, i.e. succouring the poet by means of a pledge for

[1] Punctuation, capitalisation and macrons are supplied in the citations below.
[2] Part of this is printed in *CIH* 2119.9-33.
[3] For the latter see Breatnach (1989, 21-3).

25

providing food until his circuit is completed by him; or else, the poet from a foreign territory, he is to be provided with food by the king as long as he is making his *trefocal*, i.e. the ten-day period of notice, and the ten-day period of *trefocal*, and the ten-day period of submitting pledges', *CIH* 2095.20 (cf. Meroney, 1953, 94).

As previously noted (Breatnach, 1987, 138-9) this procedure is analogous to the various stages in *athgabáil* 'distraint', viz. (1) *aurfócrae/apad* 'notice', (2) *anad* 'delay, stay of execution', (3) *tóchsal/tobach* 'removal', (4) *díthim* 'delay in pound' and (5) *lobud* 'progressive forfeiture', for which see Binchy (1973, 34-51) and Kelly (1988, 177-9).

Distraint, however, is proper to commoners, as stated in the Old Irish glossing of *Senchas Már* (cf. Breatnach, 1996, 4) in a passage on the sanctions appropriate to ecclesiastics, lords, poets and commoners:

> *Ōru suigigestar Pātraic *7 maithi fer nĒirenn in dligid-sa, is īarom con-aimdetar cīa tucht do-mbibsat a dliged do cāch fo-hich friu .i. clocc *7 salm d'eclais, gēll do flathaib, trifoclad do filedaib, aithgabāil do fēinib.*

> 'After Patrick and the nobles of the men of Ireland had established this law, it is then that they decided how they will levy their due from those who commit offences against them, i.e. bell and psalm for the church, hostages for lords, "three utterances" for poets, distraint for commoners', *CIH* 884.1 (commentary on *Cethairslicht Athgabálae*).[4]

That a *fili* could use the weapon of satire on behalf of others outside the boundaries of their *túath* is well attested in Middle Irish sources; see the passages edited and translated in Breatnach (1984). The effectiveness of satire as a means of enforcement throughout Ireland is succinctly put in the Old Irish text *Bretha Nemed Dédenach* where it is stated *Ni roich colann coimhdhilsi neinech aonchairde fon Eilg náraghar. Ite na filidh do-bongad cain nenech daigh na ccrioch nimdherg, im ná bí giall, na comhurradhus, gur fuighle cach dia ghiall gruaidhe fris na filedhoibh. ar omhan an aoire*, *CIH* 1111.19-22. This, which will require some explication, can be normalised and translated as:

> *Ní roich colainn coimdílsi n-einech. Óenchairde fon Eilg n-áragar. It é ind filid do-bongat cáin n-enech, dáig na crích n-imderg imná bí gíall ná comurradas, coro fuiglea cách día gíall grúaide frisna fileda ar omun a n-aíre.*

'The body is not as vulnerable as the face/honour. A single treaty is enforced

---

[4] Read *a ndliged* for *a dliged*, *fo-fich* for *fo-hich* and *trí focla* (an etymological equivalent of *trefocal*; cf. *CormY* 1228) for *trifoclad*. MS *gell* is to be read *gēll*, pl. of *gíall*, not *gell* 'pledge', as in Breatnach (1988, 16). For hostages see Kelly (1988, 173-6), and for 'bell and psalm' see Wiley (2001).

throughout Ireland. It is the poets who enforce the regulation of honour, because of [the existence of] the hostile territories without exchange of hostages and joint citizenship (lit. 'around which there is neither hostage nor joint citizenship'), so that everyone submits to the poets for fear of their satire, having their cheeks/honour as hostage (lit. 'by means of the hostage of his cheek').'

The key concept here is *cairde* 'treaty', an arrangement between two kingdoms which 'entitles the victim of a crime committed by a member of the other *túath* to obtain legal redress for the injury which he has suffered' (Kelly, 1988, 5).[5] While there are kingdoms which are 'hostile', i.e. which have not concluded a treaty with exchange of hostages, there is, paradoxically, throughout Ireland a single state of treaty, or means of redress, the overriding 'regulation of honour', enforced by means of satire against the more vulnerable hostage of a person's face or honour.

In spite of this, the possibility that satirising the actual offender may not always be sufficient is acknowledged. Thus a Middle Irish commentary on *trefocal* refers to satirising the kin of the offender as follows: *Is airi do-nīther trefocul do fine in cintaig ar dāig gur dīlsiget a œrad nō cor timairget hē re dliged dīa cinn; *7 mani derna in fili treocul, īcad .u.s., *7 athchur blīadna fair; *7 is ēicen apad for fine rīa trefocul amail do-berar for cintach.* 'The reason why a *trefocal* is employed against the kin of the offender is so that they may consent to his being satirised or force him to [submit to] justice instead. And if the poet does not make a *trefocal*, let him pay five *séts* and it is to be postponed for a year; and warning must be given to the kin before a *trefocal* as it is given to an offender', *CIH* 2119.30.[6]

The following *roscad* passage in *Bretha Nemed Toísech* is printed in *CIH* 2226.31-6: *Biaid menma filed ni fogra aidire, ar isi athgabail doboing do coimdeguib cert; ni cachta cethra, ni clanna ar liasa lorg, ni laimeathar airidiu naine indged for aithech nindruicc; trefocal fogra indged fora tigerna, a tri ele, tine, tenga, toibgid; togbud fora fine feochar sceo anble for flaithemuin feidm flaithemuin fine for fine for flaith falscuithe sindead; sloinnter iarmota suidiud do nach geill gruaide gabudh.* It is replete with difficulties, but it is at least certain that it concerns employing the *trefocal* procedure not only against the offender but also, in the case of a commoner, against his kin and against his lord.[7] I tentatively restore and translate as:

---

[5] For different types of *cairde* see Thurneysen (1925, 326-7) on the passage in *CIH* 792.5ff. (which belongs to *Bretha Cairdi*, tract 31 of *Senchas Már*; see Breatnach, 1996, 31-2) and Binchy (1941, 80).

[6] For the commentary at 2119.9-33 together with some preceding matter omitted in *CIH* see Meroney (1953) 122-30; my translation differs somewhat from his.

[7] For the peculiar orthography of the only complete copy of this text see Breatnach (1989a, 3).

Biaid menmae filed
ní fócra aitiri,
ar is sí athgabáil
do-boing do choimdedaib cert.
Ní cachta cethrai,
ní clanda ar lías a luirg,
ní laimethar airitiu n-aíne.
Indged for aithech n-inraicc
trefocal fócrai.
Indged fora thigernae
a trí aili.
Tein a thengad toibged,
tócbad fora fini,
feochair scéo ainbli for flaithemain;
feidm flaitheman fine
for fini, for flaith.
Falscuitheo sindad
sloindter íarmothá suidiu,
donach géill grúaide gaba.

'A poet will be mindful: he is not to give notice to a surety, for that is (belongs to) distraint, which enforces a claim by means of impoundings. He is not to imprison cattle, he is not to plant his staff before a pen, he is not to dare to undertake fasting. Let him impose on a worthy[8] commoner a *trefocal* of warning. Let him impose on his lord another three (viz., the *trefocal*). With the fire of his tongue let him enforce, let him raise [it] upon his kin, together with fierce viciousness upon the lord; the burden of the lord [and] of the kin upon the kin, upon the lord. Let scorching reviling be expressed after that if he does not get hold of cheeks of a hostage.'[9]

Although the above passage recommends against distraint *(Ní cachta cethrai...)*, and indeed against fasting (against the offender's lord?), distraint is allowed for under certain circumstances in the same text, where, several lines later we find: *Mad i tuaith i medon, gaibid in file athgabail; gaibtis do- cid im cricha imdergtha mad iar nelo a trefocuil*, CIH 2227.4, which can be restored and translated as: *Mad i túaith i medón gaibid in fili athgabáil. Gaibthius dano cid im chrícha imdergthai, mad íar n-élúd a thréfocuil* 'If it be within the kingdom, the poet takes distraint. He takes it moreover even in hostile territories if it be after evading his *trefocul*.'

---

[8] Taking this to mean that although he has committed an offence he is a person who is paradoxically 'worthy' in that he values his honour and thus will respond to the threat of satire. Alternatively, one could emend MS *nindruicc* to *inraicc* and take it as qualifying the following word, 'a fitting *trefocal*' being one that is metrically perfect (cf. p. 25 above).

[9] I take *indged* as 3sg. imperative of *ad-aig/ind-aig* (compare *ad-fét* beside *in-fét*). For *géill grúaide* (with preposed genitive) cf. *día gíall grúaide* at p. 26, third last line, above.

Elsewhere it is stated that the head of the kin may be threatened with satire, namely in *Bretha im Fuillemu Gell* (tract 23 of *Senchas Már*): *Tēchta fuillema gill cacha mnā rindas la Fēniu, mā do-roth, is dīles do suidiu āige fine cāich dara ndichet cenn a gell do rinnad, coro fuigle dia inchuib* 'The lawful pledge-interest of every woman who satirises, if it (viz., the pledge) has become forfeit, it is lawful for her to satirise the head of the kin of the person on whose behalf her pledge went security until he have submitted to adjudication for (i.e. to save) his honour', *CIH* 466.5 (see Binchy, 1938, 64).

Doubtless the threat of satire is what is in question in the section of *Críth Gablach* dealing with the *aire coisring*, who 'although a member of the *grád Fhéne*, is accorded a special status by his function as head of his kin..., whom he represents in their dealings with external authorities' (Binchy, 1941, 70), where we read: *Is é aire fine insin tobeir gell tar cenn a fine do ríg *7 senud *7 óes cherdd dia timorggain do réir*, 280-3. Mac Neill (1923, 294) takes *óes cerdd* to mean 'craftsmen', while Binchy (1941, 70) says 'the precise meaning of *óes cerdd* is doubtful, perhaps poets, who have a semi-public status'. Kelly (1988, 14, 48) is in agreement with Binchy, whereas Stacey (1994, 77-8) favours Mac Neill's interpretation. As 'craftsmen' does not make good sense here beside the authorities of king and church, Binchy's suggestion must be correct and this can be translated as 'He is the lord of a kin who gives a pledge on behalf of his kin to king and ecclesiastical authority and poets that he will force them to compliance.'

Finally, another *roscad* in *Bretha Nemed Toísech* lists all four (the offender, the kin, the head of the kin and the lord) as those against whom a poet can take action, namely, *roairlistar senca saidiugud filed fri cinntuibh fogladh* (?) *forsa a cuinncider feich for fine fria nelod for art fine, for flaith tairgilleud airibh ina treabuib tiaghuid tabair* (?) *doib dliged a leapa iar narilliud ard, CIH* 2224.32.

I would normalise and translate as: *Ro airlestar Senchae / suidigud filed / fri cinta foglaide / forsa cuindchiter féich / for fini fria n-élúd, / for art fine, for flaith: / tairgille airib, / inna treba tíagait, / tabarr doïb / dliged a leptho / íar n-áirilliud ard* 'Senchae has set out the arrangements for poets with regard to offences of wrongdoers from whom penalties are sought, [or] from the kin when they abscond, from the head of the kin, from the lord: forepledges [are given] for them, they go into their (viz. the lords') dwellings, let there be given to them the entitlements of their shelter according to noble merit.'

The last-cited passage also mentions maintenance of poets; similarly in the Middle Irish commentary at *CIH* 2095.20 cited on pp 25-6 above it is stated that a visiting poet is to be provided with food by the king as long as he is engaged in a *trefocal*. The obligation to maintain a poet is also referred to in the following passage in *Bretha Nemed Dédenach* along with further details: *Cisne tri gealla nad fuilled do flaithibh? Geall go cuigthe fria filedha foichill, geall mbiadhta go tresi, geall snaidhte – geall diongbhala fir uadh i ttig flatha, acht is in ionbodhoibh techta, ar as go cleithe tuaithe tiagaid filidh fuigheall fria forus fath, fo bhith as conn ar ecconn feith, CIH* 1125.24.

This can be restored and translated as: *Cis n-é trí gella nád fuillet do flaithib? Gell co cóicthi fri filed foichill, gell mbíadto co tresi, gell snáidteo – gell dingbála fir uad i tig flatho, acht is i n-inbadaib téchtaib, ar is co cléithe túaithe tíagait filid fuigell fri forus fáth, fo bíth as conn ar- éconn -feith* 'What are the three pledges which do not incur interest for lords? A pledge up to the end of five days for a poet's reward, a pledge for refection to the end of three days, a pledge for protection – a pledge worthy of a man of poetry in a lord's house, provided it be at lawful times, for it is to the pinnacle of the kingdom that poets go for adjudication and pronouncing on matters,[10] for it is a head that looks after a headless one.'[11]

It may be noted that the maintenance of poets, or meeting their costs, corresponds to the obligation to maintain a plaintiff until a case is settled. A number of glossed citations from Old Irish texts together with a passage of Middle Irish commentary relating to the latter are grouped together in *CIH* 1981.37–1982.36 under the heading *D'imfulung feicheman t[oicheda] for bidbaid ann so aig tobac fiach* 'Concerning a debtor/defendant being liable for the maintenance of a creditor/plaintiff here, while exacting debts/fines'.[12] By way of illustration, we can cite the last of these, namely, *For-tā a forus fuilngeadh cach cintach cēin ara-fuiregar co fosair *7 tech. *7 tene. *7 biudh. *7 tincar. co nderla co ngill *7 breith *7 fiachaib* 'There is the further enactment, let every guilty party maintain [him, viz. the plaintiff], as long as he is detained, by providing floor-covering and a dwelling and fire and food and furnishings until he discharges [his obligations] through pledge and judgement and [payment of] penalties', 1982.30.[13] Amongst the other citations we may note *cēin ara-fuirged feichem[na] fuigheall fri forus fáth* 'as long as they detain creditors/plaintiffs[14] for adjudication and pronouncing on matters', 1982.22, which contains another example of the phrase found in the citation at line 4 above, which I take as equivalent to *fri fuigell *7 forus fáth.*

The next passage to be discussed corroborates and adds to the foregoing. This has not previously been published, and the only copy I know of is in *The Book of Ballymote*, 305b48ff. where it forms part of a set of miscellaneous items on ogam, metrics and poets. It is preceded by a copy of *De Dúlib Feda* (305b10-32; edited with variants from the copy in *LL* 5320-5344 in Calder, 1917, 270-1) and a passage on rhyme and on vowels and diphthongs (305b33-47; published with comments in Thurneysen, 1933, 196-7). The latter ends with *is de asberar i mBrethaib Nemed: genmotha forfeda i fil i ndefogar na nguta* 'it is of that that it is said in *Bretha Nemed*... ' (Thurneysen omits the sentence after *Nemed*), which corresponds to *Auraicept na nÉces*, lines 1297-9 (Calder, 1917, 100). The passage below follows

---

[10] See the second citation in the next paragraph.

[11] See Binchy (1976, 20).

[12] To the cross-references in *CIH* can be added 1982.26-8 = 1112.1-2 (*Bretha Nemed Dédenach*).

[13] Ascribed in a marginal note to *Cethraimhe na T[úarastal]*, 1982m, for which see my forthcoming Companion to *Corpus Iuris Hibernici*.

[14] Expanding MS *feich-* to *feichemna* as in line 17 and at the end of line 22 (in the gloss on this citation).

on immediately from this, but it is uncertain whether the ascription to *Bretha Nemed* was intended to include it as well. Among the items which follow it are a passage on the rewards for various metres of the *filid* (306a14-27, for which see Thurneysen, 1891, 113 n1) and a passage on the rewards for various metres of the *baird* (306a38-42; published with comments in Thurneysen, 1891, 109). Thurneysen regarded the latter two as corrupt, and the same can be said for a good deal of the passage in question here; I can do no more than offer a partial translation.

(a) *arisi ambrig Iacingenn file fath fri eicsi asnes fri iarair co ochtrai crichi canaid coitectai trefocl-e focrai fict faides felmac for crica fri focra a dlig*id *ara taire ara taire ara cenn drisic i ndal a dluim.*

(b) *Tochomlud fil*ed *fri ferba findrud fri aisti fecht cen aurfocra riam co adbai flatha fes- ar tris tuili ferb fonnaid iar ndlig*iud *no atlai ba aneolus cen ḍlig*ed *dorb.*

(c) *Mad fri iarair tra is lethdam *7*7* [sic] *is lethbiatad do ca*ch *hae *7 co taire fechain ar .u.thi *7 gell *7 a iarair *7 a breth ar dech*maid.

(d) *Mad fri airchidal imm*urgu *is fech*ain *ar tris *7 is langell ar u.thi *7 biatad *7 langeall fria rer *7 lanaithni enig rig *7 landuas am*ail *bid ina cric i mmedon ina dlig*iud *o oll*amain *co focloc cona landamaib leo,*

(e) *I nindligi*ud *imm*urgu *atlui as ar .u.thi *7 facaibh coic séotu landlig*ed *naneulais co ti iar ndlig*iud

'(a)... for the narration of poetry, for demanding to the edges of a territory. He utters a proper *trefocal* of warning when (?) he sends a pupil to the border to announce his entitlements so that a *drisiuc*[15] may come to meet him ...

(b) The expedition of a poet for a fair stream of words, for a poetic occasion, without previous notice to the dwelling of the lord ... a flood of words ... according to entitlement or he goes away in ignorance without ... entitlement.

(c) If it is for the purpose of demanding, then, there is half retinue and half refection for each of them, so that consideration is completed by the end of five days, and [giving] a pledge and [making] his demand and judgement on it by the end of ten days.

(d) If it is for the purpose of [praise] poetry, however, there is consideration by the end of three days, and full pledge by the end of five days, and full refection, and a full pledge to maintain them and full entrusting of the honour of the king and full reward, as if it were inside their own territory, as the due of every grade from *ollam* to *fochloc* with their full retinues.

(e) When he has come unlawfully, however, he goes off after five days, and leaves five *séts* because of ignorant unlawfulness until he comes lawfully.'

In (a) I take *ochtrai* as a corruption of the accusative pl. of *ochair*, *trefocl-e* for

---

either *tre focla* or *trefocal*, and *fict* as a corruption of *fecht*; *ara taire ara taire* is clearly a case of dittography. As for *a dluim*, we may have to do with the genitive sg. of a word **dlom*, roughly equivalent to *dlomad* 'announcing, declaring', etc. (cf. *slond* beside *slondud*), although the only other possible example of this I know of is the dative sg. *dlum* registered in *DIL* s.v. from a poem in *Bérla na Filed*. In (b), for *findrud* (= *findsruth*) used of poetry see *DIL* F 143.14; in the light of the image of the three colours of poetry (for which see p. 25 above) it doubtless refers specifically to praise poetry. In (e) read *la indliged* for *landliged*.

Here the distinction is made between two purposes of a poet's visit, either to make a demand (with the implicit threat of satire) or to praise the ruler. In the former case (a), he is to give advance warning of his intentions and to arrange to be met at the border by a *drisiuc*; his retinue is half the normal one (c). In the latter case (b), no advance warning need be given and he goes to the dwelling of the lord of the territory; here he has his full retinue. He has five days to justify his coming for the purpose of making a demand (c) and three days when for praise (d). If he has come unlawfully, he is sent off after five days, and has to pay a penalty of five *séts* (e); 'unlawfulness' would include not observing the proper formalities for satirising; cf. the passage cited at p. 27, lines 16-18 above, where the penalty is the same.

Although not explicitly stated here, one may assume that in both cases he is met by a *drisiuc* who takes him to the lord's dwelling. This assumption is supported by two Middle Irish glosses which refer to the *drisiuc* meeting incoming poets. The first is from *Bretha Crólige* (tract 33 of *Senchas Már*): *Ar aichni na nuili naisti acin drisiuc, cona licinn fili isin crich acht iar setaib dligidh* 'Because of the fact that the *drisiuc* recognises all the metres, so that he allows no poet to enter the territory save along lawful lines', Binchy (1938, 40 §51 gl. 11).[16] The second gloss is from §19 of *Uraicecht na Ríar*, the point of which was missed by the present writer. The relevant section of this reads *nó do-roich ó thúaith ar chinn filed amach do aithne aiste* (as normalised in Breatnach, 1987, 134); the translation can now be corrected to 'or he comes out from a *túath* to meet a poet for the purpose of recognising metres'.

The elementary ability of the low-ranking *drisiuc*[17] to recognise metres means that he can tell who is or is not a poet. Outside the legal material, on the other hand, meeting and providing safe conduct for poets is one of the functions of the Ulster warriors, namely in the following passage from the Boyhood Deeds of Cú Chulainn in Recension I of *Táin Bó Cúailnge*:

> *Tecait di sudiu co Slíab Fúait. Forreccat Conall Cernach and. Do Chonall dano dorala imdegail in chóicid a llá sin, fo bíth no bíid cach láth gaile do Ultaib a láa hi Sléib Fúait fri snádud neich dothíssad co n-airchetul nó do*

---

[16]My translation differs slightly from that of Binchy.

[17]In some texts he is grouped amongst the three sub-grades of *fili*, in others amongst the bards; see Breatnach 1987, 82-3.

chomroc fri fer, combad and sin condrístá fris arná téised nech dochum nEmna cen rathugud.
'Thence they came to Slíab Fúait where they found Conall Cernach. It had fallen to Conall to guard the province that day. For each warrior of the Ulstermen spent a day in turn in Slíab Fúait, to protect anyone who came that way with poetry or with challenge to battle, so that there he might be encountered and so that no one should go unnoticed into Emain' (O'Rahilly, 1976, 21, lines 666-70).

The corresponding passage in the Middle Irish recension in the Book of Leinster is more explicit:

"Ocus in tsligi mór sa imthéit sechond, gia leth imthéit?", ar in mac bec ...
"Téit co Áth na Foraire i Sléib Fúait," ar Ibar. "Cid 'ma n-apar Áth na
Foraire in fetar-su?" "Rafetar-sa omm," bar Ibar. "Dagláech de Ultaib bís
ic foraire *7 ic forcomét and arná tíset óic nó echtranna i nUltu do fúacra
comraic forru, corop é in láech sin conairr comrac dar cend in chóicid uli.
Dá ndig dano áes dána fo dímaig a Ultaib *7 assin chóiciud, corop é conairr
séta *7 maíne dar cend aenig in chóicid dóib. Dá tí dano áes dána 'sin crich,
corop é in fer sin bas chommairge dóib co rrosset colbo Conchobuir, corop
siat a dúana-sain *7 a dréchta gabtair ar tús i nEmain ar ríchtuin."
'"And this great road which goes past us, where does it lead?" said the little boy ... "It goes to Áth na Foraire on Slíab Fúait," said Ibar. "Do you know why it is called Áth na Foraire?" " I do indeed," said Ibar. "A goodly warrior of the Ulstermen is always there, keeping watch and ward so that no warriors or strangers come to Ulster to challenge them to battle and so that he may be the champion to give battle on behalf of the whole province. And if poets leave Ulstermen and the province unsatisfied, that he may be the one to give them treasures and valuables for the honour of the province. If poets come into the land, that he may be the man who will be their surety until they reach Conchobor's couch and that their poems and songs may be the first to be recited in Emain on their arrival."' (O'Rahilly, 1967, 27, lines 990-1003).

Both versions envisage the poet being met at the border of the province of the Ulaid, and from there conducted directly to the residence of the king; while *co n-airchetul* 'with poetry' in the Old Irish version could refer to either satire or praise, it is specifically the latter which is in question in the Middle Irish version.

I conclude with a summary of the main points which have emerged. Firstly, although satire, or the threat thereof, is generally seen as an extremely effective means of enforcing claims, it is recognised that there may be some people who are impervious to it, so that it may have to be employed not only against an actual offender but also against his lord, the head of his kin and his kinsmen. Secondly, a visiting poet is to be maintained during the course of his visit, whether the purpose of that visit is for satire or praise. Thirdly, when a poet is on circuit he does not wander freely about, but is to be met at the border of a territory and taken directly to the residence of the ruler.

All of this is of importance for understanding the role of the poet in early mediaeval Ireland, and the question of the mobility of the poets is also relevant to any attempt to account for the remarkably uniform Old Irish literary language (see the remarks in *GOI* §16).

REFERENCES
Binchy, D.A. (1938): 'Bretha Crólige', *Ériu* 12, 1-77.
Binchy, D.A. (1941): *Críth Gablach*, Mediaeval and Modern Irish Series 11, Dublin.
Binchy, D.A. (1973): 'Distraint in Irish law', *Celtica* 10, 22-71.
Binchy, D.A. (1976): '*Féchem, fethem, aigne*', *Celtica* 11, 18-33.
Breatnach, Liam (1981): '"The caldron of poesy"', *Ériu* 32, 45-93.
Breatnach, Liam (1984): 'Addenda and corrigenda to "The caldron of poesy"', *Ériu* 35, 189-191.
Breatnach, Liam (1987): *Uraicecht na ríar: The poetic grades in early Irish law*, Early Irish Law Series 2, Dublin.
Breatnach, Liam (1988): 'An aoir sa ré luath', P. Ó Fiannachta (ed), *An aoir: Léachtaí Cholm Cille XVIII*, 11-19.
Breatnach, Liam (1989): 'An edition of *Amra Senáin*', D. Ó Corráin, L. Breatnach, K. McCone (eds), *Sages, saints and storytellers: Celtic studies in honour of Professor James Carney*, Maynooth, 7-31.
Breatnach, Liam (1989a): 'The first third of *Bretha Nemed toísech*', *Ériu* 40, 1-40.
Breatnach, Liam (1996): 'On the original extent of the *Senchas Már*', *Ériu* 47, 1-43.
Calder, George (1917): *Auraicept na n-éces. The scholars' primer*, Edinburgh.
Kelly, Fergus (1988): *A guide to Early Irish law*, Early Irish Law Series 3 (Dublin).
Mac Neill, Eoin (1923): 'Ancient Irish law: the law of status or franchise', *Proceedings of the Royal Irish Academy* 36C, 265-316.
Meroney, Howard (1953): 'Studies in early Irish satire: III. "Tréfhocal Fócrai"', *Journal of Celtic Studies* 2, 59-130.
O'Rahilly, Cecile (1967): *Táin Bó Cúailnge from the Book of Leinster*, Dublin.
O'Rahilly, Cecile (1976): *Táin Bó Cúailnge: recension I*, Dublin.
Stacey, Robin Chapman (1994): *The road to judgment: from custom to court in medieval Ireland and Wales*, Philadelphia.
Thurneysen, Rudolf (1891): 'Mittelirische Verslehren', *Irische Texte* 3, 1. Heft, Leipzig, 1-182.
Thurneysen, Rudolf (1925): 'Aus dem irischen Recht III', *ZCP* 15, 302-76.
Thurneysen, Rudolf (1933): 'Colmān mac Lēnēni und Senchān Torpēist', *ZCP* 19,

193-209.

Wiley, Dan M. (2001): 'The maledictory psalms', *Peritia* 15, 261-79.

ABBREVIATIONS

CIH: D.A. Binchy, *Corpus iuris Hibernici*, Dublin 1978.

CormY: Kuno Meyer, 'Sanas Cormaic', *Anecdota from Irish manuscripts* 4, Halle 1912, 1-128.

DIL: *Dictionary of the Irish Language* and *Contributions to a Dictionary ...*, Dublin 1913-75.

GOI: Rudolf Thurneysen, *A grammar of Old Irish*, Dublin 1946.

LL: R.I. Best, O. Bergin, M.A. O'Brien and A. O'Sullivan, *The Book of Leinster. I-VI* (Dublin 1954, 1956, 1957, 1965, 1967, 1983).

ZCP: *Zeitschrift für Celtische Philologie*.

THE NORSE ELEMENT IN SCOTTISH PLACE NAMES:
SYNTAX AS A CHRONOLOGICAL MARKER

Richard A.V. Cox

Traditional perception of Norse-derived place names in Gaelic Scotland is that they consist of a generic element, e.g. *Bòstadh* from Old Norse (ON) *Bólstaðr*, or a specific element followed by a generic, e.g. *Siabost* from ON *Sæ-bólstaðr* 'sea-farm'.[1] A small group of names recorded in the west of Lewis consisting of a generic followed by a specific element, however, raised the question whether they might represent an earlier or a later stratum of names, indicating, in turn, either relatively early or relatively late Norse settlement on the north-west periphery of Scotland.[2] After several recent opportunities to explore and develop some of the arguments involved,[3] it is hoped that the evidence outlined in the present paper will stimulate further, more detailed study into this aspect of Norse-Gaelic contact.

THE DISTRIBUTION OF *BURN OF* TYPE NAMES
Place names which have a similar structure to the one found in *Burn of Glendui* in Aberdeenshire and *Burn of Clashgour* in Morayshire, for example, are fairly common in some parts of Scotland. One of the reasons why the *Burn of* type name is of interest, and why its study is of importance, is that its distinctive word order raises questions about language contact and the influence of languages upon each other. However, this is just one of several types of name structure that occur within an area stretching from Aberdeenshire to St Kilda, and from Galloway to Unst in Shetland, which are

---

[1] For example, see Oftedal, Magne, 'The Village-names of Lewis in the Outer Hebrides', *Norsk tidsskrift for sprogvidenskap* 17 (1954), 363-409: 379 and 377, respectively.

[2] Cox, Richard A.V., 'Norse-Gaelic contact in the West of Lewis: the place-name evidence', in Ureland, P. Sture (ed), *Language Contact in the British Isles, Linguistische Arbeiten* 238 (Tübingen 1994), 479-94: 489-90; Richard Cox, 'The Norse Language in Celtic Scotland', *Proceedings of the 3rd Symposium of Societas Celtologica Nordica*, Oslo 1991, *Acta Universitatis Upsaliensis, Studia Celtica Upsaliensis* I (Uppsala 1994), 27-38: 38.

[3] In a lecture organised by the Seksjon for namnegransking, Institutt for nordistikk og litteraturvitskap, University of Oslo, in August 1997; in a presentation given at Trinity College Dublin, under the auspices of the Irish-Scottish Academic Initiative, in January 1998; and in a paper given at a one-day conference organised by the Scottish Place-Name Society at the University of Aberdeen, in November 1999. I am grateful to all those who contributed to discussion at these venues, and in particular to Botolv Helleland and Tom Schmidt (University of Oslo) and Åse Kari Hansen Wagner (Stavanger College), for their advice and help with references. I am also grateful to Professor Colm Ó Baoill for reading my typescript.

37

notable for their syntax.[4] Such types are not necessarily prominent in the nomenclature, as *Burn of* type names are in some areas, nor do they all belong to the same nomenclature. They are united, however, in having structures which are unusual or innovative in accordance with expected norms.

The valuable work carried out by Professor Bill Nicolaisen and published in *Scottish Studies* 3 (1959) on *Burn of* names provides a detailed analysis of the distribution and type of specific element of the 261 examples found on the 1" Ordnance Survey map.[5] The main bulk of them lie (a) in the Northern Isles (using the old county names, there are 95 in Shetland, 20 in Orkney, and 5 in Caithness) and (b) in the North-east (there are 7 in Morayshire, 22 in Banffshire, 28 in Aberdeenshire, 20 in Kincardineshire, and 54 in Angus). Of the remainder, eight lie within Central Scotland and one each in Ayrshire and Wigtownshire.[6] The type is conspicuously absent, however, from eastern (Fife and Kinross), southern (apart from the two examples in Ayrshire and Wigtownshire), western and north-western areas of Scotland. Professor Nicolaisen quickly followed this research up with an analysis in *Scottish Studies* 4 (1960) of the instance of *Water of* type names,[7] i.e. those referring specifically to watercourses (of which there are 47), such as *Water of Buchat* in Aberdeenshire and *Water of Leith* in Mid Lothian, as well as a range of similarly structured names containing initially either *Mains* (nearly 300 examples), *Mill* or *Mills* (146 examples), *Bridge* (51 examples), *Braes* (17 examples) or *Braeside* (7 examples) followed by the preposition *of*.[8] The distribution of these name types is remarkably similar to that of *Burn of* names in that the bulk of examples is found in the North-east. In contrast to the distribution of *Burn of* names, however, their presence in the North is quite light. The other main distinction is the fact that *Water of* (17 examples) and *Mains of* (14 examples) are, unlike *Burn of*, also represented in the south-west of Scotland. Otherwise, there is some variation in the representation of

---

[4] The so-called 'inversion compounds' of the south-west of Scotland are not discussed here (see for example Ekwall, Eilert, *Scandinavians and Celts in the North-west of England*, Lund and Leipzig 1918; 'Some further notes on inversion-compounds', *Studier tillägnade Axel Kock*, *Arkiv för nordisk filologi*, Tilläggsband 40 (1929), 217-22; Smyth, Alfred, *Scandinavian York and Dublin: the history and archaeology of two related Viking kingdoms*, 2 vols, Dublin 1975: vol. 1, 80-81; Nicolaisen, W.F.H., *Scottish Place-Names: their study and significance*, London 1976: 109-11; Fellows-Jensen, Gillian, 'Scandinavian Settlement in Cumbria and Dumfriesshire: the place-name evidence', in Baldwin, John R., & Ian D. Whyte (eds), *The Scandinavians in Cumbria*, Edinburgh 1985, 65-82: 72-73.

[5] Nicolaisen, W.F.H, 'The type *Burn of–* in Scottish hydronymy', in 'Notes on Scottish place-names', *Scottish Studies* 3, pt. 1 (1959), 88-102: 92-101.

[6] Nicolaisen, 'The type *Burn of-*', 94.

[7] Nicolaisen, W.F.H., 'Names containing the preposition *of*', in 'Notes on Scottish place-names', *Scottish Studies* 4, pt. 2 (1960), 187-205: 194-204.

[8] Nicolaisen, 'Names containing', 196-203.

the different generics involved in Central Scotland, but at the end of the day this variation is slight and does not appear to be very significant either numerically or geographically.

In 1965, Professor Nicolaisen then published in vol. 9 of the same journal an analysis of *Hill of* and *Loch of* names,[9] for example *Hill of Ardo* in Aberdeenshire. The distribution of the 375 *Hill of* names[10] coincides quite closely with that of *Burn of* names, with considerable representation in the Northern Isles, Caithness and the North-east, and a light scattering in Central Scotland. Of the 214 *Loch of* names, a total of 187 are found in the Northern Isles and Caithness, while the remainder are scattered over the usual area in which X *of* Y type names have come to be expected.[11]

The overall picture that emerges of the distribution of these names of similar type is one in which the Northern Isles, Caithness and the North-east are well represented and, to a lesser but nevertheless significant degree for some of the sub-types, also the south-west of Scotland. Structurally what is peculiar about these names, of course, is that they do not follow the expected Germanic syntax of qualifier + head or, in onomastic terms, specific + generic. The name, *Burn of Clashgour*, therefore, consisting as it does of a generic element followed by a genitive construction with the preposition *of* + specific element, is in contrast to the type exemplified by, for example, *Strath Burn* which follows the expected norm of specific (in the genitive or stem form) + generic.

CURRENT VIEWS ON THE PROVENANCE OF THE *BURN OF* TYPE

The main conclusion arising from Nicolaisen's research is that the provenance of the *Burn of* type name appears to be due to the influence of the outgoing language, Gaelic, on the incoming language, Scots, in areas where the latter replaced the former. Names of this type are found principally in former Gaelic language-speaking areas; on the other hand, the type does not occur in Anglian areas, nor in those areas which were anglicised at an early date; nor do they occur in areas which are still, or were until relatively recently, Gaelic speaking. The initial process in the development of this type of name in Scots is understood as one of translation, or part translation. In this way a Gaelic stream name like *Allt an t-Sluic Lèith*, literally 'the stream of the grey hollow', could be rendered into Scots as *Burn of Slock Lee* and, once established, the X *of* Y type was easily extended to the names of features other than watercourses. Given that Scots-language name forms begin appearing in the North-east from around 1220, the period of productivity of X

---

[9] Nicolaisen, W.F.H., '*Hill of–* and *Loch of–*', in 'Scottish place-names', *Scottish Studies* 9, pt. 2 (1965), 175-82.

[10] Nicolaisen, '*Hill of-* and *Loch of-*', 177.

[11] Nicolaisen, '*Hill of-* and *Loch of-*', 178.

of Y type names is seen as having taken off some time after the end of the thirteenth century.[12]

The situation in the Northern Isles appears to have been different, however, since Scots settlement there is not thought to have been earlier than the end of the fifteenth century. In addition, there was historically no Gaelic model there upon which to formulate X *of* Y type names.[13] A solution to this apparent problem was proposed earlier by Jakob Jakobsen when he suggested that names such as *Hill o' Dale* and *de Hill o' de Waters* in the Northern Isles were translations of Norse genitival compounds such as *Vatnahul* 'the hill of the waters' which had a traditional structure of specific followed by generic.[14] Considering the frequency, then, of X *of* Y type names in the Northern Isles, as well as the incidence of obscure elements (from a Scots point of view) within them, the origin of the type here perhaps lay, as Professor Nicolaisen explained, 'in the translation of Norse genitival compounds, including semi-translations in which only the generic term is rendered in Lowland Scots. From there it probably spread to other names in which only the grammatical construction was transferred into Scots, whereas the elements remained untranslated, and to new names utilising either Scots or Norse elements or both.'[15]

The immediate problem with this solution was that while X *of* Y type names in the North-east, for example, could claim a Gaelic model, e.g. *Allt an t-Sluic* 'the stream of the hollow', as antecedent, there was apparently still no syntactically suitable equivalent to be found in the Northern Isles – the structure of the proposed *Vatnahul* was straightforwardly a model for a metaphrastic *Watershill* rather than the periphrastic *de Hill o' de Waters*. The conclusion then reached was that the Gaelic model also appeared to be responsible, though indirectly, for the X *of* Y type names in the Northern Isles, and that the type had been exported northward once it had become established as a productive structure in the naming patterns of the Scots language of the North-east.[16] From current knowledge, it appeared that while the type might have been productive in the North-east from the early fourteenth century onwards, it probably did not become so in the Northern Isles until the end of the fifteenth or beginning of the sixteenth century,[17] though a few examples are attested from the 1490s.[18]

---

[12] Nicolaisen, 'The type *Burn of-* ', 97-98.

[13] Nicolaisen, 'The type *Burn of-* ', 98-99.

[14] Jakobsen, Jakob, *The place-names of Shetland*, London 1936, 5 (cited in Nicolaisen, 'The type *Burn of-* ', 100, and Nicolaisen, '*Hill of-* and *Loch of-* ', 180-81).

[15] Nicolaisen, 'The type *Burn of-* ', 100.

[16] Nicolaisen, '*Hill of-* and *Loch of-* ', 181-82: after Clouston, Storer, & Hugh Marwick in Hugh Marwick, *Orkney farm-names*, Kirkwall 1952, 241-43.

[17] Nicolaisen, 'The type *Burn of-* ', 98.

[18] Nicolaisen, '*Hill of-* and *Loch of-* ', 181.

More recently Professor Nicolaisen has brought the main arguments and conclusions of this important research together within the pages of his book, *Scottish place-names: their study and significance* (1976). More recently still, however, Nicolaisen has been upbraided for, it is claimed, leaving several questions concerning the subject unanswered. While a number of these questions do not seem to be quite to the point, the chief object of Berit Sandnes' article in *Northern Studies* 32 is to pick up the question of the absence of an appropriate local model for X *of* Y type names in the Northern Isles.[19] Sandnes draws attention to the occurrence of the X *of* Y type in English forms such as *Isle of Man* and *Isle of Wight* (*sic*) and notes that they are generally ascribed to French models, such *Île de France* and *Baie de la Seine*, and goes on to cite the Auld Alliance and close ties between the Scottish ruling class and France to support a suggested connection between the French model and the X *of* Y type in the Northern Isles. Finally, since Nicolaisen had noted that Orkney and Shetland, according to current knowledge, underwent settlement in particular from Fife and Kinross, Sandnes points out that *Burn of-* type names are absent from these areas.[20]

Sandnes also ventures in her article to find an appropriate Scandinavian model for X *of* Y type names in the Northern Isles and, after Marwick, sees in names like *Queen of Breckan* or *Queenabreckan* a probable development from a [Norse] phrasal name, *kvín á brekkunni, literally 'the enclosure at the slope', in which the qualifier is introduced by the preposition *á* 'at, or on'.[21] In conclusion, Sandnes concedes that Norse phrasal names containing a preposition 'may have eased the way for *of*-constructions' but holds that 'the underlying pattern seems to be French'.[22]

EVIDENCE FROM THE ISLE OF LEWIS

While carrying out field work on place names in the Isle of Lewis during the period 1983–85, I noted a small handful of forms which appeared to defy expected rules of syntax. An example of this initial group of names was *Beirgh Làgha* [ˌb̥ø̃ð̥'ø̃j ˈLaːɣə] and, although the name was recorded as part of a Gaelic nomenclature, it did not appear to be Gaelic in origin. The first element no doubt represented ON *bergi*, dative of neuter *berg* 'mountain, or rock' which in Lewis seems to have had a more specialised sense of

---

[19] Sandnes, Berit, 'The Bu of Orphir, Burn of Gueth – a Gaelic pattern in Orkney place-names?', *Northern Studies* 32 (1997), 125-28.

[20] In fact, the X *of* Y type construction is commonplace there, e.g. Coalton of Wemyss, Coalton of Balgonie, Milton of Balgonie, Morton of Blebo, Newton of Falkland, Hill of Beath, etc. (I am grateful to Dr Simon Taylor who kindly supplied this information.)

[21] Sandnes, 'The Bu of Orphir', 127-28; Marwick, Hugh, *The place-names of Birsay*, Aberdeen 1970, 95.

[22] Sandnes, 'The Bu of Orphir', 128.

'promontory', often with a bare, usually vertical, rock face.[23] The second element appeared to represent a weak form of the Old Norse adjective *lágr* 'low', in this instance an oblique neuter form. Semantically, this was perfectly fitting given the topography of the area concerned. However, an Old Norse reconstruction **Bergi Lága* has a structure of generic + specific, while the evidence of previously reconstructed, qualified, Old Norse names in the nomenclature showed structures of specific + generic, as for example in *Langabhat* [ˈLãŋkə ˌvaʰt] from ON *Lang-vatn* or *Langavatn* 'the long loch'. Nevertheless, the stress pattern in the Gaelic form, with full stress on the final element, indicated a structure of generic + specific and therefore supported a derivation from ON **Bergi Lága.*

The complete list of Lewis forms to date includes *Beirgh Làgha* (Garenin) from ON *Bergit Lága* 'the low promontory';[24] *Steinn Langa* [ʃtˈa ˈLãŋkə] (Doune) from ON *Steininn Langa* acc. 'the long stone';[25] *Lidh Langa* [ʟˈa ˈLãŋkə] (Doune/ Tolsta Chaolais) from ON *Hlíðin Langa* 'the long hillside';[26] *Amar Sìne* [ãmə ˈṣĩnə] (Tolsta Chaolais) from ON *Hamarinn Sýna* 'the prospect crag'; *Muile Mucal* [ˌmɪlə ˈmü̆ʰkəL] (North Shawbost) perhaps from ON *Múlinn Mykli*, or *Múlann Mykla* acc., 'the large headland'; the possible *Tomaigea Lang* [ˌtʰəmɪgˈa ˈLãŋk] (Crossbost),[27] *Sgeire Langa*[28] (Valasay),[29] *Leum Langa*[30] (NB5655 and NB5657, Ness/ North Tolsta); and the loch names: *Bhata Ciorra* [vaʰtə ˈkʰɪRə] (Tolsta Chaolais) from ON *Vatnit Kyrra* 'the calm loch', (gen.) *Bhata Leòis* [vaʰtə ˈLˈɔːʃ] (NB5153,

---

[23] Cox, Richard A.V., 'Old Norse *berg* in Hebridean place-nomenclature', in Nicolaisen, W.F.H. (ed), *Proceedings of the XIXth international congress of onomastic sciences*, Aberdeen, August 4–11, 1996, vol. 2, Aberdeen 1998, 59-65.

[24] With suffixed article – see below.

[25] Assuming a reduction of the diphthong and loss of the nasal before the lateral in weakly stressed position, cf. the nearby *A' Bheinn Leathainn* [ə ˌvã ˈlehɪnˈ] 'the broad mountain'; compare also *Lidh Langa* [ʟˈa ˈLãŋkə] from **Lìdh Langa*, from ON *Hlíðin Langa* (Note 26).

[26] Assuming reduction of the long monophthong in **Lìdh Langa* (1848 Board of Ordnance, 6 inches : 1 mile, *Lith Langa*); compare *Steinn Langa* [ʃtˈa ˈLãŋkə] from ON *Steininn Langa* (Note 25).

[27] It is conceivable that this form might originate in a Gaelic formation, **Tom Geodh Langa* (< G. *tom* 'hillock' + an Old Norse name as qualifier, perhaps **Gján Langa* 'the long cove') with intrusive schwa and reduction and, finally, loss of weakly stressed vowels.

[28] 1848 Board of Ordnance, 6 inches : 1 mile: *Sgeir a Langa*.

[29] From ON *Skerit Langa*: this is the derivation given by Donald MacAulay in 'Studying the place names of Bernera', *Transactions of the Gaelic Society of Inverness* 47 (1971–72), 313–37: *Sgeir a' Langa*, 331.

[30] 1848 Board of Ordnance, 6 inches : 1 mile: *Leum Lang*. Recorded in Magne Oftedal's notes as ˈʌeːm ˈꝉangə, i.e. [ˈLˈẽːm ˈLãŋkə].

Ness/ North Tolsta) from ON *Vatnit Ljósa* 'the bright, or clear loch',[31] (gen.) *Bhata Godha*[32] [ˌvaʰtə ˈgo-o] (NB2424, Lochs) possibly from ON *Vatnit Góða* 'the good (?i.e. productive) loch', and (gen.) *Bhatan Dìob*[33] [ˌvaʰtə ˈnʲʳᵈiːb̥] (Stornoway) from ON *Vatnit Djúpa* 'the deep loch'; in addition there are four written forms that may belong to this group: *Bhata Breidhe*[34] (NB2130, Grimersta), *Bhata Guaille*[35] (NB5460, Skigersta), *Vata choil*[36] (Back), *Vata Kolla* and *Vata-òram*[37] (North Tolsta).

One possible solution to the question of provenance was that these names were really Gaelic in origin and that Old Norse words had simply been borrowed into the Gaelic language at an earlier date and were therefore available for use in the creation of new Gaelic names. The element *berg* was certainly borrowed at some stage, yielding a feminine Gaelic noun, *beirgh*, which occurs in several names in Lewis,[38] and some of the other appellatives involved, e.g. *sgeir* 'skerry' from ON *sker* nt., are also found as loan-words in Gaelic; additionally, it appeared that there was at least one other example in the Gaelic dialect of an adjective borrowed from Old Norse, namely *brattr* 'steep', found in the name form *Bratag*, literally 'steep place'. Against this argument was the fact that one might have expected the article to occur in such a form, i.e. yielding **A' Bheirgh Làgha*, although this would not necessarily have been inevitable; also, one might have expected greater phonological adaptation of ON *langr* were it a loan-word: the final element in the forms *Steinn Langa*, *Lidh Langa* and *Tomaigea Lang* retain the original Norse cluster of velar + plosive, in contrast to the Old Norse loan-word *langa* [ˈLãyə] 'ling' (< ON *langa*) which does not; similarly, contrast the Lewis place name, *Tunga* [ˈtʰũŋkə] (< ON *Tunga* f. 'tongue of land') with local Gaelic *teanga* [ˈtʲ'əyə] 'tongue'.

As Norse creations, these forms might have represented a very early stratum of names given by Norse settlers in the Hebrides, one possibly paralleled in Norway by examples such as *Landegode* from ON *Landit Góða* 'the good land';[39] or they might have represented the pidgin language of the Norse-Gael

---

[31] Oftedal, Magne, 'Scandinavian place-names in Celtic territory: An attempt at a linguistic classification', in Andersson, T., E. Brylla & A. Rostvik (eds), *Ortnamn och Språkkontakt*, *Norna-rapporter* 17 (Uppsala 1980), 163–91: *Loch Sgeireach* [vahtə ˈL'ɔːʃ], 186.

[32] 1848 Board of Ordnance, 6 inches : 1 mile: *Loch Fadagòdha* – the *grave* accent denoting stress.

[33] MacIver, D., *Place-names of Lewis and Harris*, Stornoway 1934: *Loch vat-n dip*, 77.

[34] 1974 Ordnance Survey, 1 : 10,000: *Cnoc Fada Breidhe* – this hill is now called *Cnoc Mòr na Pàirce Glaise*.

[35] 1848 Board of Ordnance, 6 inches : 1 mile.

[36] MacIver, *Place-names*, 13: *Loch vata choil*.

[37] MacIver, *Place-names*, 17.

[38] Cox, 'Old Norse berg'.

[39] Sandnes, Jørn, & Ola Stemshaug, *Norsk Stadnamnleksikon*, Oslo 1980, 200.

of the Western Isles of the tenth century – the *gic-goc* of the Gall-Ghaidheil.[40] It appears, however, from the evidence now being collated that they in fact represent a relatively late stratum of names.

EVIDENCE FROM NORWAY

Specific elements in Scandinavian place names usually precede their generics, as in *Lang(a)vatn*, above.[41] Nevertheless several names with a structure of generic + specific, as illustrated by the example, *Landegode*, are found in Norway. A number of them contain colour adjectives: e.g. (grey) *Hamrane grå* (Årdalsheia, Rogaland),[42] *Holmengrå* (Fedje, Hordaland),[43] (blue) *Hedleblå* (Hardangervidda, Hordaland), (green) *Hadlet grøne* (Odda, Hardangervidda);[44] and with other adjectives, e.g. (beautiful, fair) *Løkenfagre* (Hylestad, Setesdal),[45] (steep) *Fossen-bratte* (Kvamskogen).[46] In some instances names have had their structures reversed over time, e.g. *Helgøya* (Mjøsa, Hedmark) is recorded as *Eyin helga* in the Middle Ages.[47] It is perhaps worth mentioning that a type of structure with which we are not dealing here is one which features strongly in Lisa Weise's monograph, *Efterstillet adjektiv i danske stednavne* (1969), which deals with superficially similar names in Denmark. In fact this study is concerned with name forms consisting almost exclusively of place name + contrastive qualifier, e.g. *Herstedvester* [hæsdæð ˈvæsdər] 'west *Hersted*', as opposed to

---

[40] Chadwick, Nora K., 'The Vikings and the western world', in [Brian Ó Cuív (ed)], *Proceedings of the international congress of Celtic Studies* 1959, Dublin 1962, 13-42: 26.

[41] Compare the modern Norwegian name, *Langvatn* (Volden, Romsdal) (Rygh, O., *Norske Gaardnavne* XIII, Kristiania 1908, 73).

[42] Hovda, Per, *Norske fiskeméd*, Oslo and Bergen 1961, 72.

[43] Sandnes and Stemshaug, *Norsk stadnamnleksikon*, 158. They also record the name form for Bohuslän.

[44] Helleland, Botolv, *Noka om stadnamn frå Hardangervidda Vest*, MA thesis (*hovedoppgave*), University of Oslo 1970, 129, who cites all these forms (those relating to notes 42-46).

[45] Hovda, Per, *Norske elvenamn*, Oslo and Bergen 1966, 74.

[46] Helleland, *Noka om stadnamn*, 129.

[47] Sandnes and Stemshaug, *Norsk stadnamnleksikon*, 149; Matras, Chr., '*Fjallið Mikla, Áin í Dal, Millum Fjarða and Urð Mans*', *Early English and Norse studies*, Brown, Arthur & Peter Foote (eds), London 1963, 141-49: 142. Compare Orkney *Eynhallow*, below. The medieval name form, *Øyin bygða* (north-west of Oslo – now Storøen, Hole, Buskerud), may have given rise to modern *Bygdø* (the name of an island off Oslo, formerly Ladegaardsøen), see Rygh, O., *Norske Gaardnavne* 5, Kristiania 1909, 5. In Denmark, *Helgeå* (Skåne) is recorded during the Viking period as *áin helga*, see Kristensen, Marius, 'Olddansk syntaks belyst af danske stednavne', *Namn och bygd* 21 (1933), 109-17: 115.

Herstedøster [hæsdæð ˈøsdər] 'east *Hersted*'. Onomastically, this sort of contrastive formation is entirely different from the *Hamrane grå* type.[48]

EVIDENCE FROM THE FAROES, THE NORTHERN ISLES AND CAITHNESS

The structure from Lewis and Norway can also be seen elsewhere. In an important article in 1963,[49] Christian Matras details a number of name structures found in the Faroes which do not correspond to the Germanic norm of specific + generic. The first of these, consisting of generic + specific, e.g. *Fjallið Lítla* 'the little mountain', corresponds to the *Hamrane grå* type of Norway and the *Beirgh Làgha* type of Lewis. But there are not just a few examples of this structure in the Faroes, they occur by the hundred. From the point of view of the reconstruction of Lewis forms, it is important to note that the syntax of these names consists of noun + suffixed article + weak declension adjective, thus *Beirgh Làgha* seems likely to derive from an ON *Bergit Lága* acc. 'the low (or, contextually, lower) promontory', *Steinn Langa* from ON *Steininn Langa* acc. 'the long stone', and *Bhata Ciorra* from ON *Vatnit Kyrra* acc. 'the calm loch'. The same structure is found in several Shetland names, e.g. *Klettin rø* 'the red rock', *Hellyina bretta* 'the steep rock' and *Hellyina wheeda* 'the white rock';[50] in several names in Orkney, e.g. *Howan-Granna* from ON *Hauginn Grœna* 'the green mound',[51] *Breckan-swarta* 'the dark slope',[52] in the island name, *Eynhallow*, from ON *Øyin Helga* 'the holy island'; and in Caithness, e.g. *Landhallow*, from *Landit Helga* 'the holy ground'.[53] There are also one or two examples from Iceland, e.g. *Fjallið eina* 'the solitary mountain', but the type is apparently uncommon there.[54]

In contrast to the undoubted antiquity of the Norwegian examples, Matras reports that many of the names of this type in the Faroes and Northern Isles are comparatively young, although some may be from the Viking Age, as for example the Orkney name, *Eynhallow*. The material from Lewis seems largely impervious to dating, although the pronunciation of the reflex of the initial

---

[48] Matras, '*Fjallið Mikla*', 142, cites the names '*Papa Stour* (and *Papa Little*)' from Shetland as parallels of *Eynhallow* in Orkney and *Eyin Helga* (*Helgøya*) in Norway, but the Shetland names are contrastive forms in which the adjectives qualify an extant, or erstwhile, name form, *Papa*.

[49] Matras, '*Fjallið Mikla*'.

[50] Jakobsen, Jakob, *The dialect and place names of Shetland – two popular lectures*, Lerwick 1897, 88–89.

[51] Marwick, *Place-names of Birsay*, 91.

[52] Matras, '*Fjallið Mikla*', 144.

[53] Matras, '*Fjallið Mikla*', 142 and 144; Ekwall, *Scandinavians and Celts*, 60; Thorson, Per, 'Stadnamn med norrønt upphav i Nord-Skotland', *Fram daa, Frendar* 6 (19590, 29-40: 38. Other Caithness examples include *Clavey Green* from ON *kleifin grœna* 'the green cliff', *Quoynee* from ON *kvíin nýja* 'the new enclosure', see Thorson, 'Stadnamn', 32 and 34, respectively.

[54] Matras, '*Fjallið Mikla*', 145.

cluster of ON *steinn* in one of the examples indicates that at least that name was not borrowed early on in the Viking period.[55] The fact that examples of this structure are found in Lewis, however, must indicate that it was a generally productive one at least before the decline of Norse speech there.

Another structure discussed by Matras is already familiar to us from the suggested derivation of *Queenabreckan* in Orkney from ON **kvín á brekkunni*. According to Matras, this type, consisting of 'a substantive in the form of a common appellative (usually with the definite article) followed by a prepositional phrase which defines the locality, occurs in the Faroes by the thousand', e.g. *Tangin á Barmi, Gjóvin á Oyggj, Áin í Rók*.[56] In Orkney, names such as *Queenabreckan* and *Queenamoan* (from ON *kvín á móinn* 'the fold on the heath'[57]) are taken to have this structure;[58] indeed, as indicated earlier, Marwick assumes this type to be the basis of X *of* Y names there and states that 'As ON *á* passes reg[ularly] in Ork[ney] and Shet[land] into *ō*, it is practically certain that *o'* in the general modern usage *John o' Breck, Willie o' Skaill* ... is the ON *á* rather than the Scots *o'* – a contraction of *of*'.[59] As far as the dating of the structure is concerned, Matras says that written sources indicate only that the type was common two centuries ago in the Faroes, and that he would envisage that the oldest of these names would go back to the Middle Ages, and a few to the Viking Age.[60]

EVIDENCE FROM ST KILDA

This phrasal structure does not seem to be present in Lewis, although it is uncertain how much evidence might survive phonetically. There may be some evidence in St Kilda, however. The Rev. Kenneth Macaulay's *History of St Kilda* (1764) contains several place names including a number which appear to have structures similar to those under discussion.[61] The possible meanings of these names have previously been discussed by Alf Sommerfelt in 1952

---

[55] The initial cluster of ON *steinn* yields G. [ʃt']-, while earlier ON **stainn*, before raising of the diphthong, yields G. [st]- (Oftedal, Magne, 'Norse *steinn* in Hebridean place-names', *Fróðskaparrit* 13 (1964), 225-34: especially 229–32).

[56] Matras, '*Fjallið Mikla*', 145.

[57] Marwick, *Orkney farm-names*, 113.

[58] Matras is more guarded, perhaps in view of Nicolaisen's work: 'this type corresponds to the very common formations found in Orkney and Shetland [...] A thorough study of this Shetland-Orkney type has been made by W.F.H. Nicolaisen, who shows that the names accord with Scottish forms based on Gaelic prototypes. Whatever the final answer may be, it is hardly possible to dissociate the Faeroese names [...] from the similar forms in Orkney and Shetland. It is the same *Sprachgefühl* that has found expression in all three groups of islands.' Matras, '*Fjallið Mikla*', 147.

[59] Marwick, Hugh, *The Orkney Norn*, Oxford 1929, 1, *s.v. A*.

[60] Matras, '*Fjallið Mikla*', 146.

[61] Macaulay, Kenneth, *The history of St. Kilda*, London 1764.

and by A.B. Taylor in 1968.[62] The names of relevance here are *Tober Childa Chalda*,[63] *Multum agria*, *Multum favere* or *Multum fodere*, *Queen o Scot*, *Land dotteros* or the *Doctor's ground*, *Multum taurus* and *Lan-phalin* or *Paul's division*.[64]

The form *Tober Childa Chalda* has been recognised as consisting of the Gaelic word for 'well' (*tobar*), and the Norse words for 'well' (*kelda*) and 'cold' (*kaldr*).[65] The development of this name would seem to have been as follows: initially we have an Old Norse name, *Keldan Kalda* 'the cold well' with an onomastic structure of generic + specific and a syntactic structure of noun + suffixed article + weak declension adjective – familiar to us from the Faroes, the Northern Isles and Lewis; subsequently this form would have been borrowed at some stage into Gaelic and later used as the specific in the creation of a new Gaelic name, namely **Tobar Cealda Calda* 'the well of **Cealda Calda*'.[66] It would have been no impediment to this process of development whether or not the borrowed Norse name was semantically transparent to the Gaelic speakers who created the new name. The initial *chs* in the given form of the name have understandably been taken to represent Gaelic lenition, but the question may not be quite so clear cut. Firstly, it is uncertain how sure we can be of Macaulay's spellings: for two other well names, he gives the forms *Tobirnimbuadh* and *Toberi Clerich*[67] which would seem to contain specifics in the genitive plural (i.e. *nam buadh* 'of the virtues') and in the genitive singular (i.e. *a' Chlèirich* 'of the cleric'), respectively; but lenition of the specific in the latter has not been shown. On the other hand, lenition of a personal name does appear to have been shown in

---

[62] Sommerfelt, 'Further notes on Norse-Gaelic contacts', *Norsk tidsskrift for sprogvidenskap* 16 (1952), 375-76; Taylor, A.B., 'The Norsemen in St. Kilda', *Saga-Book of the Viking Society* 17, pts 2-3 (1967-68), 116-44: 127–29 – both cited in Coates, Richard, *The place-names of St Kilda – nomina hirtensia*, Lampeter 1990: especially 148-52.

[63] Macaulay, *History of St. Kilda*, 101 (cited in Sommerfelt, 'Further notes', 375).

[64] Macaulay writes: 'Among the best of these [arable plots] are the divisions called *Multum agria*, *Multum taurus*, *Multum favere*, or *Multum fodere*, *Queen o Scot*, *Land dotteros*, or the *Doctor's ground*, *Lan-phalin* or *Paul's division*' (*History of St. Kilda*, 33, cited in Sommerfelt, 'Further notes', 375). Macaulay's 1765 edition, *A Voyage to, and History of St. Kilda*, published in Dublin, reads '*Lan-vhalin* or *Paul's division*' (p. 30).

[65] Taylor, 'The Norsemen in St. Kilda', 126. *Tober Childa Chalda* is not the provenance of the name *St Kilda*, which is the result of a miscopying and misplacing of the name of another island or group of islands, *Skildar*, see Taylor, 'The Norsemen of St. Kilda', 135-37. The Gaelic name for St Kilda, modern *Hiort*, is no doubt derived from Norse, cf. the form *Hirtir*, plural of *hjǫrtr* 'stag', of the Norse sagas, see Taylor 'The Norsemen of St. Kilda', 120-23.

[66] Cf. the possible development of the name *Tomaigea Lang*, Note 27.

[67] Macaulay, *History of St. Kilda*, 93 and 99, respectively (cited in Sommerfelt, 'Further notes', 375). For the former, Martin, Martin, *A late voyage to St. Kilda*, London 1698, 24, gives *Toubir-nim buey*.

47

the name *Lan-phalin*, a form perhaps for Gaelic *Lann Phàilìn* 'Paul's (here in a diminutive form) enclosure' – or 'division', after Macaulay. Secondly, while Old Norse loan-names in comparatively young Gaelic creations are often lenited, lenition does not take place internally within those loan-names. Is it possible then that we should take Macaulay's form to be for **Tobar Chealda Calda*?

The form *Multum agria* appears to consist of a similar structure, if Carl Marstrander's derivation from ON *moldu magru* dat. 'the barren ground, or earth' is correct,[68] although this would not appear to be consistent with Macaulay's claim that the name refers to one of the best arable plots on St Kilda.[69] For the specific in the form *Multum favere* or *fodere*, Marstrander suggests a derivation from ON *fagr* 'fair' which, if correct, gives another example of the same structure.[70] The name *Queen o Scot*, however, is fascinating in that it may provide an example of the phrasal or prepositional structure so common in the Faroes and the Northern Isles. A possible derivation for this form, as A.B. Taylor notes,[71] might consist of initial *Kvín á-* 'the enclosure at, or by-' + a place name.

Finally, the form *Land dotteros* may contain ON *land* followed by a specific with genitive *-s*. Taylor rejects any connection with 'doctor' in spite of the alternative name, the *Doctor's ground*; instead he notes the possibility of ON *dóttir* having a genitive in *-s*.[72] If indeed this name does consist of a generic-initial genitive construction – and the form *Multum taurus* may do also[73] – it reflects the structure represented in Orkney by the forms, *Kuikobba* (1329), i.e. *Kví Kobba*, 'Kobbi's sheep-pen'[74] and *Quybernardis* (1492) 'Bernard's sheep-pen'.[75] This structure of generic + genitive personal or occupational name is also attested in Shetland, e.g. *Gjopoba* 'the ravine of the *papa*, or clerics'[76] and in the Faroes where, according to Matras, all the names are young and date from the seventeenth to nineteenth centuries: the oldest recorded example there is *Urð Mans* (1619) 'Mand's scree'.[77] The last of Macaulay's forms, *Lan-phalin*, by virtue of the comparison with *Land*

---

[68] Sommerfelt, 'Further notes', 376, note 1, although Sommerfelt suggests a dative ON *akri* 'tilled ground' for the second element. The name is recorded by Martin, *A late voyage*, 29, as *Multus Agris*.

[69] See note 64.

[70] Sommerfelt, 'Further notes', 376.

[71] Taylor, 'The Norsemen in St. Kilda', 128.

[72] Taylor, 'The Norsemen in St. Kilda', 128-29.

[73] Although Marstrander suggests a derivation with ON *þurr* 'dry'. The name is recorded by Martin, *A late voyage*, 29, as *Multa Terra*.

[74] Matras, '*Fjallið Mikla*', 148.

[75] Matras, '*Fjallið Mikla*', 148; Marwick, *Orkney farm-names*, 91.

[76] Jakobsen, Jacob, *The place-names of Shetland*, 173; Ekwall, *Scandinavians and Celts*, 59.

[77] Matras, '*Fjallið Mikla*', 149.

dotteros, has also been thought to contain ON *land*;[78] however, considering the alternative form,[79] *Paul's division*, this may simply be a rendering of Gaelic *Lann Phàilin*, literally 'Paul's enclosure', as suggested earlier. As far as this particular structure of generic + genitive name in Norse is concerned, Matras, unaware of its possibly wider geographical spread, was wary of linking occurrences on the one hand in Orkney and on the other in the Faroes, arguing that the similarity may be of a more incidental character and 'be due for example to the general post-positional use of the appellative gen[itive] in West Norse'.[80]

CONCLUSION

In spite of the difficulties of interpretation presented by these St Kildan names, it seems likely that the bulk of them, along with the examples from Lewis, represent relatively late Norse names with generic-initial structures similar to those found in the Faroes, in the Northern Isles and in Caithness, and that they are not only evidence for the linguistic continuum that we can expect to have lasted for a considerable period of time over the Atlantic area, but that they are to some extent also characteristic of it.

In addition, while one might argue for a Gaelic model for the origin of X *of* Y type names in the North-east and in other parts of Scotland which allow for such a model on the basis of a suitable sub-stratum, it is submitted that the provenance of the type as found at least in the North of Scotland and in the Northern Isles, if not elsewhere, should be reconsidered in light of the plentiful evidence which suggests that there was indeed a perfectly adequate Scandinavian model for the development of X *of* Y type names there and that it existed within a context of a growing tradition of generic-initial naming structures.

PHONETIC NOTE

Palatisation is shown by a superscript slash, e.g. [t'].
[ʟ'] and [ɴ'] are palatals.
[ʟ] is a velarised dental and [ʀ] a velarised alveolar trill.
Svarabhakti vowels, with stress reflecting that of the preceding vowel, are shown by a *grave* accent, e.g. [b̥øð'ø̀j ˡʟaːɣə].

---

[78] Sommerfelt, 'Further notes', 376; Taylor, 'The Norsemen in St. Kilda', 129: 'Perhaps originally ON *Páls-land*, 'Paul's land.'
[79] Some of Macaulay's alternative forms appear to be aliases, others, as here, to be translations (whether of his own or not is another matter).
[80] Matras, '*Fjallið Mikla*', 149.

GAELIC MILITARY HISTORY
AND THE LATER BREHON LAW COMMENTARIES

Katharine Simms

The establishment of the Irish Scottish Academic Initiative was prompted by the undeniable fact that the literature and history of Scotland and Ireland have many aspects that are best studied in common. In the field of Celtic studies, we have of course a common cultural heritage in medieval Gaelic literature, well demonstrated in the *Fiannaigheacht* material discussed by Professor Donald Meek; but it is also true that each country can offer the other certain unique resources, and unique expertise. As a historian of Gaelic Ireland in the later middle ages, I am deeply envious not only of Scotland's possession of the early sixteenth-century manuscript anthology, the Book of the Dean of Lismore, but of the Scottish scholars who have the ability to decipher the poems it contains, because many of those poems are not merely verse dealing with the early modern court of the earl of Argyll or lays of Fionn mac Cumhaill. In that unique manuscript are also copies of thirteenth-, fourteenth-and fifteenth-century poems addressed to Irish chieftains by well-known bards which are not only as yet unedited, to the best of my knowledge, but to me are quite unreadable. They include poems associated with the court of Cathal Croibhdhearg Ó Conchobhair, king of Connacht (1196-1224) – 'Lá dar shuidh ceathrar re ceird' certainly, and perhaps also 'Go meala a Chathail do chrios' and 'Ionmhain maol da [mel?] an sgian'.[1] There are also poems associated with the Clontarf cycle, about Brian Bóraimhe's famous victory over the Vikings: 'Dá shleigh ag Murchadh mac Fhloinn' and 'Dursan toisg Dhonnchaidh mhic Bhriain'.[2] There are unpublished poems attributed with greater or lesser probability to the fourteenth-century Munster authors, Gofraidh Fionn Ó Dálaigh, and Gearóid Iarla, third earl of Desmond.[3] Even

---

[1] Book of the Dean of Lismore, Nat. Lib. Scot., Adv. MS 72/1/37, pp. 101, 269, 310. See diplomatic text in Quiggin, Edmund Crosby (ed), *Poems from the Book of the Dean of Lismore*, Cambridge 1937, 36, 38, 83.

[2] Book of the Dean, pp. 65, 310 (Quiggin, *Poems*, 55, 83) – a longer version of the latter poem is found in TCD MS 1381 (H.5.9), p. 18 where a concluding verse claims authorship by 'Cam Cluana' [Ó Dubhagáin], d. 1394 – see O'Donovan, John (ed), *Annals of the kingdom of Ireland by the Four Masters* [henceforth *AFM*], 7 vols, Dublin 1851-4, vol. 4, 732.

[3] In addition to poems unsatisfactorily edited in Cameron, Alexander (ed), *Reliquiae Celticae I*, Edinburgh 1892, and M'Lauchlan, Thomas (ed), *The Dean of Lismore's Book*, Edinburgh 1862, 'Do níthear líonta don líon' and 'Maith do hoileadh Gormlaith ghearr' are attributed to Gofraidh Fionn, the former particularly unconvincingly, Book of

more tantalising to me as a historian are the poems 'Geall do chuir *lir ayet er nail*' addressed to the thirteenth-century Munster chief, Conchobhar son of Eoghan Ó Caoimh, and attributed to the well-known bard Giolla Brighde Beag Mac Con Midhe, and the acephalous poem addressed to Tadhg Ó Ruairc, king of Bréifne (d. 1376 or 1435), '... *ard la rechtazow re Braivin*'.[4] In each of these latter cases, it is clear that the phonetic transcription using English script but based on Scottish Gaelic pronunciation, which is the most characteristic feature of the Book of the Dean of Lismore, made it impossible for the learned Professor Quiggin even to reconstruct the original text of the first lines. All the more helpless are interested Irish historians without the expertise of the Scottish scholars.

On the other hand, in Dublin and particularly at the hands of Professor Liam Breatnach in Trinity College, much work has recently been done on the Old Irish law tracts, whose description of early Irish society has a comparative value for Scottish scholars also. In an article on 'The lordship of the Isles', Dr John Bannerman wrote:

> Many of the constituent elements in the prevailing kin-based structure of society [in the lordship of the Isles], in terms of both organisation and law, derive from a pre-twelfth century situation and their fullest expression in written form is often to be found in the seventh- and eighth-century law tracts.'[5]

Since the publication of that article in 1977, the society depicted in Old Irish law tracts has become much more accessible through the publication of Fergus Kelly's *Guide to early Irish law* and *Early Irish farming*.[6] However, the actual brehon law manuscripts as we have them today were copied out in Irish law schools in the fifteenth and sixteenth centuries, with the original Old Irish texts embedded in a series of interlinear glosses dating from the ninth to the twelfth century, and interspersed with longer passages of commentary dating from the eleventh to the sixteenth century. Professor Daniel Binchy, editor of the *Corpus iuris Hibernici*, was very dismissive of the historical value of such later passages of commentary added to the original

---

the Dean, 53, 165 (Quiggin, *Poems*, 47, 66); and 'Mairg do chuirfeadh geall a mnaoi' and 'Tar isteach a dhreoláin bhig' are attributed to 'Gearóid Iarla', Book of the Dean, 11, 303 (Quiggin, *Poems*, 76, 82).

[4] Book of the Dean, 8, 226 (Quiggin, *Poems*, 51, 56).

[5] Bannerman, John, 'The lordship of the Isles' in Brown, Jennifer (ed), *Scottish society in the 15th century*, Edinburgh 1977, 239.

[6] Volumes III and IV in Dublin Institute for Advanced Studies, School of Celtic Studies *Early Irish law series*, Dublin 1988, 1997.

tracts.[7] However, I have recently argued that rather than judging them as primarily intended to explain and interpret the sense of the original Old Irish text, they deserve closer scrutiny in their own right:

> that is, that [the commentarists] were not even trying to explain Early Irish law, but rather to extend its principles into a system that had a contemporary relevance for their own day. At the same time, we are dealing in their work with the legal theory of the schools, with systems rather than the practical reality of recent enactments or judge's precedents. ... [T]he relationship between the theory of the law-schools and the custom of the people was not a one-to-one correspondence and ... the commentaries would only form one of a whole range of sources that would have to be scrutinised and weighed against each other before a clearer picture of the day-to-day realities of Irish society could be obtained.[8]

A reassessment of the value of these commentaries gives us a new source descriptive of Irish social customs, a source relevant to the Ireland of the high middle ages from the eleventh to the sixteenth century (depending on the date of the particular passage of commentary); material, therefore, which may be capable of providing better parallels to Scottish society in the later medieval period than the original Old Irish tracts themselves.

One aspect of society about which the later Brehon law commentaries have quite a lot to say is military service. It is now generally accepted that the Old Irish law tracts were composed by churchmen, and on the whole, they rather avoided the subject of warfare. They were particularly hostile to the men they named the 'sons of death', the *fiana* or *díbergaig,* pagan or semi-pagan cult warriors who had dedicated their lives to the practice of martial arts.[9] A well-known passage in the Old Irish law of sick-maintenance, *Bretha créeige,* denies special treatment to the druid, the cult warrior and the satirist, saying 'neither their dignity nor their sacred character nor their rights nor their [cropped hair] make any increase in [the standard of] their sick-maintenance... for it is more fitting in the sight of God to repudiate them than to protect

---

[7] Binchy, Daniel, 'The linguistic and historical value of the Irish law tracts', *Proceedings of the British Academy* 9 (1943), 33.

[8] Simms, Katharine, 'The contents of later commentaries on the brehon law tracts', *Ériu* 49 (1998), 24, 26.

[9] Sharpe, Richard, 'Hiberno-Latin *laicus*, Irish *láech*, and the devil's men', *Ériu* 30 (1979), 75-92.

them.'[10] This in itself demonstrates a contradiction between the 'dignity, sacred character and rights' accorded to these people by secular society, and the repudiation of them by church lawyers, suggesting that the lawyers' standpoint in the Old Irish period cannot always be taken as typical of society at large. What is even more interesting is that the commentary added to the passage subsequently during the high middle ages, instead of condemning the druid, the berserker and the satirist, praise them for defending the borders of their country from attack or intrusion:

> Even though they have not the property [qualification] of a *bóaire*, the attendance fee of a *bóaire* may be due to them [for the following reasons]: for the avenging of outrages on territory and race by the *aire échta*; and for the magic mist which the druid sends across the border into the midst of the [enemy] host so that they enter not the territory to do damage; for the knowledge of all the metres [classes of poems] which the lampooner possesses, so that he allows no poet to enter the territory save along lawful lines.'[11]

The reason for this reversal of sympathies seems to be that the three different periods at which the Brehon law tracts were composed, that of Old Irish text, Old to Middle Irish glosses, and Middle to Early Modern Irish commentaries correspond to three different environments in which Irish legal studies were cultivated. Liam Breatnach has provided much evidence that in the Old Irish period the authors of the tracts could be actual clerics and monks, equally at home in Latin canon law and the scriptures, which influenced their exposition of Old Irish customary law.[12]

During the tenth to twelfth centuries, at a time when many of the interlinear glosses were added to the law-tracts, authority within the Irish Church had passed to a considerable extent into the hands of laymen holding church office by hereditary right, and inside the church schools we can see a swing towards

---

[10] Binchy, Daniel (ed), '*Bretha crólige*', *Ériu* 12 (1934-38), 41; McCone, Kim, *Pagan past and Christian present in Early Irish literature*, Maynooth 1990, 223.

[11] Binchy, '*Bretha Crólige*', 41.

[12] Breatnach, Liam, 'Canon law and secular law in early Ireland: the significance of *Bretha Nemed*', *Peritia* 3 (1984), 439-59; 'The ecclesiastical element in the Old-Irish legal tract *Cáin Fhuithirbe*', *Peritia* 5 (1986), 36-52; 'On the glossing of Early Irish law-texts, fragmentary texts, and some aspects of the laws relating to dogs', Ahlqvist, Anders *et al.* (eds), *Celtica Helsingiensia. Proceedings from a symposium on Celtic Studies, Societas Scientiarum Fennica, Commentationes Humanarum Litterarum* 107, Helsinki 1996, 11-20; and see Ó Corráin, Donnchadh, Liam Breatnach & Aidan Breen, 'The laws of the Irish', *Peritia* 3 (1984), 382-438.

the use of Irish rather than Latin and towards the study of secular history and secular learning.[13] James Kenney, who compiled the magnificent *Sources for the early history of Ireland* points to this period as the time in which many Latin texts were translated into Irish,[14] including the Irish annals themselves, which become more interested in secular and military matters. This partial laicisation of Irish vernacular scholarship was increased after the church reform of the twelfth century, and the arrival of the English, when native learning, including the study of Irish law, passed completely into the hands of laymen,[15] hereditary brehons attached to the courts of local chieftains whose interest in the law tracts focussed on more secular themes than were dwelt on by the clerics who originally composed them. The most prominent of all the later medieval brehon lawyer families, the MacEgans, originated as secular landowners in Uí Mhaine and are recorded as taking an active part in military forays in that area during the thirteenth and early fourteenth centuries, at least one of these incidents postdating their involvement in legal studies.[16]

Typical of the increased detail on military matters in the later period is a passage of commentary which occurs in the *Cetharslicht athgabála* ('The four ways of distraint'), one of the basic texts making up the *Senchas már*, the great traditional compilation of Old Irish law. Commenting on the original tract's statement that three days' notice is necessary before distraining a man's property for failure to answer the hosting-summons, the commentary tells us that a king might summon three kinds of hosting: firstly, every landowner to legislate or parley; secondly, every shield to plunder; thirdly, every head to a battle.[17] The first phrase, 'every landowner to legislate or parley', meant that when the king needed a ceremonial show of force to attend him to the frontier of his land, where he would meet the neighbouring king similarly attended, to parley and legislate for relations between the territories, only the heads of the noble landowning households need attend him, though they would have to

---

[13] Simms, Katharine, 'An Eaglais agus filí na scol', Ó Fiannachta, Pádraig (ed), *An dán díreach, Léachtaí Cholm Cille* 24, Maigh Nuad 1994, pp. 22-3; 'Literacy and the Irish bards' in Pryce, Huw (ed), *Literacy in medieval Celtic societies*, Cambridge 1998, 240-1.

[14] Kenney, James, *The sources for the early history of Ireland: ecclesiastical. An introduction and guide*, New York 1929, reprint Dublin 1978, 10-11, 732-3.

[15] Simms, Katharine, 'The brehons of later medieval Ireland' in Hogan, Daire & W.N. Osborough (eds), *Brehons, serjeants and attorneys*, Dublin 1990, 51-76.

[16] Simms, 'The brehons', pp. 58-9.

[17] Binchy, Daniel (ed.), *Corpus iuris hibernici* [henceforth *CIH*], 6 vols continuously paginated, Dublin 1978, 381, 889, 1687; commentary on the *Cetharslicht athgabála* in Hancock, W. N., *et al.* (eds) *Ancient laws of Ireland* [henceforth *ALI*], 6 vols, Dublin 1865-1901, 1, 156-9.

come fully armed, because, as the annals often record, such meetings frequently broke up in disorder and became the scene for assassinations.[18]

'Every shield to plunder' apparently meant that when a hostile expedition against another territory was planned, the heads of households would come accompanied by their adult sons and all the warriors in the community would be mobilised. It would have referred in particular to the noble grades as shield-carrying, since nobles' sons were ceremonially presented with a spear and shield[19] when they finished their period of fosterage at the age of fourteen or seventeen years, after which in the early period they might spend another seven years or so in a *fian*, or warrior-band, living off the hunt, practising the martial arts and plaguing, or even plundering, the settled community. From the tenth to the twelfth centuries the *fiana*, who had pagan associations, seem to have been phased out, and the activities of young warriors are described by the Irish annals in two ways, either as *glaslaith* – apparently young amateur fighters, who served only when there was a war on, and were thus inexperienced and vulnerable, or as *ceithirne* – war-bands, who became increasingly mercenary in character as time went on.[20]

The third type of hosting, 'every head to battle', is specifically said to include the *grád tuaithe*, the common freemen. These men are thus distinguished from those who bear shields, and interestingly the armed Irishmen in contemporary illustrations to the twelfth-century works of Giraldus Cambrensis are not shown as carrying shields.[21]

Another long passage of commentary or commentaries written on the tract known as *Lebar Aicle* illustrates both the interest of later lawyers in military matters and their extremely systematised academic approach. It deals with the penalties for *meath slóighidh* or failure to turn out for hosting-duty. One version, found in the legal miscellany T.C.D. 1337, or H.3.18, tells us that failure to respond to the king's summons to war was fined at the rate of a cow for every commoner absent, three cows for each minor nobleman defaulting, a *cumal* (literally a slave-girl, otherwise a unit of value equivalent to perhaps thirty-five acres of land),[22] for a great lord who failed to turn up, two *cumals*

---

[18] Simms, Katharine, *From kings to warlords: the changing political structure of Gaelic Ireland in the later middle ages*, Woodbridge 1987, 64-5, 73.

[19] See Quin, Ernest Gordon, *et al.* (eds) *Royal Irish Academy: Dictionary of the Irish language*, Dublin 1913-76 reprinted as compact edition, Dublin 1983, under 'gaisce'.

[20] Quin, *Dictionary, sub verb.*; Simms, Katharine, 'Gaelic warfare in the middle ages', Bartlett, Thomas & Keith Jeffery (eds), *A military history of Ireland*, Cambridge 1996, 100-106.

[21] E.g. O'Meara, John Joseph (ed), *Gerald of Wales: the history and topography of Ireland*, Harmondsworth 1982, 107.

[22] Mac Niocaill, Gearóid, 'Tír cumaile', *Ériu* 22 (1971), 84 n. 10.

from the king of a *tuath*, four *cumals* from an over-king and seven *cumals* from the king of a province, who failed to join the army of the high-king. If the king of a *tuath* had duly summoned his people to war in the high-king's name, but his subjects failed to turn out, then the people are liable to pay the fine to their own ruler, but only if he *had* issued the hosting-summons. It is the king and not his subjects who must pay the fine to the high-king if no summons was issued. The summons must give the participants three days' notice to collect shoes and armour, and no hosting lasts longer than three days, or the period of notice should be equal in length to the period of military service.[23]

While the reference to a high-king with authority to summon a provincial king to war appears to date this text to the eleventh or twelfth century, a period to which the bulk of the commentaries may belong, it is interesting that the overking's agents are expected to know with some precision how many commoners should have turned up, in order for the system of fines to work. In this case we can compare the specific penalties mentioned in the legal commentary with penalties recorded for failure of hosting-duty in Irish tracts and English state papers in the late medieval and early modern period.

The closest parallel is found in an explanation of the fiscal rights of MacCarthy Mór given as an introduction to the government's survey of the late earl of Clancare's lordship in 1597:

> Garemsloaeg [*gairm shluaigh* 'the hosting summons'] is a risinge upon a warninge given of all the able men of the countrye everye man to be furnished with sufficient weapon and three dayes victuals, and for every defalt to be fyned at a choyce cowe or xx[s] old money, but such of the countrye as were his ennemies would neyther pay nor yeald to any such fyne or risinge.[24]

Here at the very end of the sixteenth century we have the three-day period implied as the normal duration for a hosting, the responsibility of those summoned for their own arming and provisioning, and the fine of one cow for every commoner absent. There is also, however, an admission that this is a theoretical right of lordship, not always enforceable. The 1565 agreement between MacCarthy Mór and O'Sullivan Beare distinguishes between a general obligation on this leading vassal chief to turn out with all his forces when summoned to war, and a more precise duty to contribute to the lordship's permanent military establishment, expressed as a quota assessed by

---

[23] *CIH*, 723-4; Simms, 'The contents of later commentaries', 26-7.
[24] Butler, William F.T., *Gleanings from Irish history*, London 1925, 20.

land area, and it is in connection with this more easily defined obligation that a fine for each missing man is mentioned:

> Sir Owen ought to find continually five galloglasses or five kerne out of every quarter of land arable, inhabited and manured in his country, 'to be afore the guard of the said Earl's person'; and in default of every such galloglasse or kerne to pay 6s. 8d. sterling or one beef, at the Earl's choice.[25]

An agreement between O'Donnell and MacSweeny of Fanad, preserved in the early sixteenth-century Book of the MacSweenys but referred by it back to the late fourteenth century, resembled the arrangement with O'Sullivan in that the number of soldiers was assessed by land area:

> ... this is how the levy was made: two gallowglasses for each quarter of land, and two cows for each gallowglass deficient, that is, one cow for the man himself, and one for his equipment. And Clann Suibhne say they are responsible for these as follows, that for each man equipped with a coat of mail and a breastplate [*scaball*, or pisane], another should have a jack and a helmet; that there should be no forfeit for a helmet deficient except the gallowglass's brain [dashed out for want of it]; and no fine for a missing axe except a shilling, nor for a spear, except a groat, which shilling and groat the Constable [MacSweeny Fanad himself] should get, and O Domhnaill had no claim to make for either.'[26]

In the MacSweeny's family chronicle this is referred to as the imposition for the first time of 'rising-out' (*eirge amach*) and 'hosting' (*sluaigedh*) on the family, rather than the maintenance of a standing force, as in the O'Sullivan agreement, but since MacSweeny's followers were galloglass, and the title of Constable of O'Donnell's army was hereditarily vested in the Lord of Fanad, the distinction in this case may not have been clear to the participants themselves. Earlier in this account O'Donnell is said to have granted the same MacSweeny billeting-rights from the rest of Tír Conaill for 120 axes as *buannacht bona* ('basic' or peacetime billeting).[27] If we take it that the lordship of Fanad was reckoned as containing 60 quarters of arable land, these 120 axemen may have been identical with the galloglass followers

[25] Brewer, J.S., & W. Bullen (eds), *Calendar of the Carew manuscripts 1515-75*, London 1867, 366.

[26] Walsh, Paul (ed), *Leabhar Chlainne Suibhne*, Dublin 1920, 45.

[27] Walsh, *Leabhar Chlainne Suibhne*, 42-3.

MacSweeny must bring to his overlord's hosting. For the end of the sixteenth century the rental of Red Hugh O'Donnell states:

> MacSweeny Fanad gave him ... 10 marks for the support of bonaghts. And he sent to the battlefield 120 galloglasses with armour, and should any of them lack armour he was fined one beef.
> MacSweeny na dTuath rendered the same.
> MacSweeny of Tír Boghaine sent 60 galloglasses with armour, and of these he sent the man to carry the armour and stone (?) of Colmcille free of charge.[28]

In this extract the reference to an additional money payment for the support of 'bonaghts' or hired mercenaries, makes it clear that the quotas imposed on the MacSweenys are seen as their 'hosting-duty'. Galloglass were professional soldiers, who expected wages, and, as we have seen, were billeted at the expense of O'Donnell's other subjects. The observation that the man who carried Colmcille's relics was free of charge implies the others received their wages from O'Donnell. Neither the brehon lawyer's three-day limit on the duration of the hosting, nor the stipulation that subjects coming to the hosting should bring their own provisions apply in this case.

'The Right of O'Neill', a tract dating in its present form to the mid-sixteenth century or later, but clearly containing passages originally composed at many different periods from the twelfth century onwards,[29] varies its treatment of hosting duty from one section to another, from one vassal-chief to another. Sometimes a quota is set, at other times the lord's brehon had a free hand to fix a penalty appropriate to the circumstances:

> The lordship of Ó Néill over the Feara Manach ... a hosting of two hundred men; and if those two hundred should not come, a cow for every man lacking of them; and two in-calf cows for every cow that is not delivered. And if Mag Uidhir himself should come on hosting without his people, he shall receive half the fine ...
> The right of Ó Néill from Uí Eachach Uladh: that they come in full muster, and if they should not come Ó Néill shall have from them what his own judge shall award.[30]

---

[28] I have used here John O'Donovan's translation in Royal Irish Academy 'Ordnance Survey' MS, Strongroom 14/B/7, pp. 423-5, collated with the original Irish text in Cambridge Additional MS 2766/20/7.

[29] Simms, *From kings to warlords*, 3.

[30] Dillon, Myles (ed), 'Ceart Uí Néill', *Studia Celtica* 1 (1966), 7, 9.

The passage about Maguire is of interest. On the one hand it deals with the situation where the local king is prepared to join his overlord's hosting, but his people will not follow him, which is mentioned in the brehon law commentary referred to above, while on the other hand it links the fine for men missing from the muster to a precise quota, which in other sixteenth-century texts seems often associated with the use of mercenary soldiers. It seems therefore almost humorously appropriate to learn that in the course of the Nine Years War (1594-1603):

> M'Guire in the late wars did hire and wage the greatest part of his soldiers out of Connaught and out of the Breny O'Reilly, and made his own countrymen feed them and pay them, and therefore the jury enquiring of escheats found only two freeholders in this country, besides Hugh M'Guire himself to have been slain in the late rebellion.[31]

Three-day hostings, for which the subjects must bring their own food and equipment are mentioned in an indenture between Fearganainm O'Carroll and Lord Leonard Grey, 12 June 1538, which also refers to a longer six week hosting and the additional duty of maintaining the overlord's own mercenaries. The Latin text of articles 3, 4 and 5 may be summarised as follows:

> 3. On the occasion of every 'general hosting' declared by the King's Deputy and Council, Fearganainm and his successors should furnish the Deputy of the day with 12 good horsemen and 24 good kerne, well-equipped for war, with food-supplies for 40 days, and at his own costs and expenses they should attend and serve the commands of the Lord Deputy.
> 4. Moreover O'Carroll grants for himself and his successors, that he and they, when required after reasonable warning, will attend the King's Deputy with all their forces to any small journey or expedition at their own costs and expenses, with food-supplies for three days.
> 5. Furthermore, the King's Deputy will have annually for three months of every year provisioning for 80 galloglasses in the territory of Ely O'Carroll, levied by the reigning O'Carroll of the day.[32]

Although the time-limit mentioned in article 3 might seem reminiscent of medieval English 'knight service', references to expeditions lasting forty days

---

[31] Morley, Henry (ed), *Ireland under Elizabeth and James I*, London 1890, 370.
[32] Betham, William, *Irish antiquarian researches*, 1, Dublin 1827, 105-8.

or six weeks also occur in Irish sources from the Old Irish poem on the rights of the Airgialla, dating about the turn of the eighth century,[33] to prose tracts on the rights of O'Kelly and MacDermot from the high middle ages,[34] while the chief sub-kings under O'Conor, king of Connacht in some undefined period just before or after the Norman invasion were considered bound to indefinite 'service of [expedition and hosting], hostages and escort (*fecht 7 sluaigeadh 7 géillsine 7 coimhdeacht*) and to accompany him at every need on payment of a stipend (*do chiond tuarustail*).'[35]

Another passage of commentary on the Old Irish clause on *meath slóighidh* which occurs in the tract known as *Lebar Aicle* applies the penalty for *meath slóighidh* directly to the question of clientship. Base clients (*daerchéli*) of commoner rank are liable for a fine (*smacht*) if they refuse to go on hosting, or if they withdraw afterwards. Free clients (*saerchéli*) of commoner rank are to pay twice as much as the base ones. Base and free clients of noble rank pay fines (*smachta*) for refusal to go on hosting and honour-price (*enechlann*) for withdrawing subsequently. *Smacht*, we are told, is calculated in relation to the status of the person paying the fine, whereas *enechlann* (honor-price) relates to the status of the person to whom the fine is paid, and is consequently a heavier punishment, because, as the jurist explains, it is worse for the patron to be deserted by his men in enemy territory, than if they had refused to go with him in the first place. Nobles are fined more than commoners because their absence is a greater hindrance to the hosting. If a patron withdraws together with his clients, the patron and the clients are jointly liable for the fine. In the case of clients who do not come in the first place, their fines are collected from their lord, just as he would receive compensation for attacks on their property. The profit from such fines is to be shared, half going to the supreme commander of the hosting, envisaged as the provincial king, and the other half divided in thirds, one going to the immediate commander of the defaulter (in some versions called the *rí tuaithe* or local king), one to the next

---

[33] O Daly, Máirín (ed), 'A poem on the Airgialla', *Ériu* 16 (1952), 181-2, 186. On dating of this text see Byrne, Francis John, *Irish kings and high kings*, London 1973, 115-16.

[34] On O'Kelly see O'Donovan, John (ed), *The tribes and customs of Hy-Many*, Dublin 1843, repr. Cork 1976, 66-7. For the date of this tract see article by Ní Mhaonaigh, Máire, in Owen, Morfydd (ed) *Nosa Ua Maine* (Aberystwyth forthcoming). On MacDermot see Ní Shéaghdha, Nessa (ed) 'The rights of Mac Diarmada' in *Celtica* 6 (1963), 159, 165. For the date of this prose tract see Simms, Katharine, 'Gabh umad a Fheidhlimidh', *Ériu* 31 (1980), 145.

[35] Dillon, Myles (ed.), 'The inauguration of O'Conor' in Watt, John, *et al.* (eds), *Medieval studies presented to Aubrey Gwynn*, Dublin 1961, 190-1, 198. Although it is preserved in a 17th-cent. manuscript, the prototype of this tract may have been originally composed 12th-15th cent., see Simms, 'Gabh umad', 139-44. The words in square brackets replace the single word 'raid' found in Dillon's translation.

highest commander under the provincial king, and the last third to be split among any intermediate ranks.[36]

The Old Irish text of 'Córas Béscnai' ('The regulation of proper behaviour') refers to *slóiged* or *slógad* as one of a list of obligations comprehended in the term *manchuine* – the personal service due from a client,[37] originally meaning the service of a monk, or ecclesiastical tenant, naturally enough, if we see the Old Irish texts as the work of clerics concerned principally with church rulers who had accepted free landowners into their patronage. Another tract, the 'Cáin Sóerraith' ('The law of free fief') tells us that free or noble clients, who bound themselves to a lord for a term of seven years at a time only, owed their patron *manchuine*, glossed as a supply of men for harvest-work, fort-building or hosting-duty,[38] while base-clients, the lesser landowners who bound themselves to a patron for life, are also said to owe their lord escort to public assemblies and on expeditions to avenge their lord's wrongs (*dál ocus dígail*), and liability for the local military service known as 'attack and ward' '*fuba ocus ruba*'.[39] This is particularly significant, because the *fuba* and *ruba* which are here described as owed by the base-client to his personal lord, are elsewhere said to be owed by every landowner, including female heiresses, as a public duty which the king had the power to enforce by seizing the property of subjects who defaulted.[40]

This relates to a question raised by Susan Reynolds in her major criticism of the conventional interpretation of feudalism, *Fiefs and vassals*.[41] When a chief vassal is summoned to war and his tenants follow him, are they turning out because they owe this duty to their immediate lord, or to the king? In the latter case, their immediate lord's function is merely to command them in battle, just as their kin-head would do if they were not clients to a lord. The late brehon law commentaries seem fairly clear that when a chief vassal submits to the local king, he loses control over matters of peace and war, and

---

[36] *CIH*, 330-1, 1169-70, 2156-7; *A.L.I.* vol. 3, 496; see Simms, 'The contents of later commentaries', 28-9. The use of the term *rí tuaithe*, rather than *toísech* or 'chieftain' and the generally conservative terminology of this passage may be an indication of pre-Norman date.

[37] *CIH*, 525.

[38] *CIH*, 1770; Thurneysen, Rudolf, 'Aus dem irischen Recht II. Das Frei-Lehen' in *Zeitschrift für celtische Philologie [Z.C.P.]*, 15 (1925), 240.

[39] *CIH*, 486; Thurneysen, Rudolf, 'Aus dem irischen Recht I. Das Unfrei-Lehen' in *Z.C.P.* 14 (1923), 364-5; Kelly, Fergus, *A guide to early Irish law*, Dublin 1988, 31.

[40] Dillon, Myles, 'Relationship and the law of inheritance' in Binchy, Daniel (ed), *Studies in early Irish law*, Dublin 1936, 139, 155, 157; Binchy, Daniel, 'Distraint in Irish law', *Celtica* 10 (1973), 39-40; *CIH*, 381, 1687.

[41] Reynolds, Susan, *Fiefs and vassals*, Oxford 1994. For an interesting discussion of her approach, see Wormald, Patrick, in the *Times literary supplement*, 10 March 1995, 12.

the military service of his subjects is owed directly to the king, and if that local king submits to a higher authority, the ordinary subjects owe their military allegiance to that higher authority, not to the intermediate lord.

According to the glosses, the duty of 'attack' or *fuba* was rather like the English duty of 'hue and cry'. It obliged landowners to turn out in force to resist raids by pirates, rustlers or wolf-packs, monastic tenants being obliged to go wolf-hunting once a week in winter and summer, every three days in spring and autumn.[42] The Book of the Dean of Lismore contains a poem by Giolla Críost Táilliúr in praise of John Stewart as he prepares to make war on a wolf-pack.[43] The duty of 'ward' or *ruba* involved standing guard on ridges or peninsulas, passes through mountain or forest and the frontiers generally.[44]

A fifteenth-century bardic poem to the chieftain Hugh Magennis whose territory included the Newry Pass, the main entrance into Eastern Ulster, gives us some idea of just how unpleasant this guard-duty could be, in the Irish climate. Magennis is depicted symbolically as watching the track of every sailor and horseman from the Ards Peninsula to the Hill of Howth, standing guard in cold weather, walking by night alone, his hand clasping his sword hilt or his slender spear. However long the winter night, he doesn't take his hand from his horse's rein, he doesn't shelter his head beneath the roof of a house – 'Much danger, little sleep is the burden laid upon Hugh of the cold-edged weapon, it was ever the custom of the heroes before him, in the interests of guarding Ulster.[45]

Ruba, the duty of guarding the passes, can be viewed as a primitive equivalent of the feudal castleward, the duty of vassals to send men at regular intervals to take turns in garrisoning the lord's defensive castle in the locality. The Irish did eventually build castles and place wards in them by the late fourteenth and fifteenth centuries, but this was a development which followed the appearance of standing troops of mercenary soldiers. Already in the eleventh century an extended commentary on the Munster law tract, *Uraicecht Becc* ('the Little Primer'), speaks of the household of a great king as including foreign mercenaries, men of high status, protected by the same honour-price as the king himself, so presumably we should see these as early examples of the Scottish galloglass chieftains. At the same time the commentary refers to native mercenaries of lower status, who may be seen as forerunners of the

---

[42] *CIH*, pp. 487, l. 3; 1687, ll. 25-37; 1788, l. 8; *ALI*, vol. 1, 160-1; vol. 2, 268-71.

[43] Watson, William J. (ed), *Scottish verse from the Book of the Dean of Lismore*, Edinburgh 1937, 176-9.

[44] See note 42 above.

[45] Mac Cionnaith, Láimhbheartach (eag), *Dioghluim dána*, Dublin 1938, repr. 1969, no. 96, qq. 10-16.

kerns of the later middle ages. Some of these mercenaries were living in the king's house, we are told, and some were billeted out among his subjects.[46]

From the mid-ninth century onwards the major Irish kings had begun to reinforce their own armies by using Viking armies, mixed Hiberno-Norse troops or Scots from the Western Highlands and Islands, sometimes as political allies, sometimes, it would seem, as hired mercenaries, the first reference to Scottish commanders in the army of the king of Tír Conaill coming as early as 975, to be followed by similar entries in the eleventh century.[47] By the late tenth century we hear also of native Irish bands of mercenaries, apparently not very large bands, since the 'king-mercenary of all Ireland', Cathal mac Fogartaich, whose death is recorded in the Annals of Innisfallen under the year 968, is described as commanding a hundred armed men, each with a large warrior's shield at his side.[48] Brian Ború in his struggle against the Viking settlers and his meteoric rise to take the high-kingship of Ireland was served by two kinds of mercenaries, amsu, the term used of Cathal mac Fogartaich's followers, and suatrich (Old Norse svartleggi), a word normally applied to the heavy-armoured Viking footsoldiers.[49] At Clontarf, in his final battle against the Norsemen, we are told Brian's forces included at least one Scottish commander, the mórmhair or earl of Marr, while the early twelfth-century propaganda narrative about this battle claims Brian's army was reinforced by ten mórmhair leading troops of Norse soldiers in Brian's service.[50] The concept of Irish mercenary captains of noble birth who roam from one lordship to another looking for employment seems to feature in the Modern Irish law-tract of Giolla na Naomh mac Duinnshléibhe Mhic Aodhagáin c. 1300 A.D.[51] Here they are portrayed as travelling with a troop of followers and a herd of cattle, a grouping known from the late fourteenth to the seventeenth century as a 'creaght' or caoraigheacht,[52] a word for which I have searched in vain in Dwelly's dictionary of Scots-

---

[46] ALI 5, 72-5; CIH 653, 1607, 2323. I am indebted to Professor Liam Breatnach for an estimated eleventh-century date for this commentary.

[47] Mac Airt, Seán & Gearóid Mac Niocaill (eds), The annals of Ulster [AU], Dublin 1983, 308, 314*, 322*, 326, 336, 392, 394, 408, 418, 428, 448*; Stokes, Whitley (ed), The annals of Tigernach [Ann. Tig.], Revue celtique 1895-7, reprinted in two vols, Felinfach 1993, vol. 2, new pagination, 231*, 313-14* (asterisks mark entries which may refer to mercenaries).

[48] Mac Airt, Seán (ed), The annals of Innisfallen [AI], 158; Todd, James Henthorne (ed), The war of the Gaedhil with the Gaill, London 1867, 74.

[49] AI, 164, 166. See Quin, R.I.A. Dictionary, sub verb.

[50] AU, 448; Todd, The war, 168.

[51] CIH, 691-2; Mac Niocaill, Gearóid, 'A propos du vocabulaire social irlandais du bas moyen age', Études Celtiques 12 (1971), 512-46.

[52] Simms, Katharine, 'Nomadry in medieval Ireland', Peritia 5 (1986), 379-91.

Gaelic.[53] In this case they would seek grazing-rights from the patron who brought them into his employ. At other times mercenaries were billeted on the lord's subjects or tenants.

Quartering-rights had existed in early Irish society long before the use of hired mercenaries became common. The Old Irish law tracts tell us that every landowner inherited the public duty of *congbáil* or maintenance, along with his obligations to tribute and hosting-duty, though, not altogether unexpectedly in view of the clerical origins of the Old Irish law tracts in their written form, the commentary applies this right to the benefit of the Church as much as the king. When a Church synod was held in a particular neighbourhood, it says, or the abbot came on circuit with the relics, the local landowners must provide the ecclesiastics and their retinue with food and lodgings. Similarly the muster of the countryside for attack and ward, *fuba 7 ruba*, must be similarly billeted, and the assemblies of the king for legislation or parleys.[54] As in other similar passages, the needs of the aggressive hosting for war, the *slóiged*, are passed over in silence.

In the eleventh and twelfth centuries, however, after the introduction of mercenaries into the warfare of the Irish kings, billeting-rights became much more onerous. It was not that the mercenaries themselves formed such a large proportion of the Irish king's army as yet. A fascinating poem in the Book of Leinster, 'Cert cech ríg oo réil', describes the hosting of the high-king of the north, the king of Aileach, as it goes into battle. The forces of Tír Conaill and Cairbre (in modern terms, Donegal and Sligo) are to be on his right hand, those of the modern Derry on his left, his own people of Inishowen and Tyrone fight with him, the people from Fermanagh and Monaghan fight in front of him, and his foreign and palace mercenaries guard his back. More than anything else, this is a description of the geographical layout of the subject territories of Aileach, but it contains the assumption that mercenary troops form as yet only a small proportion of an over-king's army.[55]

On the other hand the military service owed by a king's natural subjects, or vassal territories, was transformed in the eleventh and twelfth centuries by a new element in the contract of submission, the payment by the king of a retaining fee or 'wages', called *innarrad* or *tuarastal*, both words used of the wages paid to mercenary soldiers.

---

[53] Dwelly, however, does give *caorachd*, as does Maclennan in his dictionary in senses ('stock, cattle and sheep; a raid, a cattle raid') which correspond to part of the semantic range of Irish *caoraigheacht* (see DIL, *cáeraigecht*).

[54] *CIH*, 381, 1687.

[55] O'Donoghue, Tadhg, 'Cert cech ríg co réil' in Bergin, Osborn & Carl Marstrander (eds), *Miscellany presented to Kuno Meyer*, Halle 1912, 258-77.

For instance in 1070, according to the *Annals of Inisfallen*, Mac Gilla Pátraic of Ossory submitted to Tairdelbach Ua Briain king of Munster and received a very large stipend (*innarrad*) of valuables and riches.[56] In 1166 Ruaidri Ua Conchobuir, king of Connacht and Ireland, gave 4,000 cows as a retainer (*tuarastal*) to the men of Dublin, 240 cows and 200 coloured garments to the men of Tír Conaill, 300 cows to the king of Airgialla, 25 horses to the king of Ossory, 70 horses to the king of Cork and so forth.[57] As I have argued in my book *From kings to warlords*, the combined evidence of the *Book of rights*, the verse sections of the *Book of Fenagh* and the tract on the inauguration of Ó Conchobhair[58] indicates that acceptance of such a stipend or *tuarastal* meant the submitting chief entered a quasi-mercenary contract, obliging him to respond with his forces to an overlord's hosting summons whenever called on, without customary limitations as to the season of the year or the duration of the expedition. In return the overlord might undertake to pay wages to the fighting men if they followed him on a campaign far from their own homeland, and he provided for them by billeting these armies on the inhabitants of other territories subject to him, sometimes quartering them forcibly on church lands.[59] Under these new arrangements we hear of campaigns by the high-kings in the twelfth century which lasted for three months or six months at a time, and of armies being billeted on subject territories for spells of a fortnight or a month.

It is frustrating that all the more informative passages in the legal commentaries, in which one can sense real regulations that affect real people, seem to belong to the earlier range of dates from the eleventh to the thirteenth century. Later passages of commentary from the fifteenth or sixteenth century are more theoretical in focus, and deal with such subjects as the six grounds for claiming lawful possession,[60] or the application of the right of seniority in inheritance.[61]

However, the earlier passages with their vivid descriptions of the concerns and conditions of life in the courts of kings who were contemporary with, for example, MacBeth, have surely more to offer the interested enquirer than has yet been acknowledged. And the best of it all is, they are readily available in English translation – because the objections to the reliability of the editions and translations of the Old Irish tracts in the nineteenth-century edition of the *Ancient laws of Ireland* do not apply with nearly such force in the case of the

---

[56] *AI*, 226.
[57] *Ann. Tig. s.a.* 1166.
[58] See above, note 35.
[59] Simms, *From kings to warlords*, 100-103, 118.
[60] Simms, 'The contents of later commentaries', 30-2.
[61] *A.L.I.* vol. 4, 372-3, n. 1; Simms, *From kings to warlords*, 48-9.

Middle and Early Modern Irish commentaries of which I speak. My constant practice has been to riffle through the pages of this venerable edition looking for long passages in small print, since that is how the editors identified commentary. They were not always correct, however, and sometimes printed Old Irish passages in small print as if they were late commentary. When I have found something that particularly interests me from the point of view of content by this method, I am able to enquire as to the date and status of the passage from my Trinity College colleague, Professor Liam Breatnach. When Liam Breatnach's forthcoming detailed catalogue of the contents of D.A. Binchy's diplomatic edition of the *Corpus juris Hibernici* appears, this information will be available to all. A period of much richer understanding of Gaelic society is about to dawn.

THE GAELIC OF ISLAY, A NORTH CHANNEL DIALECT?

James Grant

INTRODUCTION

The Gaelic of Islay is regarded by many Scottish Gaelic speakers as an eccentric south-western dialect, while some Scottish Gaelic scholars have classified it as belonging to a 'peripheral' group of dialects. The main aim of this paper is to consider to which group of dialects the Gaelic of Islay truly belongs, not just in the context of Scotland, but in the context of all the dialects of Gaelic found in Scotland, Ireland and the Isle of Man. This paper is illustrated by a series of maps showing the distribution of features for the areas of the Gaelic-speaking world on which the *Linguistic Atlas and Survey of Irish Dialects* (LASID) and the *Survey of the Gaelic Dialects of Scotland* (SGDS) provide information. Those areas of Scotland, Ireland and the Isle of Man, for the purposes of this paper, will be referred to as the 'Greater Gaidhealtachd'. For the sake of clarity and in order to avoid having a plethora of forms, the orthography used in the maps will be that of Scottish Gaelic alone. In order more fully to understand Islay's dialect relationships, it is necessary to know something about its geographical position and its history.

The Island of Islay lies only 24 miles from the Antrim coast and only 19 miles from Rathlin. From Islay the Irish coastline from Antrim to Inishowen is visible on most days, and at night the lights of cars can be seen moving along the Antrim coast. Being so close to Ireland, Islay was one of the first places in Scotland in which Gaelic was spoken. The first Gaelic speakers known to have inhabited Islay were the Dál Riata. During the fifth century the Dál Riata, from their base in Co. Antrim, expanded their kingdom across the North Channel to encompass the islands and mainland districts of Argyll. Islay was therefore part of a political unit which spanned the North Channel and this was to be a recurrent feature in its history.

The Scottish Dál Riata seem to have lost their territories in Antrim after the Battle of Magh Rath in 637, but eventually expanded eastwards to take over the whole of mainland Scotland. The Annals of the Four Masters record that in the year 835 Gofraid mac Fergusa (a leader of the Airgialla from Armagh) was invited over to Scotland by King Cináed mac Ailpín in order to reinforce the western flank of his kingdom. Gofraid, at the time of his death in 851, seems to have held sway over the islands of Argyll (including Islay), but by the end of the ninth century many of the islands and coastal districts of Scotland had fallen under the control of the Norse. The Hebrides were eventually ruled from the Isle of Man as part of a Norse sub-kingdom, known as the 'Kingdom of Sodor and Man'.

This situation lasted until the twelfth century when a descendant of Gofraid, Somhairle mac Ghille Bhrìghde, wrested control of most of the islands and mainland districts of Argyll from the Norse. Somhairle's grandson was

69

Dòmhnall, and his descendants the MacDonalds, whose court was at Finlaggan in Islay, began to build up their territories into what became known as the 'Lordship of the Isles'. By the year 1411 they controlled about a fifth of the land area of Scotland and also Rathlin and the Glens of Antrim in Ireland.

The Lordship of the Isles was, at the beginning of the fifteenth century, the most autonomous part of Gaeldom. The Lordship was regarded as a threat to the Scottish crown due to the extent of its autonomy and consequently the Lord was forfeited of his territories and powers in 1493. However, most of the constituent clans of the Lordship were allowed to retain control of their lands in return for loyalty to the Scottish crown. The most powerful amongst these clans was the branch of the MacDonalds known as the *Clann Iain Mhòir* in Gaelic and the 'MacDonalds of Dunnyveg and the Glens' in English. By 1565 this branch of the MacDonalds controlled Islay, Colonsay, South Jura, Gigha, Kintyre, Rathlin, the Glens of Antrim and the Route. They too came to be regarded as a threat to the Scottish Crown and the chief was forfeited of his Scottish lands in 1594. Kintyre was planted with Lowland Protestant settlers and Islay, along with most of the other clan lands, came into the possession of various branches of the Campbells.

Islay was taken out of the realms of clan politics in 1726, when it was bought by a merchant proprietor, Daniel Campbell of Shawfield. Although Islay was no longer part of the same political entity as Rathlin and the Glens of Antrim, family and trade ties between the two areas remained strong until the twentieth century. My Islay informants told me that the main social event of the year for Islay people, up until the time of the First World War, was the Ballycastle Fair. They also told me that the Islay people had no problem understanding the Gaelic of Rathlin and the Glens of Antrim (although they do have problems understanding the Gaelic of the Northern Hebrides).

FEATURES OF THE GAELIC OF ISLAY

The centre of the Scottish Gaelic-speaking world now lies in the islands of the Northern Hebrides: Lewis, Harris, North Uist, Skye, Benbecula, South Uist and Barra. Amongst Scottish Gaelic speakers there seems to be a tacit agreement that Gaelic as spoken in and around the central districts of this island group should be accepted for most purposes as the standard form of the language. This is particularly apparent in broadcasting, where broadcasters, no matter their origin, seem unconsciously to adopt the pronunciations and usages which they think common to this area. It follows that any pronunciations or usages which diverge from those found in the Northern Hebrides are regarded by many Scottish Gaelic speakers as aberrant or eccentric. The following eleven features, which are characteristic of the Gaelic of Islay, would tend to be regarded in this way by most Scottish Gaelic speakers. Furthermore, most Scottish Gaelic speakers on hearing these features would tend to assume that they were features unique to that dialect. Some of the following features are also amongst those which have led to a number of scholars characterising the Gaelic of Islay as belonging to a 'peripheral' grouping of dialects.

FEATURE 1: TREATMENT OF INITIAL *SR*

In most dialects of Scottish Gaelic and Manx, where orthographic *sr* is found in word initial position, such as in the words *sràid*, *sròn* and *srannadh*, an intrusive *t* sound is introduced between the *s* and *r* (O'Rahilly 1972, 137). In Irish, according to Ó Baoill (1978, 152), this intrusive *t* is not normally found and the historical pronunciation of *sr* is maintained. In the Islay dialect of Scottish Gaelic the intrusive *t* is never found in natural speech. Although the pronunciation without intrusive *t* sounds unnatural or hypercorrect to most Scottish Gaelic speakers, it is by no means limited to Islay: it is found in all parts of Argyll and Arran, apart from Tiree, Coll and Ardgour (Grannd 2000, 51) and is also found throughout Perthshire (SGDS, Question 800).

Could the occurrence of intrusive *t* in the Isle of Man and the northern three-quarters of the Scottish Gaidhealtachd and its absence from most of Argyll provide us with some clues to the origins of this innovation in pronunciation? At the beginning of the twelfth century much of the northern mainland of Scotland and all of the islands from Man to Shetland were under Norse control. The islands lying to the west of Scotland had become part of the Norse sub-kingdom of Sodor and Man, ruled from Man. During the course of the century Somhairle mac Ghille Bhrighde, who is portrayed in Gaelic sources as a champion of the Gaels, fought to wrest control of territories within Argyll from Norse control. In 1156 Somhairle defeated Godred, King of Sodor and Man, in a sea battle fought off the north-west coast of Islay, after which Godred ceded control of those islands lying between Man and Ardnamurchan, while retaining control over the other islands (MacDonald 1978, 21). According to the Red Book of Clanranald, Somhairle also drove the Norse northwards out of mainland Argyll 'across the River Shiel' (Cameron 1894, 155). At the present day the River Shiel forms a significant dialectal boundary: immediately to the south of this (in Ardnamurchan) Gaelic speakers pronounce initial *sr* without intrusive *t*, while immediately to the north of the river (in Moidart) intrusive *t* is found. History tells us that the islands and seaboard north of Ardnamurchan (as well as Man) were under Norse control for a longer period than most of Argyll and its islands. Could this be the factor which led to the development of intrusive *t* in those districts?

Map 1 shows those areas of the Greater Gaidhealtachd in which forms with or without intrusive *t* are found.

Treatment of initial *sr*

MAP 1

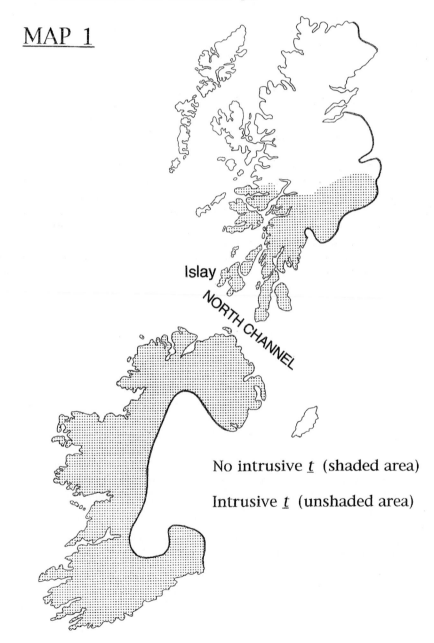

Islay

NORTH CHANNEL

No intrusive <u>t</u> (shaded area)

Intrusive <u>t</u> (unshaded area)

FEATURE 2: TREATMENT OF POSTVOCALIC BROAD *RT*

In most dialects of Scottish Gaelic, where orthographic *rt* is found immediately following a stressed broad vowel, such as in the words *ceart* and *ort*, an intrusive *s* sound is found between the *r* and *t* and sometimes completely replaces the *r*. Ó Baoill (1978, 53) says that 'pronunciations like these do not occur in Irish' while Broderick (1984) shows that such pronunciations do not occur in Manx.

The Gaelic of Islay agrees with Irish and Manx in this respect, for postvocalic broad *rt* in Islay is generally realized without intrusive *s*. On testing throughout the rest of Argyll and Arran for the pronunciation of *ceart* and *ort,* only my informants in Gigha, Kintyre and Arran gave me forms without intrusive *s*.

While I obtained forms with intrusive *s* in Jura and South Knapdale, SGDS, Question 174 obtained forms without intrusive *s* when testing for the pronunciation of *ceart* in these districts. This would suggest that usage in Jura and South Knapdale is mixed. Outwith South Argyll and Arran, SGDS records forms without intrusive *s* at only one other point in Scotland, namely Braemore, Caithness, in the far north of the Scottish mainland.

Map 2 shows those areas of the greater Gaidhealtachd in which forms with or without intrusive *s* are found.

Treatment of postvocalic broad *rt*

<u>MAP 2</u>

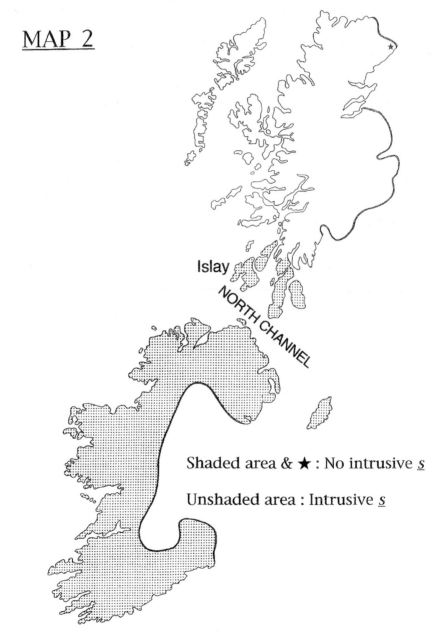

Islay

NORTH CHANNEL

Shaded area & ★ : No intrusive *s*

Unshaded area : Intrusive *s*

FEATURE 3: TREATMENT OF STRESSED *A* BEFORE ORIGINAL LONG *M*

In the Gaelic of Islay, words containing stressed *a* or *o* before original long *m* (such as in *trom* 'heavy', *cam* 'squint' and *àm* 'time') are always pronounced in the historical fashion, with the vowel realized as a short monophthong and the *m* as a long consonant. To most Scottish Gaelic speakers this pronunciation again sounds unnatural or hypercorrect. This is because the great majority of Scottish Gaelic speakers pronounce such words with the *m* realized as a short consonant and the preceding vowel realized as a diphthong.

On testing throughout Argyll and Arran, I found that the three test words cited above were pronounced without diphthongization on the Argyll mainland from Loch Leven southwards and also in the islands of Lismore, Luing, Colonsay, Jura, Gigha and Arran. In addition to these districts, SGDS, testing with the same words (Questions 33, 144 and 871), recorded forms without diphthongization in the island of Easdale and in the easternmost part of the Isle of Mull. They also recorded forms without diphthongization throughout Perthshire and Aberdeenshire. Forms with both a long final consonant preceded by a short monophthong and a short final consonant preceded by a half-long monophthong were recorded in those districts, with no clear pattern being revealed.

Broderick 1984, 59 records a variety of pronunciations of the word *cam* in Manx, but none with diphthongization of the vowel.

The word *am* 'time' is pronounced without diphthongization throughout Ulster and also in Omeath, Co. Louth, Leinster. It is also pronounced without diphthongization throughout Connacht, but generally pronounced with diphthongization in Munster (LASID, Question 919).

It can be seen that the North Channel lies almost at the centre of that area of the Greater Gaidhealtachd in which forms without diphthongization are found.

Map 3 shows where forms with or without diphthongization are found.

Treatment of stressed *a* before original long *m*

MAP 3

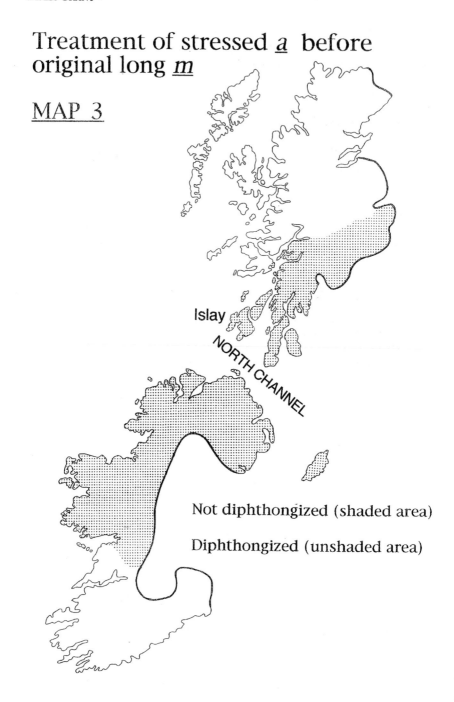

Islay

NORTH CHANNEL

Not diphthongized (shaded area)

Diphthongized (unshaded area)

FEATURE 4: TREATMENT OF OLD IRISH *IG*

In Modern Scottish Gaelic orthography, the Old Irish ending *-ig* is represented by *ich*. This reflects the fact that, in most dialects of Modern Scottish Gaelic, Old Irish *ig* is realized with a final fricative, as /ix'/. Some examples of words in which this occurs are *coilich* 'cockerels', *balaich* 'boys' and *bodaich* 'old men'.

In Manx 'cockerels' is spelled *collee* and Broderick 1984, 89 records that the ending there is pronounced /i/. The Modern Irish spelling of 'cockerels' is *coiligh* and LASID, Question 81 records that the ending is realized as /i/ almost everywhere in Ulster, and as /i/ or /i:/ in all parts of Connacht apart from in Co. Roscommon and in the south western and north eastern parts of Co. Galway. In the rest of Ireland, it is mostly realized as /ig'/ or /ə/.

In the Gaelic of Islay, the Old Irish ending *-ig* is generally realized without the final fricative and is pronounced /i/. Testing throughout Argyll and Arran for the pronunciation of *balaich* and *bodaich*, I found that the realization of this ending as /i/ was limited to only Islay, Gigha, Kintyre and Arran. SGDS, Question 72, testing for the pronunciation of *balaich*, confirms that the realization of this ending as /i/ is found in no other part of the Scottish Gaidhealtachd.

Although the Islay realization of Old Irish *-ig* tends to be regarded within Scotland as something rather unique, it can be seen that this is something which Islay shares with approximately a third of the Greater Gaidhealtachd.

Map 4 shows where the forms /i/ and /i:/ are found.

Treatment of Old Irish *ig*

MAP 4

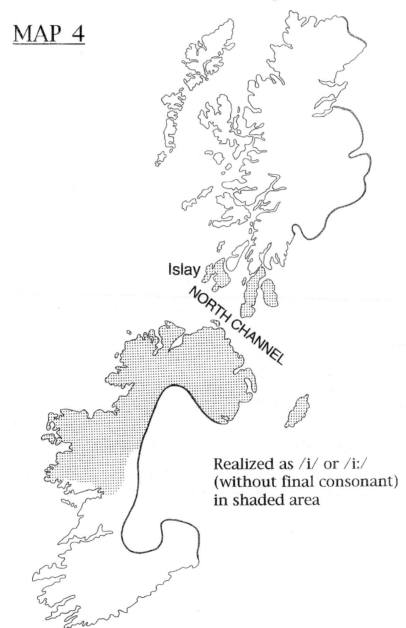

Islay

NORTH CHANNEL

Realized as /i/ or /i:/
(without final consonant)
in shaded area

FEATURE 5: TREATMENT OF POSTVOCALIC BROAD *MH* + CONSONANT

In most dialects of Scottish Gaelic, Irish and Manx (according to the evidence of LASID, Question 905/ Map 231 and SGDS, Question 736) where orthographic *mh* is found following a stressed vowel but immediately preceding a consonant, such as in the word *samhradh* 'summer', the *mh* is usually vocalized. This means that *samhradh* is most commonly pronounced as /saurəɣ/ (with nasalization of the first vowel being very common in Scotland).

In Islay, *mh* in this position is always pronounced as /v/, so *samhradh* is pronounced as /sɛvərəɣ/. Islay has taken this tendency further and added /v/ in this position in at least one word where there is no historical reason for its presence. I refer to the word *dannsadh* 'dancing' which is normally pronounced /dɛvəsəɣ/ in Islay. The word *dannsadh* seems to be a borrowing from the French *dannser* and is normally pronounced /dãũsəɣ/ in Scottish Gaelic. The Gaelic speakers of Islay, on analogy with words such as *samhradh* seem to have adapted this word to suit their own sound system.

Testing throughout Argyll and Arran using the words *samhradh* and *dannsadh*, I obtained forms with /v/ in both words from my informants in only Islay, Colonsay, South Jura, Gigha, Kintyre and Arran. SGDS, surveying all of the Scottish Gaidhealtachd, found that such a pronunciation of *samhradh* was limited to the same area.

Outwith Scotland, forms with /v/ in words of this type seem to be mostly limited to those districts of Ireland closest to Islay and Kintyre: Rathlin and the Glens of Antrim. Holmer 1942 records /savrəɣ/ and /davsəɣ/ for *samhradh* and *dannsadh* in Rathlin, while Holmer 1940 records /savrə/ and /davsə/ in the Glens of Antrim. Outside this area there are only two sporadic occurrences of *samhradh* with /v/: in Rosmuck and Letterfrack in Co. Galway (LASID, Question 905/Map 231).

It is very interesting that the districts of the Greater Gaidhealtachd in which this feature is found largely correspond with the lands which were in clan times under the influence of that branch of the MacDonalds known as the *Clann Iain Mhòir* whose lands lay on both sides of the North Channel.

Map 5a shows those districts of the Greater Gaidhealtachd in which forms with /v/ have been found, while Map 5b shows those areas which were c.1565 under the control of the *Clann Iain Mhòir*.

Treatment of postvocalic broad
mh + consonant

<u>MAP 5a</u>

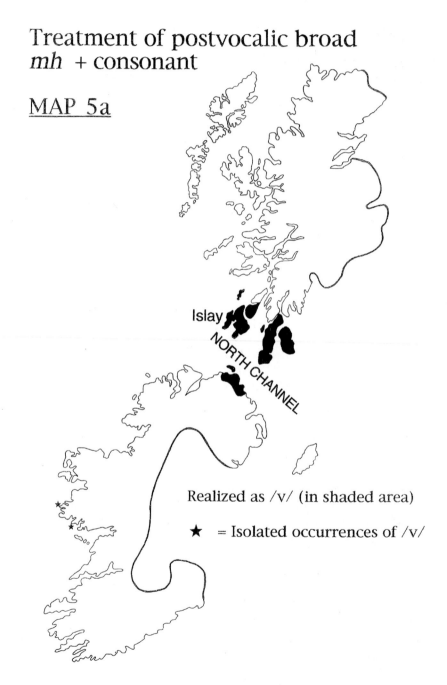

Realized as /v/ (in shaded area)

★ = Isolated occurrences of /v/

Districts under control of the
Clann Iain Mhòir c.1565
(Shaded area)

MAP 5b

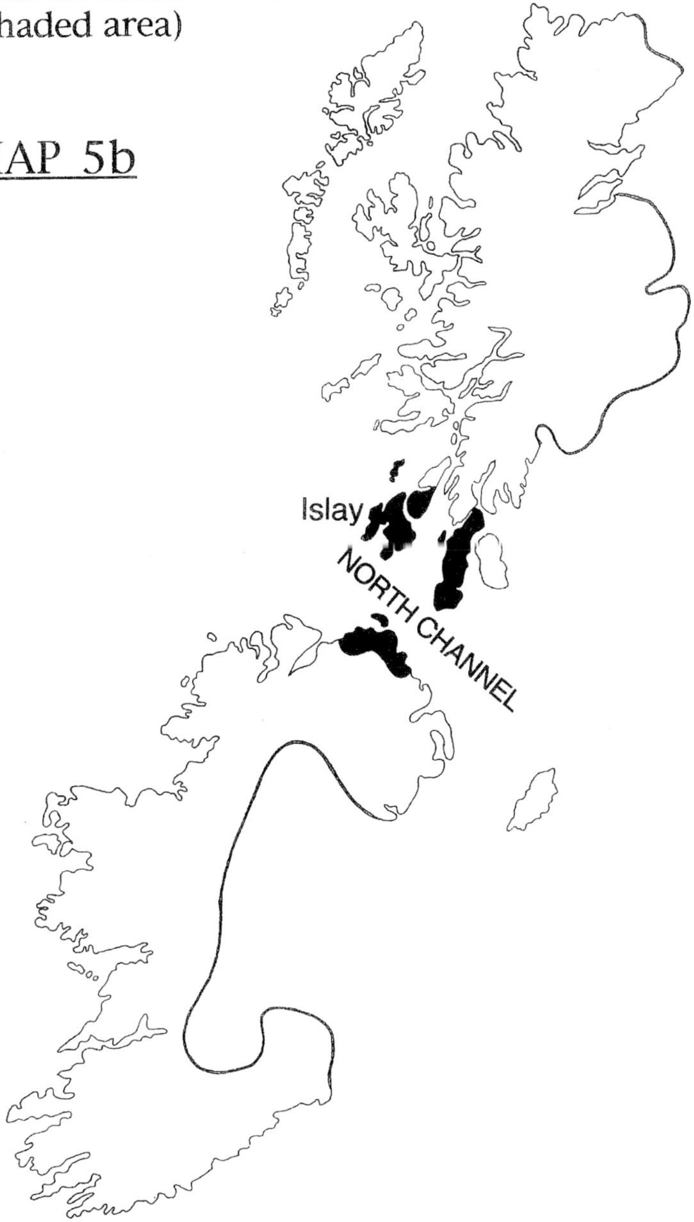

Islay

NORTH CHANNEL

FEATURE 6: *GU ROBH MATH AGAD* NORMAL FOR 'THANK YOU'

The expression normally used in Irish for 'thank you' is *go raibh maith agat*. This also seems to be the case in Manx, for Kneen (1970, 73) gives only *gura mie ayd* for 'thank you'.

The expression normally used by most Scottish Gaelic speakers for 'thank you' is *tapadh leat*. In Islay, however, the expression normally used for 'thank you' is *gu robh math agad*. This to most Scottish Gaelic speakers would be regarded as an Irish expression.

On asking my informants throughout Argyll and Arran to translate the phrase 'thank you', I found that *gu robh math agad* was the expression normally used in Colonsay, Jura, Gigha, Arran, Kintyre, Knapdale, Cowal, Lochgair and Ford. Informants in the rest of Argyll told me that the expression they would normally use was *taing dhuit*. Although my informants in Tiree and Lismore used *taing dhuit*, they told me that *gu robh math agad* was used by previous generations of Gaelic speakers in those locations, so the use of *gu robh math agad* for 'thank you' must have been more widespread in Scotland at one time.

Map 6 shows those areas of the Greater Gaidhealtachd in which *gu robh math agad/go raibh maith agat/ gura mie ayd* is the expression normally used for 'thank you'.

gu robh math agad normal for
'thank you' (in shaded area)

MAP 6

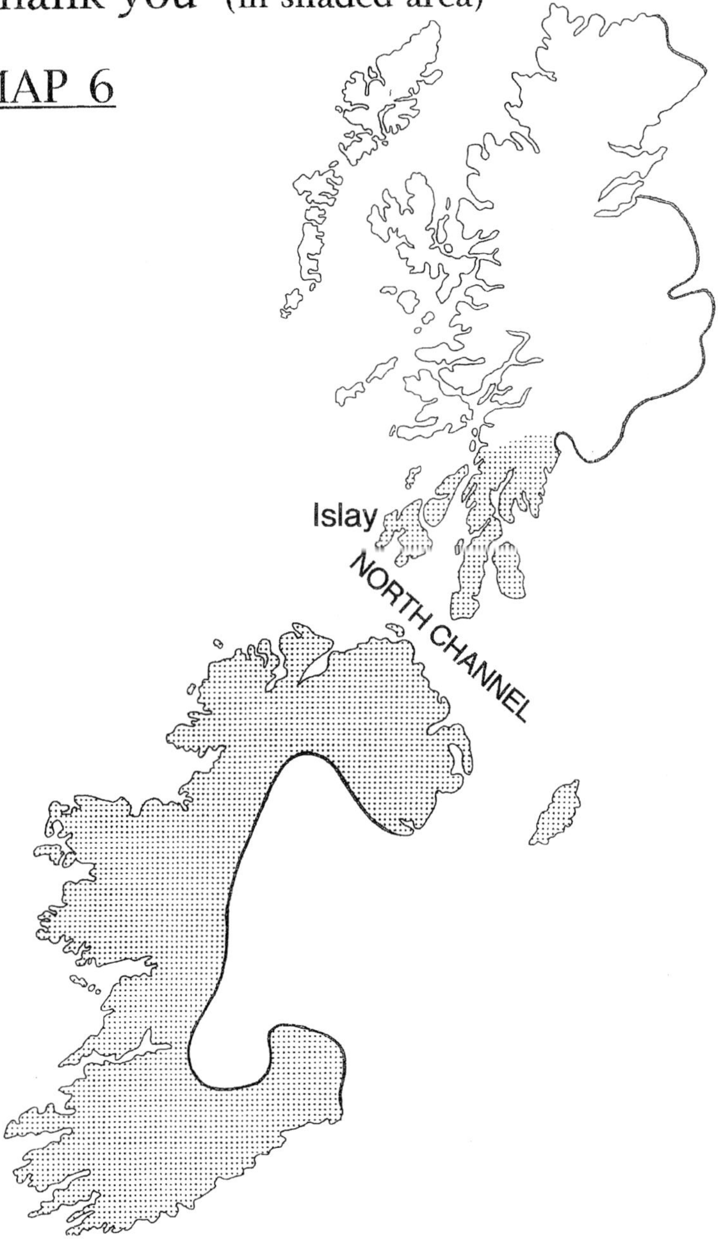

Islay

NORTH CHANNEL

Feature 7: *a' tabhann* normal for 'barking of dog'

In Islay, the word normally used for 'barking' (of a dog) is *a' tabhann*. This can be quite confusing for Gaelic speakers in the Northern Hebrides, where this word is generally understood as meaning 'offering'. In most dialects of Scottish Gaelic the word normally used for 'barking' (of a dog) is *a' comhartaich* although in the dialect of my home district, Strathspey, Inverness-shire, the word normally used is *a' sgeamhann*.

On asking my informants throughout Argyll and Arran to translate the phrase 'The dog is barking', I found that *a' .tabhann* was the word normally used in mainland Argyll as far north as Taynuilt and Dalmally and also in the following islands: Colonsay, Jura, Luing, Gigha and Arran.

LASID, Question 28/Map 11, shows that in Irish *ag tafann* is found for 'barking' throughout Ulster, in Omeath, Co Louth and throughout most of Connacht, apart from Co. Roscommon and the eastern half of Co. Galway, where forms of *ag sclamhairt* are found. (This seems to be related to a word found in Islay, *a' sglamhadh*, which is used with the meaning of a dog 'barking and snapping at one's heels'). In northern and eastern Munster the word used is *ag sceamhail*, which seems to be related to the word used in Strathspey. In South Munster the word used is *ag amhastraigh*. Broderick (1984, 207) records that the word used in Manx is *gounstyrnee*, which he believes is closely related to *ag amhastraigh*.

It can be seen from Map 7 that the North Channel lies close to the centre of the area of the Greater Gaidhealtachd in which *a' tabhann/a' tafann* is the word normally used for 'barking of dog'.

a' tabhann normal for 'barking of dog' (in shaded area)

MAP 7

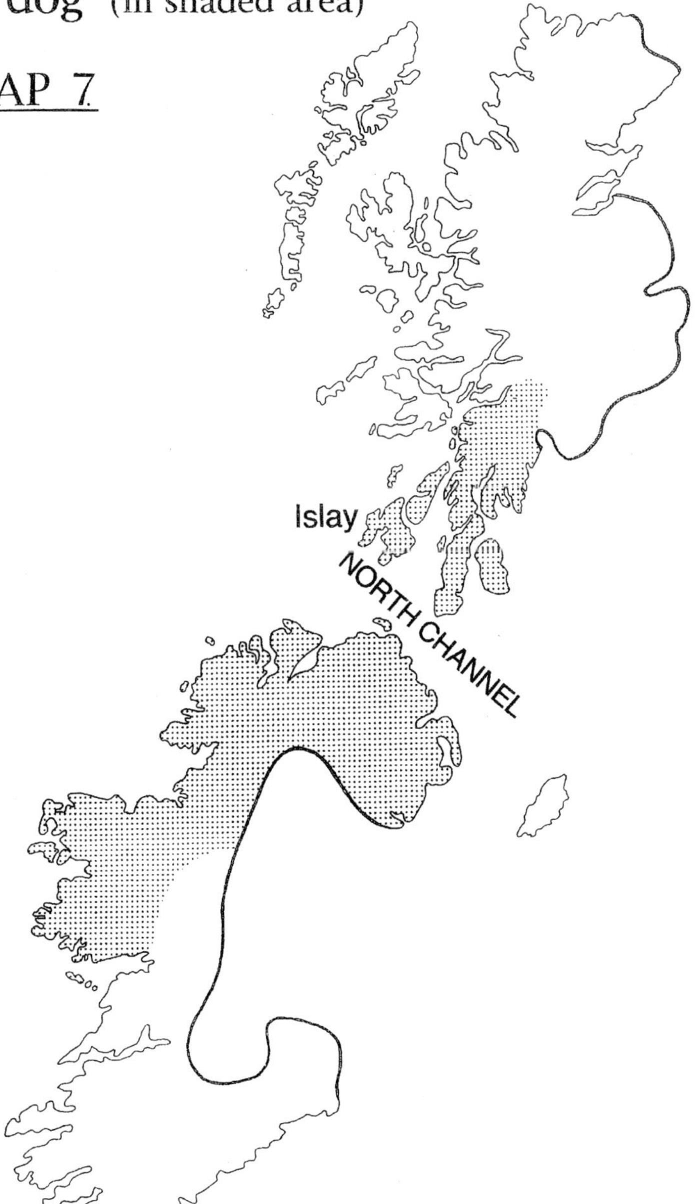

Islay

NORTH CHANNEL

FEATURE 8: *MOTHAICH* VERB NORMALLY USED FOR 'FEEL'

In Islay, the verb normally used for 'feel' is *mothaich*. In most dialects of Scottish Gaelic the verb normally used is *fairich*, although Ó Murchú (1989, 339) records *faithnich* for 'feel' in East Perthshire.

On asking my informants throughout Argyll and Arran to translate the phrase 'I'm feeling tired', I found that the verb *mothaich* was used in the same area as *a' tabhann* (in mainland Argyll from Taynuilt and Dalmally southwards, and also in the islands of Colonsay, Jura, Luing, Gigha and Arran).

In Irish *mothaigh* is used for 'feel' throughout Ulster, and in Omeath, Co. Louth. In Connacht, *mothaigh* is found in only Co. Sligo, Co Roscommon and the north-easternmost part of Co. Galway. It is also found in Munster, in an area on the Cork/Kerry border immediately to the north of Bantry Bay. In most of Connacht and Munster the verb used is *airigh*, which is clearly related to the Scottish *fairich*. The other verb found is *braith*, the use of which is mostly limited to South West Kerry (LASID, Question 421/ Map 131).

Broderick (1984, 192) records *gennaghtyn* and *gennagh* for 'feeling' in Manx. This is clearly related to the verb *faithnich* recorded in East Perthshire by Ó Murchú.

Map 8 shows those areas of the Greater Gaidhealtachd in which *mothaich/mothaigh* is the verb normally used for 'feel'.

mothaich verb normally used
for 'feel' (in shaded area)

MAP 8

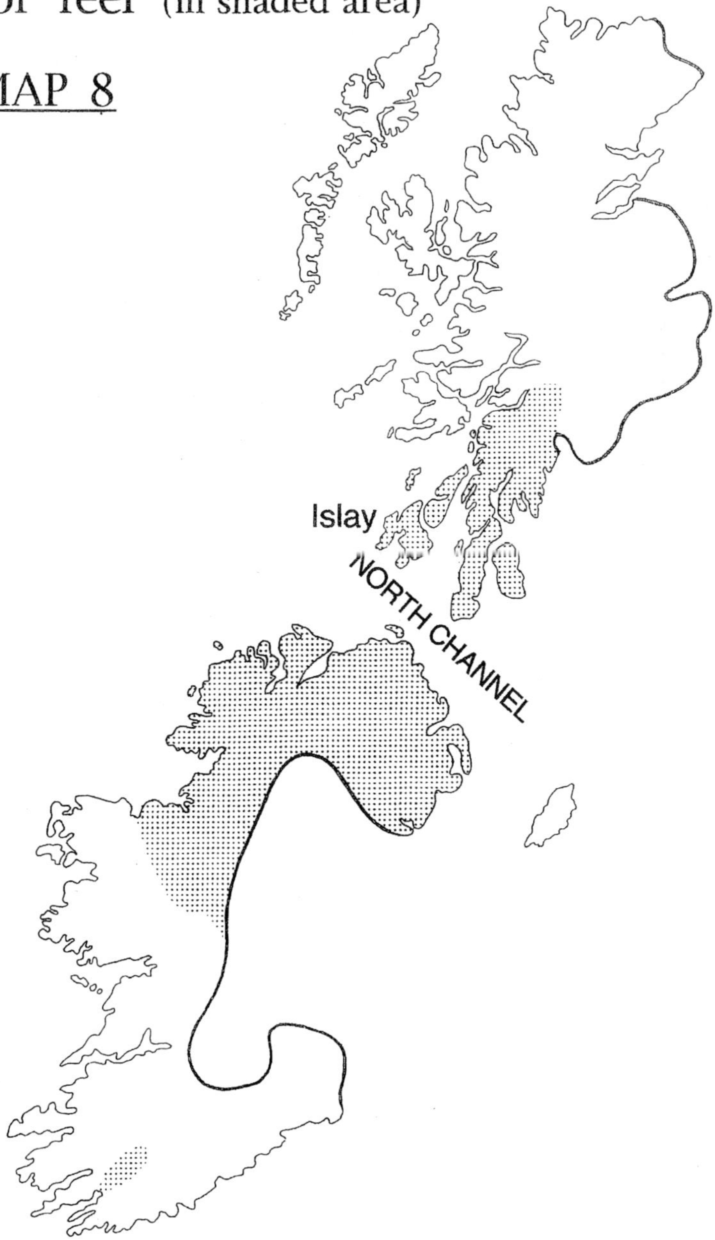

Islay

NORTH CHANNEL

FEATURE 9: *DRÙIN* VERB NORMALLY USED FOR 'CLOSE'

In Scottish Gaelic, the verb most commonly used for 'close' (imperative form) is *dùin*. On asking my informants throughout Argyll and Arran to translate the phrase 'Close the door', I found that *dùin* was the verb normally used throughout the northern and eastern parts of Argyll, while all my informants in Arran, Kintyre and Knapdale responded with the verb *druid*.

In Islay, neither of these forms is in normal use for 'close', the form normally used being *drùin*, which is clearly a hybrid form combining features of both the verbs *druid* and *dùin*. I also obtained this form in the islands of Colonsay, Jura and Gigha and in the mainland district of Mid-Argyll at Lochgair.

Although I obtained *druid* from all my informants in Knapdale, SGDS, Question 359, in trying to establish the quality of the first vowel in the verbal noun *dùnadh*, recorded the form *drùnadh* there. As SGDS was principally a phonological study and the fieldworkers were trying to establish the type of vowel sound used (not the word normally used) it is difficult to tell how this form was elicited, but it would not be surprising if usage is mixed in Knapdale.

In Manx, the only verb recorded for 'close' is *doon*. This is the form given by Kneen (1970, 65) and Broderick (1984, 126).

In Irish, two verbs are in common use for 'close': they are *dún* (sometimes found in the form *dúin*) and *druid*. The verb *dún* is used throughout Munster while *druid* is used throughout Ulster. The verb *dún* is also used in most of the southern half of Connacht while *druid* is used in most of the northern half, although at some points in the northern part of Co. Mayo both verbs are recorded as being used side by side (LASID, Question 487/Map 144).

When considering the two main verbs used in Gaelic for 'close' (*dùin* and *druid*) it is apparent that Islay lies in a transition zone between the use of these two verbs which is situated to the north of the North Channel. Another transition zone between the use of the same two verbs seems to be found in the northern part of Co. Mayo where *dún* and *druid* are found side by side.

This is one of the clearest illustrations of what must have been much more apparent to our ancestors: when the different varieties of vernacular Gaelic are examined we find that we are not dealing with three separate languages, but a series of dialects of what is essentially the same language which shade into one another as one moves from the north of Scotland to the south of Ireland.

Map 9 shows those areas of the Greater Gaidhealtachd in which the three principal forms are found.

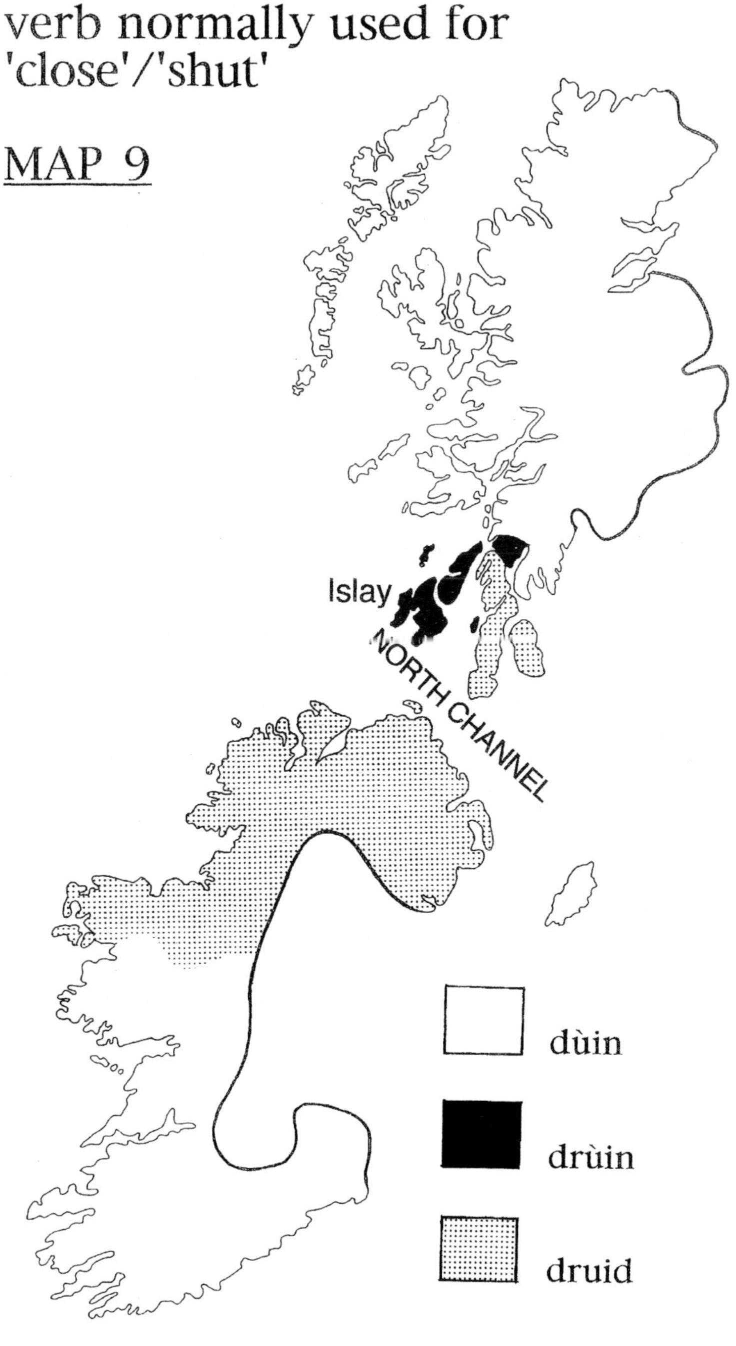

verb normally used for 'close'/'shut'

MAP 9

Islay

NORTH CHANNEL

☐	dùin
■	drùin
▨	druid

FEATURE 10: *BALLAN* NORMAL FOR 'COW'S TEAT'

In most dialects of Scottish Gaelic, the word normally used for 'cow's teat' is *sine*. This is not the case in Islay, however, for the word normally used there is *ballan*.

On asking my informants throughout Argyll and Arran to translate 'cow's teat', I found that outwith Islay *ballan* was used with this meaning in only Colonsay, Jura, Gigha, Arran, Knapdale and Kintyre.

LASID, Question 49/Map 18, shows that the use of *ballán* with this meaning in Ireland is largely limited to Ulster and Omeath, Co. Louth. There are two isolated occurrences of *ballán* in Connacht, in Achill and the Curraun Peninsula of Co Mayo, which probably occur due to migration from Ulster to that area in the seventeenth century (Ó Dochartaigh 1987, 8). In the rest of Connacht and Munster only *sine* is recorded. Broderick (1984, 394) records *sheeintyn* for 'teats' in Man.

It can be seen from this that the use of *ballan/ballán* with the meaning 'cow's teat', within the greater Gaelic world, is largely limited to that area lying on either side of the North Channel.

Map 10 shows those areas of the Greater Gaidhealtachd in which *ballan/ballán* or *sine* are the words normally used for 'cow's teat'.

'cow's teat'

<u>Map 10</u>

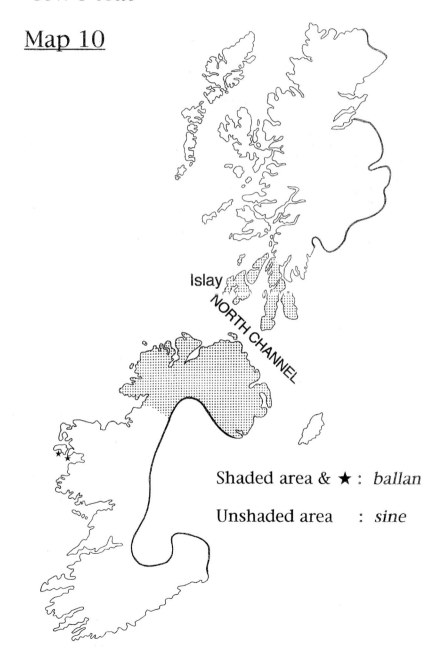

Shaded area & ★ : *ballan*

Unshaded area : *sine*

FEATURE 11: AG ÈIREACHD

In Scottish Gaelic, the normal form taken by the verbal noun of *èirich* 'rise' is *ag èirigh*. The form normally found in Irish is *ag éirí*, while Broderick (1984, 197) shows that Manx has a similar form, *girree*.

In the Gaelic of Islay the form always taken by the verbal noun of *èirich* is *ag èireachd* with a final stop consonant. On asking my informants throughout Argyll and Arran to translate the phrase 'The sun is rising', I obtained the form with final stop *ag èireachd* in only Colonsay and Jura. Although I obtained the form *ag èirigh* from my informants in Kintyre and Arran, Ó Baoill (1978, 77) states that the form with final stop has been recorded in both these districts.

The form normally found in Ireland is *ag éirí*, but the form with final stop *ag éireacht* has been recorded in Rathlin (Holmer 1942, 190) and the Glens of Antrim (Holmer 1940, 112).

It would appear from this that the form with final stop, *ag èireachd/ag éireacht* is, within the Greater Gaidhealtachd, limited to those districts which lie on each side of the North Channel. Again, the districts in which this feature is found correspond closely with those which were in clan times under the influence of the *Clann Iain Mhòir*.

Map 11 shows those areas of the Greater Gaidhealtachd in which the form with final stop, *ag èireachd/ag éireacht* have been found.

'rising' = *ag èireach<u>d</u>* (in shaded area)

MAP 11

Islay

NORTH CHANNEL

CONCLUSION

The distribution of only 11 of those features which are characteristic of Islay Gaelic has been examined here. When we take a list of 89 such features, we discover that only eight other districts of the Gaelic world share over 50% of those features with Islay: Colonsay, Jura, Gigha, Kintyre, Arran, Tayvallich and South Knapdale in Scotland, and Rathlin in Ireland. Although data for only 83 of the 89 features exists for Rathlin, it still shares (by the same calculations) 57.2% of these features with Islay, which is more than both Tayvallich and South Knapdale in Scotland, districts for which we have data for all 89 features (Grannd 2000, 63).

If we do the same calculation for some of the other Scottish islands we find that Skye shares 7.1% of those features with Islay, while Lewis shares only 2.8%. It is therefore not surprising that speakers of Islay Gaelic have difficulty in understanding Gaelic speakers from the Northern Hebrides, while, as my informants told me, Islay people had no difficulty in understanding Gaelic speakers from Rathlin. They also told me that previous generations of Islay people had no difficulty in understanding Gaelic speakers from the Glens of Antrim. In this context, it would have been interesting to have had data for the same 89 features for the Glens of Antrim.

It seems clear that, when Gaelic was still widely spoken in all places between the far north of Scotland and the far south of Ireland, a Gaelic speaker travelling between those two points would have only noticed a series of dialects of the same language gradually shading into one another. The fragmentation of the Gaelic world, the evolution of nation states and the consequent evolution of separate standard forms of the language obscures that fact from us today.

It is clear that the Gaelic of Islay shares some features with the whole of Ireland which are rare in Scotland. Islay also shares many features with the northern half of Ireland, with Ulster in particular, which are rare in Scotland. Islay Gaelic shares many features with those districts of the Gaelic world which lie on each side of the North Channel. In the Gaelic world some of those features seem to be very much restricted to the vicinity of the North Channel. One of the closest dialects to Islay, according to the criteria used here, is that of the Island of Rathlin, which lies to the south of the North Channel.

For the purposes of Gaelic dialectology it would seem helpful to set aside the labels 'Scottish' and 'Irish' and consider the place which the Gaelic dialect of Islay occupies in the wider context of the continuum of dialects of Gaelic which at one time existed, unbroken by the intrusion of English or Scots, between Cape Wrath in Scotland and Cape Clear in Ireland. In this context, the Gaelic of Islay can be seen to belong to a group of related dialects which at one time existed, in the vicinity of and on both sides of the North Channel. From the perspective of the Greater Gaidhealtachd, it therefore seems fair to classify the Gaelic of Islay as belonging to a North Channel group of dialects.

BIBLIOGRAPHY

Broderick, George (1984), *A handbook of Late Spoken Manx* 2, Tübingen.

Cameron, Alexander (1894), *Reliquiae Celticae* 2, Inverness.

Grannd, Seumas (2000), *The Gaelic of Islay: a comparative study*, Aberdeen.

Holmer, Nils M. (1940), *The Irish dialect spoken in the Glens of Antrim*, Dublin.

Holmer, Nils M. (1942), *The Irish dialect in Rathlin Island, County Antrim*, Dublin.

Kneen, J.J. (1970), *English-Manx pronouncing dictionary*, Douglas.

MacDonald, Donald John (1978), *Clan Donald*, Loanhead.

Ó Baoill, Colm (1978), *Contributions to a comparative study of Ulster Irish and Scottish Gaelic*, Belfast.

Ó Dochartaigh, Cathair (1987), *Dialects of Ulster Irish*, Belfast.

Ó Dochartaigh, Cathair (ed, 1994-7), *Survey of the Gaelic dialects of Scotland*, 5 vols., Dublin.

Ó Murchú, Máirtín (1989), *East Perthshire Gaelic*, Dublin.

O'Rahilly, Thomas F. (1972), *Irish dialects past and present*, Dublin.

Wagner, Heinrich & Ó Baoill, Colm, (eds, 1958-69): *Linguistic atlas and survey of the Irish Dialects*, 4 vols., Dublin.

THE BARDIC POET AS TEACHER, STUDENT AND CRITIC
A CONTEXT FOR THE GRAMMATICAL TRACTS

Damian McManus

In his well-known account of the 'poetical Seminary or School', published in the preface to the *Memoirs of the Marquis of Clanricarde* in 1772, Thomas O'Sullevane provides us with some very interesting information regarding the nature of the bardic training school and the routine activities of its members, teaching staff and students alike.[1] The schools, he tells us, were equal in number to the families that followed the calling and were often frequented by students from remote parts, who desired to be at a distance from relations etc. who might interrupt their study. The qualifications required of a student were reading, writing, and a strong memory. On registration the students were examined and assigned to classes or grades in accordance with their age, ability and previous schooling, if any. The training method involved the assignment to each of these classes of subjects suitable to their ability, the metre to be used being determined, and its requirements outlined in detail, by the professor(s).[2] Each student worked alone on the topic in the privacy and darkness of his own apartment and later, when lights had been brought in, committed his piece to writing. The classes then reassembled and the scholars submitted their work to the masters for correction. Depending on how well they had done they were then assigned a fresh topic or invited to work again on the original one. They worked in the dark, according to O'Sullevane, in order to avoid the distractions 'which Light and the variety of Objects represented thereby commonly occasions', the complexity of the work requiring their full and undivided attention. The course lasted six or seven years before a 'Mastery or the last Degree was conferred' and on breaking up in March each year the scholars returned to their own countries, each with an 'Attestation of his Behaviour and Capacity from the chief Professors'.

Though dating from the early eighteenth century, many of the details of O'Sullevane's account can be confirmed by the works of the poets

---

[1] For extracts from the text of O'Sullevane's account see Bergin's introductory lecture on bardic poetry in *IBP*, 3ff., 5-7. On its authorship see Flower, 1953, 15-16. I would like to express my thanks to Professors Cathal Ó Háinle and Liam Breatnach and, in particular, to Dr Eoin Mac Cárthaigh, for reading through a draft of this paper and suggesting numerous improvements. For any error remaining I alone am responsible.

[2] I take O'Sullevane's 'Syllables, Quartans, Concord, Correspondence, Termination and Union, each of which were restrain'd by peculiar rules' to refer respectively to syllable count, quatrain structure, rhyme (*comhardadh*), consonance, *dúnadh* and alliteration (*uaim*).

themselves. His explanation of the reason for composing in the dark, for example, is backed up by the well-known late 16th- or early 17th-century poem *Cuimseach sin, a Fhearghail Óig* 'This is comfortable, O Fearghal Óg' (*IBP* no. 27), in which Fear Flatha Ó Gnímh takes Fearghal Óg Mac an Bhaird to task for boasting that he had composed a poem on horseback. Typically, Ó Gnímh appeals to tradition and names a number of early masters of the craft – Donnchadh Mór Ó Dálaigh, Giolla Brighde Mac Con Midhe, Aonghus Mac Cearbhaill Bhuidhe (Ó Dálaigh),[3] Aonghus Ruadh Ó Dálaigh, Gofraidh Fionn Ó Dálaigh, Tadhg Óg Ó hUiginn, Eoghan Mág Craith (an tÓrthóir, see fn. 47) and a son of Cearbhall Buidhe Ó Dálaigh (Sgolb) – whose custom it was to compose in the darkness (*dorchacht*) of a secluded hut (*both dhiamhair*). Indeed O'Sullevane could be paraphrasing Ó Gnímh's explanation as to why he composes in the dark: *Misi féin dá ndearnoinn dán, / maith leam – lughoide ar seachrán – / bac ar ghriangha um theachta as-teagh, / leaptha diamhra 'gar ndídean. Eadrom is eatoil ghlana / muna n-iadhoinn m'aphradha, / mar dhlaoi díona ar lés an laoi / díogha dom ghrés do-ghéntaoi* 'As for myself, should I make a poem, I like – a thing which keeps me from error – a barrier to keep out the sunlight, and dim couches to guard me. If I did not close my eyelids between me and the bright rays as a protecting veil against the daylight, it would ruin my artistry' (qq 9-10).

Bardic poetry provides many references to the apartment (*both, dánbhoth*) and bed (*leaba*) of O'Sullevane's account,[4] and the building in which these

---

[3] See the discussion of this poet in McManus (2000a 72-4).

[4] For examples of *both, dánbhoth*, usually but not invariably appearing together with the verbal noun *luighe* 'lying' or the noun *leaba* 'bed', see Fearghal Óg Mac an Bhaird's farewell to the Munster schools, *Slán agaibh, a fhiora Mumhan* (*IBP* no. 7: *'Na mbothaibh do bhínn im luighe, / mo lucht cumainn, cead a luadh* 'it is right to mention my friends, in whose huts I used to lie', q 7ab); Tadhg Óg Ó hUiginn's († 1448) elegy on his brother Fearghal, *Anocht sgaoilid na sgola* 'Tonight the schools disperse' (*IBP* no. 38), which refers to both beds (*leabtha*) and huts; *Aonar dhamhsa eidir dhaoinibh* 'I am alone among men' (*IBP* no. 42) where the *teach luighe* is described as a *dánbhoth ór dhoichealgtha sinn* 'poetic hut from which we could not be beguiled' (q 6c); Fear Flatha Ó Gnímh's *Tairnig éigse fhuinn Gaoidheal* 'Irish poetry has come to an end' (*DiD* no. 115.5c: *i leabthaibh both*); Ó Maoil Chiaráin's elegy on his son Fearchor, *Tugadh oirne easbhaidh mhór* (Breatnach, 1942: *a bhoth a ndéanadh an dán* 'O hut, wherein he was wont to make his poetry, q 42); and Ó'n Cháinte's *Mór an feidhm deilbh an dána* 'The composition of poetry is a great task' (McKenna, 1951), which refers to the works of the seven grades of poets as being worthy of their composition in a *dánbhoth* (*fiu an dánbhoth* (*sic leg.* for *daghbhoth*), *a chara, a ccradh*, 9c; see fn. 37 below). The *dánbhoth* (rhyming, as in the last example as well as *IBP* 42.6, with *ánroth* 'second highest grade of poet') appears again in *IGT* ii 354 (= iii 729 and *BST* 213.25-6) in a quatrain which summarises neatly O'Sullevane's depiction of the 'rich Farmers of the Country' providing for the 'Subsistence of the Academy': *Bronnaidh a ghroigh*

were housed, O'Sullevane's 'snug, low Hut', is referred to in the anonymous (probably 17th-century) nostalgic poem, *Aonar dhamhsa eidir dhaoinibh* (see fn. 4), as one of the three forges (*teora ceardcha*) of the bardic academy, viz. the *Teach luighe ar lochta samhla* 'the house of reclining for such as we'.[5]

That students travelled long distances to attend bardic schools, and that they attended several, is also confirmed by the poets themselves. In the late sixteenth century, for example, Eochaidh Ó hEodhasa found himself at odds with his patron, Aodh Mág Uidhir († 1600), because of his decision to absent himself from Aodh's court in Fermanagh in order to engage in further study at some unspecified school or schools in Munster.[6] The dilemma in which this poet's eagerness to pursue his studies (*toil na hoileamhna*) and perfect his art[7] placed him is teased out in his well-known poem *A-tám i gcás idir dhá chomhairle* (see fn. 6), composed in a highly demanding and very ornate metre (*droighneach*). The bulk of the poem is given over to a portrayal of the lavishness of Maguire's court and of Maguire's own generosity, all of which the poet desperately misses, but the message has a sting in it which Ó hEodhasa cleverly buries in extravagant eulogy, designed to serve as an anaesthetic to it.[8] It is simple and to the point: I have embarked on this

---

go górdhaith ,/ do scoil ollaimh nó ánraith / dtlún gel do-rò don righfhlaith / fer 'gá línbhraith dhó i ndánbhoith 'He readily bestows his steeds on the school of an *ollamh* or an *ánrath*; a fine poem will be given to the prince in return; a man will compose it for him in a poetic hut.'

5   Elsewhere we read of the *trí tighe i dtá an Ghaoidhealg* 'the three houses of Classical Irish' (*Mór an feidhm deilbh an dána*, see fn. 4; q 16). For a discussion of this poem see below.

6   See Carney's excellent discussion in his *The Irish bardic poet*, 20-21. Ó hEodhasa refers to Munster twice in the poem *Atám i gcás idir dhá chomhairle* 'I am caught between two (conflicting) counsels' (*DiD* no. 70, and *ISP* p. 72ff.: *Measaim triall... ó sheanmhaigh shíothMhumhan* 'I consider leaving the old plain of peaceful Munster' and *Dá n-anar san ríoMhumhain* 'If I stay in royal Munster', qq 3ab and 6b).

7   See his bitter remark on the consequence of his stay in Munster in his famous, though as yet unpublished, poem *Mór an t-ainm ollamh flatha* 'Great is the title *ollamh* to a prince', *Book of O'Conor Don*, fol 214a, 13d: *meath na healadhna a hóradh* 'perfecting art (merely) results in its decline'. For a discussion of this and related poems see Carney (1967, 22-26), Breatnach (1983, passim) and Ó Háinle (2000, 15-16).

8   The same device is employed again by Ó hEodhasa in his unpublished poem to Cú Chonnacht Óg Mág Uidhir († 1608), *Fada óm intinn a hamharc* 'Far from my mind's eye is her vision' (*Book of O'Conor Don*, fol 252a), which in the present writer's view is one of the finest of all bardic compositions. Here Ó hEodhasa, writing from his sickbed in Fermanagh, is tormented (as in the related poem *Fúar liom an adhaigh-se dh'Aodh* 'Too cold I deem this night for Hugh', *IBP* no. 29) by fear for the safety of his patron on his military campaign in the south of Ireland, but his main preoccupation in the poem to Cú Chonnacht is with finding a diplomatic way of declining the invitation to join him. The discomfort of the campaign would not trouble him, he says, if only he

course of study and I will complete it. This dedication to his art may have
been the cause of the difficulties which Ó hEodhasa experienced later at
Maguire's court; indeed his decision to stay in Munster must be viewed in
the light of his strong contention later, in his famous poem, *Mór an t-ainm
ollamh flatha* (see fn. 7) that an *ollamh flatha* needs to be by his prince's
side, to be at hand at all times to provide counselling etc. It did, however,
stand him in good stead as a poet, and it is noted in the elegy to him by an
unknown poet, *Fogus orchra don éigsi* 'Decay is near to Poesy' (*IBP* no. 48),
where his pursuit of learning is likened to the bee's pursuit of nectar (qq 9-
10). Indeed when defending his own skills in *Mór an t-ainm ollamh flatha*, Ó
hEodhasa describes his learning as the 'choice of true bees' and confirms
that he has studied widely: *Ag gaibhnibh glanta ar gcearda / fuaras
faighreadh drithleanda / a leath Mhogha, a mínleath Chuinn, / togha
fírbheach ar bhfoghluim* 'At the hands of the purifying smiths of our craft I
got a sparkling tempering, both in the southern and in the fine northern half
of Ireland; my learning is the choice of true bees' (q 14),[9] and the very same

---

could be by his lord's side (*Gidh eadh nír annsa liom-sa / bheith aige san éigion-sa /
síon gum thaobhlot a dtoigh nocht / fa aonbhrot re Coin Connacht. Ní éigeorainn gaoth
do ghnáth / chugam tre chumhdach mbéalsgáth / ná sreath braon re bruach mo phill /
re taobh í Dhuach a ndoininn. Ní thuigfinn m'imshníomh ná m'olc / ar ghualainn mhic
Con Connacht / ag roinn aoinphill dúinn is dó / ní shaoilfinn m'úidh ar annró. Dobudh
bruighne na botha / dobudh fíon na fuarshrotha / dobudh clúimh thais cearchaill
criadh / re hais í ghealChuinn Gailian.* 'Nonetheless I would have no problem being
with him in those dire straits with the cold piercing me in a roofless abode, were I under
the one blanket with Cú Chonnacht. Were I by the side of Daoi's heir I would not
complain of the wind piercing me through the cover of an open tent nor of the raindrops
spilling around my pillow's edge. I would be oblivious to anxiety and discomfort by the
shoulder of the son of Cú Chonnacht; were both of us sharing a single bed I shouldn't
think that my attention would be distracted by hardship. Tents would be like palaces
and cold streams of water like wine; pillows of clay would be like soft down were I by
the side of the heir of fair Conn of Gailian.'). But the sting comes in the closing
quatrain in which the poet points out that though he is in spirit, at least, by Maguire's
side in the southwest of Ireland, Cú Chonnacht, if he knew how bad things were for the
poet, would not ask him to actually join him in Munster (*A rinn iarthair inse Gréag / gé
a-tú a bhfochair mic Mairgréag / ód-chí ar seise a dheacra damh / meise ar eachtra ní
iarfadh*).

[9] Here and elsewhere the school is likened to a forge, the professors being the smiths, the
students the material (*adhbhar*) moulded by them into works of art. The curriculum
may also be referred to metaphorically as a 'sea of knowledge' or a 'sea of Irish' (*muir/
lionnmhuir/téachtmhuir an iomhais/ na Gaoidheilge*), as a 'dark ocean' (*aigéan
dorcha*), as a 'purifying river of knowledge' (*sruth ionnalta an iomhais*) or as 'lakes of
learning' (*linnte fis/forais*) which the poet must navigate (*snámh, tomhas, asgnamh*)
successfully. Examples will be found in *Mór an t-ainm ollamh flatha* (q 15), *Mór an
feidhm deilbh an dána* (qq 2, 7, 19-20), *A fhir shealbhas duit an dán* 'O friend who lays
claim to the art of poetry' (qq 27-28), *Créad dá sealbhainn damh an dán* 'What if I do

analogy is made by Piaras Feiritéar in a poem (*Oide a ndréachtaibh an dreasfháil* 'The *dreasfháil* (?) is a master in compositions') in which he lists all the schools visited by the Scottish poet Maol Domhnaigh Ó Muirgheasáin in the mid-seventeenth century: *Gadaidh bláith gach blátha a-muig / don bheich is meadh Maol Domhnaigh* 'he steals the nectar (?) from every flower outside, Maol Domhnaigh is similar to a bee' (O'Rahilly, 1942, q 10ab). There is probably no better example of a poet's circuit of schools than this one.[10]

Studying with different masters of poetry would doubtless have been an enriching experience for any young poet and many refer to it as such. We have just seen Ó hEodhasa's reference to the 'purifying smiths of our craft', viz. the teachers with whom he studied, in *Mór an t-ainm ollamh flatha*. In an earlier poem, *Anois molfam Mág Uidhir* 'Now I will praise Maguire' (*Maguire* no. 23), he apologises to Cú Chonnacht Mág Uidhir († 1589) for the delay in composing praise poetry for him. Ó hEodhasa's excuse is that he was waiting until he was sufficiently well trained (*ollamh d'fhilidh, fortail bhfoghlama, ullamh d'ealathain*). To 'ripen his learning' (*aipdhioghadh m'fhoghlomae*) he attended several schools and studied with a number of professors of poetry with the result that he now feels up to the task (*beiti tend as m'oige ass / gach oide as ferr dá bhfuarass* 'I can be sure of my poetry since I got the best teachers', q 22cd). Again, in the poem *Th'áire, a chumhthaigh, réd chomhrádh* (see fn. 9), in which Fearghal Óg Mac an Bhaird defends himself against alleged criticism of his skill by Flaithrí Ó Maolchonaire, the poet makes the point: *Tarla ó oidibh Innsi hAirt / cruaidh im cheird fuai[r a faghairt]* 'My tempered[11] art has in it a steel-like quality acquired from the professors of Ireland' (q 7ab). Tadhg (mac Dáire) Mac Bruaideadha's measured response to the Connacht lady, Síle, who found fault with his historical knowledge, will be found in his poem *Dob fhearr mo sheachna, a Shíle* 'It had been better to leave me alone, O Síle' (*AiD* no. 41).

---

make claim to the poetic art?' (q 4; for the last three poems see McKenna, 1951) and *Th'aire, a chumhthaigh, red chomhrádh* 'Be careful of what you say, my friend' (*DBM* no. 25, q 8).

[10] Elsewhere we read of scholars from the five provinces of Ireland (*scolaidhe na gcóig gcúigeadh*) attending the Ó Dálaigh bardic school in Baile Uí Dhálaigh in Cork (*Bean dá chumhadh críoch Ealla* 'Críoch Ealla is a woman of two sorrows', *DiD* no. 73, q 14d).

[11] For *faghairt* here compare *faighreadh* in Ó hEodhasa's *Mór an t-ainm ollamh flatha* (quoted above), *Do faighreadh ....meise* in the next quotation cited, and the following apology for not composing in the Classical language: *ní thugsam dhóibh – ní díoth soin – / foighreadh i nGaoidhilg grianaigh* 'I have not given them a tempering in grand literary language' from the poem *A fhir léaghtha an leabhráin bhig* 'O reader of the small book', *DBM* no. 12, q 5ab.

Tadhg says: *Do faighreadh – feirrde m'aigneadh – / meise, a bhaisréidh bhrághaidgheal, / – nach mealltair go hollamh ionn – / i gceardchaibh ollamh Éirionn* 'I was trained (lit. 'burned, tempered') in the smithies of Éire's sages; that has perfected my mind so that I do not easily make blunders, O smooth hand and fair bosom' (q 8). Similarly, in his appraisal of his own skills in a complex field, an appraisal which brought the wrath of a former student down on him (see below), Fear Feasa Ó'n Cháinte mentions, among other things, the fact that he had studied widely: *Do iarras go foirfe ar gceird, / na trí tighe a tá an Ghaoidheilg;*[12] *mairg dan dualas déagsoin ruinn, / ní ar éansgoil fhuaras m'fhoghluim* 'I have gone carefully into all my profession, the three mansions of [Classical] Irish; 'twill go hard with anyone who has to face me for I have acquired my learning in many schools' (*Mór an feidhm deilbh an dána*, see fn. 4; q 16).

Reading, writing and a strong memory were the qualifications required of a student according to O'Sullevane and the first two of these skills are in danger of being underestimated by those who would contend that the 'nature of bardic teaching and training ... was largely oral' (Ó Cuív 1980, 27) or that the grammatical tracts are 'mere museums' of an oral tradition (Murphy, 1953, 190; see McManus, 1996, 181), while the last, the strong memory, is seen to offer support to this understanding of the nature of the bard's profession. In the context in which it occurs O'Sullevane's 'strong memory' might be understood to be a requirement for the composition of a bardic poem as outlined by him, i.e. that it was composed in the dark and not committed to writing until it was finished. Memory would undoubtedly be a factor here in the case of a long poem, but it would be short-term memory, as the poem was committed to writing on composition, and anyone who has composed a bardic poem in strict metre will know that memorising it is the least of one's problems; getting the metre right and expressing oneself clearly is the major task. Furthermore, in a poem already referred to, *Aonar dhamhsa eidir dhaoinibh,* the 'three forges' of the bardic school are identified as (1) *teach meabhraighthe ar mac bhfuirmhidh*[13] 'the house of memorising of our *meic fhuirmhidh* ('second grade of student', see fn. 37), (2) *teach luighe ar lochta samhla* 'the house of reclining for such as we', and (3) *teach breithimh (sic leg.) gach gréasa gloin* 'the house of the critic of each fine work' (qq 5-7). Here memorising (1) and composition (2) are kept apart and the *teach meabhraighthe,* said to be an *áit oiris d'ógbhuidhnibh* 'a trysting-place for youthful companies', sounds more like the counterpart of a modern university library than anything else. We know that the poet's

---

[12] On the lack of alliteration in the first line and the faulty grammar in the second see fn. 55 below.

[13] *Sic leg.*, see Armstrong, 1981, 721, note 60.

training was practical in its orientation and that he could achieve a high standard in his profession by emulating his predecessors, especially those who had gained notoriety for their skill and fluency in the medium. Innovation, experimentation and the development of an individual style were not encouraged in the way that imitation was,[14] so that the emphasis in training will undoubtedly have been on a detailed study of the works of master poets.[15] This much is stated in the preface to the first of the grammatical tracts where we are told: *dlighidh aithne ar reanna 7 úaithne 7 úama 7 chomhardadh ... 7 dlighidh sé ceangal doéilighthi 7 deismireachd iomdha do bheith aigi orra sin ó ughdaraibh 7 ó shaoithibh an dána, do shuidhioghadh a n-aibeóradh* 'he (the trainee poet) is obliged to know *rinn/airdrinn* rhymes, consonance, alliteration and perfect rhyme ... and he should have a firm grasp of these and plentiful examples of them taken from the authors and learned men of poetry, in order to substantiate what he might say' (*IGT* i §2). The poets, no doubt, memorised countless quatrains of verse, the structure of bardic metre being a great asset to the memorising process,[16] but any comfort that an acknowledgment of the role of memory in their profession might be seen to offer to the 'oral tradition' theory is seriously undermined by the countless references to books (i.e. to O'Sullevane's reading and writing) in the poetry itself.

Direct references to books studied in the course of a poet's training will be found, for example, in Maolmhuire Mág Craith's 14th-century poem *Mairg*

---

[14] In fact they are strongly discouraged in Ó Gnímh's criticism of Mac an Bhaird in *Cuimseach sin, a Fhearghail Óig*.

[15] In the mini-contention between Fear Feasa Ó'n Cháinte and Gofraidh Mac an Bhaird to be discussed below, for example, Mac an Bhaird wonders at Ó'n Cháinte not having learned humility from a couplet which he should have come across in his studies, *neach féin go mór dá mholadh / céim as lór dá lochtughadh* 'for a man to praise himself highly is a step sufficient to bring him blame'. The couplet will be found in q 7cd of the poem *Créad agaibh aoidhigh i gcéin* 'Whence comes it that ye have guests from afar', *IBP* no. 20, by the famous Muireadhach Albanach Ó Dálaigh. Ó Dálaigh was one of the poets who was carefully studied in the schools, to judge by the number of quotations of his works in the grammatical tracts, see McManus 1997. Elsewhere (in Fear Flatha Ó Gnímh's early 17th-century *Mairg do-chuaidh re ceird ndúthchais* 'Alas for him who has followed his family profession', *IBP* no. 28) we read of the poets 'discussing the compositions of their ancestors' (*labhairt ar oigdhe a n-aithreadh*, q 2c).

[16] The fact that the profession was hereditary and that poets were *leisin ndán druim ar druim* 'engaged in poetry from generation to generation,' as Gofraidh Fionn Ó Dálaigh puts it (*Madh fiafraidheach budh feasach* 'If one be given to questioning one grows wise', McKenna, 1947, q 51c) in his challenge to their learning, meant of course that they would have been hearing poetry read and recited since early childhood and would have memorised much of it in that way.

chaitheas dlús re dhalta 'Alas that anyone should take pains with his student' (*DiD* no. 104), in which the poet upbraids Gofraidh Fionn Ó Dálaigh for not giving due recognition to the training he (Ó Dálaigh) had received at the Mág Craith school of poetry (*ionann leabhair do léaghmaois / 'gun mhóroide do mhún sinn* 'we read the same books with the great teacher who taught us', q 7bc) and again in Fear Feasa Ó'n Cháinte's 17th-century *Créad dá sealbhainn damh an dán* (see fn. 9) in which the poet defends his skill and training against the criticism of a former pupil (see further below): *Ní dhéanabh* (leg. *dhiongan* ?) *cainnt seachas sain / go bhfuilim inghill ionntaibh / na leabhair do léaghadh liom* 'I content myself with saying that I am well versed in the books that I have read', q 7). Later in the same poem three of these works are named, viz. the *Treasfhocal*, q 32, the *Agallamh* and the *Uraiceapt*, q 33. Elsewhere bardic poetry abounds with references to books read by the poets, in particular *seinleabhair* 'ancient books' (sometimes *seinleabhair seanchaidh* 'ancient books of the *seanchaidh* 'historian', i.e. traditional law, charters, annals, rolls of kings, genealogies etc.) to whose authority the poet appeals in asserting the claims to kingship of his patrons,[17] books containing the prophecies of the saints in which the fame of the patron was foreseen,[18] books containing accounts of the feats of valour or generosity or of the fame of the patron's ancestors,[19]

---

[17] In his poem *Díleas breith do bhreith le seilbh* 'It is right to judge in favour of possession' (*AiD* no. 17), for example, Tadhg Óg Ó hUiginn asserts the authority of books as repositories of ancient tradition to which the poet should refer in making claims for his patron and to which he should give new and fresh form in his own work (*Breath na leabhar is lé a-tám* 'I will abide by the judgment of the books' and *i mbeirt naoidhe is cóir an chairt* 'the charter (found in ancient books) should be set forth in ever-fresh form', qq 2a and 3d). Further appeals to *breath/rádh/glór/iúl na (sein)leabhar* will be found in secular verse at *AiD* 31.20, 44.2, *DiD* 100.14c, *LCAB* 9.17, *LB* 19.5, 32.25, *O'Reilly* 8.27, *Táinig an Croibhdhearg go Cruachain* (*Book of O'Conor Don*, fol. 314a, q 29), *Cia rer fuirgheadh feis Teamhrach, Irish Texts* ii p. 96, q 6, and in religious verse at *AiD* 75.7 and 76.2, to mention but a few examples. Note in particular the rhyming pair *(sein)leabhar : deimhneaghadh* in the context of books as authorities (*AiD* 44.2, 75.7, 76.2, *DiD* 84.24, *LB* 19.5).

[18] See for example *LCAB* 17.20, *O'Reilly* 12.3, *Maguire* 20.11.

[19] In *DiD* 102.15, for example, we are told that the deeds of generosity of Síol Suibhne can be followed *i seinleabhraibh eoil*, and the poet goes on to recount a story testifying (*sgéal fiadhnaighthe*) to that generosity, while the fame of the Uí Thuathail as recorded in ancient books is what ensures that Sadhbh Ní Thuathail, wife of Aodh (mac Seaáin) Ó Broin, has flocks of importunate poets on her doorstep (*clú a sean isna seinleabhraibh / do bhean bú don bhanLaighnigh* 'the fame of her ancestors in ancient books has deprived this Leinsterwoman of (many) cows', *LB* 7.42cd). In Muireadhach Albanach Ó Dálaigh's poem to Cathal Croibhdhearg Ó Conchobhair (*Tabhrum an Cháisg ar Chathal* 'Let us spend Easter with Cathal', *IBP* 23), on the other hand, the statement that Cathal is frequently mentioned in books (*Minic luaittear i leabhraibh /*

books containing stories drawn upon by the poet as exempla (*(uir)sgéala*) or evidence to substantiate a point he is making.[20] In our earliest *Duanaire*, or (family) poem-book, the fourteenth-century *Book of Magauran*, we hear of the poet's duty to read such stories,[21] and when a poet offers his patron immortal fame (*clú, bladh, ainm, tairm*) in return for fleeting wealth,[22] that

---

oidhre taoibhgheal Toirrdhealbhaigh, q 25) appears, from the context, to refer to contemporary praise poetry to him.

[20] See, for example, *O'Reilly* 6.17, 19.2 and *TD* 24.18. In singing the praises of Marta Staford, wife of Sir Henry O'Neill, Fear Flatha Ó Gnímh turns to his books to substantiate his claim that Irishmen have always fancied foreign women as partners in marriage: *Báin inghen Sgáil go sgéimh ngloin, / Nar inghen Lóigh, 'nar leabhraibh, / techt na mban gcéibhfhionn gcnistiogh / go magh Éireann innistior* 'Báin, daughter of Sgál of fair complexion and Nar, daughter of Lógh; in our books we are told that these fair-haired, soft-skinned women came to Ireland [from overseas]' (from the poem *Mná tar muir, maith le Gaoidheal* (sic leg.?) 'Irishmen like women from overseas' *LCAB* no. 30, q 3) while Brian Mac an Bhaird, author of *Ní ar aois roinntear rath buanna* 'A mercenary's success does not depend on age' (Ó Foghlú, 1992, 109), finds support in learned books for his contention that age is not a man's greatest asset (*Fríoth i leabhraibh le lucht eóluis / nach aois is mó fhoghnus d'fhior*, q 2).

[21] *Sloinnfidh mé dod mhalaigh dhuinn / blagh sgeoil do sgríobhadh romhainn; / sgéal léaghthar mar as dual dúinn / do ghéabhfthar uam man ionnhnúdh* 'I will tell thy dark brow a piece of a story written of old, a story which we (poets) have to read; thou shalt hear it; it is about envy' (*Do fhóir Dia dobrón ó mBriuin* 'God has healed the sorrows of the scions of Brión', *Magauran* no. 24, q 13).

[22] See, for example, Tadhg Dall Ó hUiginn's formulation of this standard contrast in his poem *Maith an ceannaighe Cormac* 'A good merchant is Cormac' (*TD* no. 31): *Féach an fearr iomlaoid oile, / ná an mhoirn shuthain shíorroidhe, / téid don fhlaith ionfhuair fhaoilidh, / ar mhaith ndiombuain ndíomhaoinigh. Gearr do mhairfeadh na maoine, / bhronntar le flaith Formaoile, / 's budh buain na molta ar marthain, / dá ghruaidh chorcra chomharthaigh.* 'Behold is there any better exchange than the lasting enduring honour that goes to the pleasant, kindly chieftain in return for vain transitory wealth. Not for long would the riches given by Fermoyle's lord remain, but the praise of his noble, ruddy countenance shall endure eternally.' (qq 4-5). A similar sentiment is found in Fear Flatha Ó Gnímh's *Ná maith dhúinn t'fhiach, a Énrí* 'Do not abandon your claims against me, O Henry' (*LCAB* no. 22): *Diombuan i ndiaidh gach flatha / seóid oile acht an ealatha / a mionnmhasail nó a gcradh chreach / ní mhar d'ionnmhusaibh h'aithreach. 'Na ndiaidh ar dhumhaidh sealga / caidhid coin sluaigh Seinealga? / na cluana caidhid a sguir? / 's mairid duana 'na ndeaghuidh.* 'Shortlived after every prince are all valuables with the exception of art. Nothing of your ancestors' treasured mazers or plundered booty survive today. Now after their passing on, where on the hunting course are the hounds of the host of old Ealga, and where are the steeds of their meadows? And yet their poems survive them' (qq 9 and 10). The immortality of praise is given beautiful and clever expression in Donnchadh Ó Muirghiosa's *Dá rann déag mo dhúthracht d'Aodh* 'Twelve quatrains are my offering to Aodh' (*LB* no. 6): *Is é an moladh oighri as fhearr / bhias choidhche ar fhearuibh Éireann; / scél a n-aghaidh eóil nach fuil, / maraidh go deóidh an domhuin* 'Praise is the greatest heir the men of

immortality is the poet's praises, fashioned and fixed in strict verse and recorded in books which will long outlive poet and patron alike.[23]

Of all the 'books' the poets studied, the most important were undoubtedly those containing the works of the master-poets they strove to emulate.[24] The anonymous author of the elegy on Eochaidh Ó hEodhasa, *Fogus orchra don éigsi* 'Decay is near to Poesy' (*IBP* no. 48), gives expression to this process of study and emulation when he says of Ó hEodhasa that 'he went through the writings of the schools' (*do-chuaidh tré screaptraibh na scol*, q 6a), seeking out the very best that was available (*óradh ughdar an léighinn* 'the gilding of the authors of learning') which he then brought into his own verse ('*na dhán as-teach go ttabhair*, q 9). Echoes of earlier poems are well known in bardic verse[25] and are ample testimony to this aspect of the trainee poets'

Ireland will ever possess; it is no contradiction of fact to say that it will survive until the end of time' (q 3).

[23] See, for example, *Bheith dá laoidhibh i leabhraibh / i ndiaidh mheic mheic Toirdhealbhaigh, / buaine leam ná cogail chruidh / mar gheall don bhogfhuil Bhrianaigh* 'That his lays be recorded in books [and survive long] after the grandson of Toirdhealbhach is, in my opinon, a more permanent testimony to the kindly race of Brian than hoarding cattle could secure' (from Lochlainn Óg Ó Dálaigh's *Léigidh dhamh mo Dhomhnall féin* 'Leave to me my own Domhnall', *IBP* no. 19, q 20) and *Sgéala h'oirbheart is t'fhéile / uaisle crú do chaithréime / ad dhiaidh dá deighleanmhain d'fhior / biaidh a seinleabhruibh sruitheadh. A bhfad a-nonn budh núidhe / m'fhighe ag iomrádh t'fhortúine;* 'The tales of your valour, your generosity, the nobility of the blood in your battle-roll, these being traced by a man when you are gone, will be found in the old books of the ancients. In distant times to come my verse celebrating your fame will still be fresh' (*Gabh mo shuirghe, a ua Émuinn*, qq 12-13, Carney, 1955, 268, 273).

[24] Emulation by patrons of their ancestors' liberality towards, or respect for, poets is, of course, the counterpart to the poets' emulation of the master-poets themselves. For a fine example see Cú Chonnacht Ó Fialáin's *Bheith re dán dlighidh ollamh* 'An ollamh is entitled to practice the craft of poetry,' addressed to Tomás Mág Uidhir (*Book of O'Conor Don*, fol. 246b): *Do bhrethaibh na rígh roimhe / na heirgedh úa ar n-Áodhuine / rugadh breth dho úaisligh ionn / fa sech lé huaislib Eirionn. Ni rachaid rioghradh Bhanbha / a n-aghaidh na healadhna / do-gabhair gach áon ór fhás / 'na mháor tabhaigh ar Thomás* 'Let the descendant of our Aodh not distance himself from decisions made by kings before him; many a decision made by the nobility of Ireland ennobled us. The dynasties of Ireland will not oppose the men of art; [the example of] each of Tomás's ancestors can be called upon to exact payment of dues from him' (qq 19 and 23). Another fine example is the following final quatrain from a now lost poem, *I dTeamhraigh ríoghthar rí Éireann* 'The king of Ireland is inaugurated in Tara': *A Í Bhríain, a bhranáin Chaisil, / cuimhnigh an teagusg tug mé, / gan bheith ar seól na ríogh romhad, / ná bíodh 'na sgeól orad é* 'O descendant of Brian, O hero of Cashel, remember the instruction I have given you; let it not be said of you that you did not follow the custom of kings before you' (see *BST* 210.1-3/12a25-7/42b1-2).

[25] See P. Breatnach's important study 'Traidisiún na haithrise liteartha i bhfilíocht chlasaiceach na Gaeilge' in Breatnach, 1997, 1-63.

studies, while the greatest testimony to the care and detail with which the
master-poets were read is, of course, that of the grammatical and syntactical
tracts, which abound with citations from the verse of what we may
reasonably call the 'golden era' of bardic poetry, viz. the thirteenth to
fifteenth centuries, illustrating, for the most part, the correct use of the
classical language (McManus 1996 and 1997). Direct references to earlier
poets and their works are also found in the poetry itself. We have already
seen Ó Gnímh's appeal in *Cuimseach sin, a Fhearghail Óig* to the example
of eight former masters, all of whom fall within that 'golden era', and it
seems clear from what he says in this poem that he was very familiar with
two late thirteenth- or early fourteenth-century poems on the 'palace' built by
Aodh Ó Conchobhair at Cluain Fraoich, viz. *Tomhus mhúir Chruachna i
gCluain Fraoich* (*DiD* no. 119) and *An tú a-rís, a ráith Teamhrach*?
(Quiggin, 1913, and see McManus, 2000a, 72-4).[26] Elsewhere we find
Eochaidh Ó hEodhasa referring to, and comparing his own situation with,
Brian Ruadh mac Meic Con Midhe's refusal to compose verse for Énrí Ó
Néill († 1489) until he was fully trained (*sgagtha*, see below) and could offer
his patron 'the flower of his art' (*sgaith a ealadhan*, Maguire 23.9-12),
which Ó hEodhasa had no doubt read, and in another poem by the same
author (*Conradh do cheanglus re hAodh*, ed. Breatnach, 1993) we read of the
poetry of Gofraidh Fionn Ó Dálaigh (fourteenth century) being recited
(*gabhadh*) in Enniskillen in the late sixteenth century, and of Ó hEodhasa's
ability, despite not yet having completed his training, to explain to a young
Aodh Mág Uidhir the circumstances of Ó Dálaigh's contract with
Conchobhar Ó Briain († 1328), as outlined in Ó Dálaigh's poem *Teach
carad do-chiu folamh* 'I see the house of a friend empty' (*DiD* no. 116).[27] In

---

[26] It is worth noting here too that Ó Gnímh's main criticism of Mac an Bhaird is the
latter's failure to follow the example of his predecessors in the manner of composition
of his poem, expressed with loaded irony in the phrase *dol tar a riaghail d'ágh ort* 'you
had the fortune to stray from their practice' (or 'rule', q 6c). Bergin defends Fearghal
Óg's 'breach of etiquette' on the grounds that his poems 'have a natural grace and
charm beyond the miracles of technique admired and imitated in the schools', but this
gift of the muse, acknowledged at the outset by Ó Gnímh in the line *fuarois tiodhloicthi
ón Tríonóid* 'thou hast gotten gifts from the Trinity' (q 1b), plays second fiddle in
bardic tradition to the skills acquired by training.

[27] The relevant part of Ó Dálaigh's poem (*Conradh do-rónsam a-raon,/ is inn i n-aois dá
mhacaomh*; / – *a-tá tuirse ar gcúl dom char*, / *san toigh-se dún ga dhéanamh. Is eadh
do bhí do-san de*, / *rann ar gach nduain dar ndáin-ne*; / *each gach bliadhna do bhí
dhamh*; / *rí Liamhna nocha locfadh*. 'We both made a contract in this house when we
were young men – sadness brings the recollection to me. He secured a quatrain in every
duan I composed and I got a horse every year in return; the king of Liamhain would
never fail [to meet his part of the bargain]', *DiD* 116.20-21) is summarised by Ó
hEodhasa as follows: '*Each gach bliadhna – buan an bhreath – / d'Ú Dhálaigh –
díochra an t-eineach – / do bheireadh saorbharr sluaigh Fáil / ar an aonrann uaidh*

the same area a little later (circa 1608) Fearghal Óg Mac an Bhaird could also call on the example of Gofraidh Fionn Ó Dálaigh in defence of the composition of a full-blown elegy in strict verse (*oige iomshlán ... do Ghaoidhilg ghréasaigh*) for a hunting hound (*Teasda easgcara an fhiadhaigh* 'The enemy of game is dead', *DiD* no. 118), in this case the celebrated Ábhartach, hound of Cú Chonnacht Óg Mág Uidhir († 1608).[28] The details Mac an Bhaird furnishes regarding the death of Mág Carthaigh's hound (qq 13-15) show that he was familiar with Ó Dálaigh's elegy, so much so, indeed, that he could model[29] his own work on it (*Do chumas don choin-se thoir / marbhna do Ghaoidhilg ghréasaigh / mar chéadmharbhna na con thiar* 'For this hound in the east I have composed an elegy in ornate classical Irish, like that earlier elegy for the hound in the west', q 19abc). Again, in seeking payment for his *duan na Feirsde*, with which its author assures Aodh (mac Maghnusa) Ó Domhnaill lasting fame,[30] Uilliam Óg Mac an Bhaird has no hesitation in comparing his work with a 'famous' poem which he refers to as *Duan oirdhearc an eich bhuidhe*, composed apparently for Cathal Croibhdhearg Ó Conchobhair: *Duan oirdhearc an eich bhuidhe / duan Croibhdheirg ar gCruachai-ne, / duan na Feirsde - as togha trom - / ga meisde a cora i cconchloinn?* 'What harm is it to compare the famous *duan an eich bhuidhe* ('*duan* of the yellow steed'), composed for Croibhdhearg

---

d'fhagháil' 'A horse every year (it was a lasting judgement) was given to Ó Dálaigh (fervent the liberality) by the noble scion of the host of Fál in return for receiving the single stave from him' q 7. Of course Ó hEodhasa was consciously emulating Ó Dálaigh in that he too, as a young man, was seeking, and secured, a similar arrangement with a young prince (Aodh Mág Uidhir is always Aodh in the poem, never Mág Uidhir).

[28] Brian Ó Corcráin's *Rí con Éireann Ábhartach* 'Ábhartach is the king of the hounds of Ireland' (*DiD* no. 112) celebrates the same hound.

[29] The phrase he uses is *snáthghlanfaidh sionn a samhail* 'I will embroider its likeness' (q 18d). The elegy in question may be the (unpublished) poem *Slán dona saoithibh sealga* 'Good-bye to the masters of the hunt' (Franciscan Library A25, page 166). This poem has no ascription in the manuscript but it is an elegy on the hound of Diarmaid (mac Cormaic mhic Dhomhnaill) Mág Carthaigh († 1368), to whom Gofraidh addresses the poem *Fa ngníomhradh measdar meic ríogh* 'Princes are judged by their deeds' (*DiD* no. 91). It is quoted twice in the grammatical/syntactical tracts (*IGT* iii 251 = q 17cd and *BST* 189.19/8a3/Da29 = q 11cd) and there are clear echoes between the two poems. Thus, Fearghal Óg refers to Ábhartach as *easgcara an fhiadhaigh* 'the enemy of game' while Diarmaid's hound is called the *neamhchara* of the *fiadhach* and the *biodhbha d'fhiadhach Éireann*. Similarly, the opening theme of both poems is the same, namely that the death of the hound in question has removed any threat to the game of Ireland, who now enjoy freedom to roam as they please throughout the country.

[30] *Acc sin duit a Ui Dhomhnaill / duain far féchadh firfhoghlaim / bh*era (leg. méraidh) i ndéoidh do dhola / ag denamh eoil th'engnamha* 'Here, Ó Domhnaill, is a *duan* which bears witness to true learning and which will live on after your death, recording your deeds of valour' (*Grés dearbhtha duan na Feirsde*, NLI G 167, p. 129, q 45).

from our Cruachain, with *duan na Feirsde*, a serious choice [for comparison]?' (q 44). And finally, poets could, of course, go much further back in time in their pursuit of suitable models for their works. This is the case, for example, with Tadhg (mac Dáire) Mac Bruaideadha in his well-known but as yet not satisfactorily edited 'Instructions' to Donnchadh Ó Briain, fourth Earl of Thomond, *Mór a-tá ar theagasg flatha* 'Much depends on the instruction of a prince'. Mac Bruaideadha compares his *teagasg* with that of Torna to Niall, Morann to Fearadhach Fionn Fachtnach, Cormac to Cairbre Lifeachair, Fítheal to Cormac, Ciothruadh to Conn Céadchathach and Feircheirt to Labhraidh Loingseach, and expresses the wish that his patron may enjoy the same good fortune as that secured for former kings of Ireland by their poets (*Buaidh ríoghradh rátha Logha / go mbé ar mac meic Donnchadha, / drem rer mínigheadh mór bhfonn, / tre ghlór ríghfhileadh romham*).[31]

We have seen above that the bardic poet offered his patron immortality of fame in his verse, and throughout the bardic period the offer of immortal fame is a recurring element in the bardic sales-pitch. The Church, which was working in the same market and selling a similar product, immortality of the soul, may from time to time have denounced the bardic eulogy as worldly and false but the poets were very skilful in defending their work, and could call on no less a figure than Colam Cille for support for their profession.[32] But how could they guarantee immortal fame and, in particular, how could they broadcast it, for, as one poet puts it, 'fame is of no value unless

---

[31] From University College Oxford, MS 103, 58 r ff. q 19. Mac Bruaideadha gives prominence to the role of the poet as instructor and counsellor of his patron in this poem, just as Ó hEodhasa does in his *Mór an t-ainm ollamh flatha*. This being the case one cannot help wondering whether q 11 of the former poem (*Gach rí riamh ó ré na sean / do bhíodh leis leannán fileadh, / ós cionn fhírfheithmhe an iuil ghlain, / badh stiúir dhírighthe dá dhúthaigh* 'Since ancient times every king has had his poet-partner in charge of providing good husbanding of knowledge and acting as a guiding rudder for his territory') and q 25 of the latter (*D'fhiachaibh ollaimh, is iul fíor, / bheith láimh re longphort airdríogh; / sdiuir dhírighthe ós cóir re a chois, / a ndóigh fhírfheithmhe an eolais* 'Among the obligations of an ollamh is to be close to the fortress of a chief; it is right that he have a rudder for guidance with him for the true husbanding of knowledge', Breatnach, 1983, 65) constitute another example of the influence of one poet's work on that of another. See Breatnach, 1997, 59.

[32] See Giolla Brighde Mac Con Midhe's *A theachtaire tig ón Róimh* 'O messenger who comes from Rome' (*GBMC*, no. 18), the poem *Damhaidh dúind cóir, a chléirche* 'Grant us justice, O clerics' (Ó Cuív, 1971), Fearghal Mac Eochadha's *Briseadh riaghla ró molta* 'Excess of praise is a breach of rule' (*LB* no. 26) and *A lucht chumas bréag san dán* 'O ye who fashion lies in verse' by An Pearsún Riabhach (*Measgra Dánta*, no. 21). On Colam Cille in this context see Ó Cuív, 1968.

broadcast' (*ní maith clú gan chraobhsgaoileadh*)?[33] The answer lies not in the poem's first life, its formal recitation by a *reacaire* in the chief's court, no matter how great the gathering of nobles for the occasion, nor indeed in its second, as a prized work of art recorded in the chief's family *duanaire* or poem book. The real broadcasting engine was the poem's third life, and it was here that outstanding quality was the guarantee of success. The chief might retain a copy of the poem in his possession but the intellectual property belonged to the schools, and poems of top quality were guaranteed a high profile on the school circuit for as long as bardic poetry was studied.[34] What greater promise of immortal fame than the guarantee, backed up by quality training and skill, that a poem singing the praises of a chief's nobility, valour, generosity and good looks would be studied in detail again and again by trained and trainee poets alike in the bardic schools of Ireland and Gaelic Scotland?

The broadcast and the guarantee of fame are implicit, for example, in Seaán Ó Clumháin's well-known poem to the young prince Aodh Ó Conchobhair († 1309), *Dorn idir dán is dásacht* 'A fist is all that stands between learning and madness' (*DiD* no. 84). When Ó Clumháin assures Ó Conchobhair that the latter's forbearance in the face of extreme provocation and his willingness to forgive an act of inexcusable arrogance will secure similar treatment from patrons of their poets, and the praises of poets to come for himself (*maithfidh rí, a dhonnabhraigh dheis, / ní d'ollamhnaibh ar th'aithreis* and *budh é luagh ar léigis linn / duan gach éigis i nÉirinn*; qq 15cd, 16cd), the guarantee lies both in Ó Clumháin's broadcasting skills and in the exemplary behaviour he is broadcasting. Not surprisingly, citations in the grammatical tracts (for which see McManus, 1997 and de Brún, 1998) are evidence that this poem was studied closely in the schools,[35] where it came to be known, affectionately (?), as *laoidh an duirn* 'the lay of the fist'.

---

[33] From *Mithidh th'athdhúsgadh, a Aodh* 'It is time to stir yourself up, O Aodh' by Uilliam Óg Mac an Bhaird, NLI G 167, p. 164, q 8d).

[34] In this the high-quality bardic poem was not unlike today's pioneering article published in a Festschrift to celebrate the work of an established scholar. The original lecture and the honorand's leather-bound copy correspond to the first and second life of the poem, but its reception by the discipline is the guarantee of its success as a work of scholarship.

[35] Three couplets and two whole quatrains from the poem are cited in the tracts: 14cd = *BST* 220.28/12b5/43a9; 18cd = *BST* 225.20; 24cd = *IGT* ii 1324; 42a-d = *IGT* ii 583; 43a-d = *BST* 15a10-11/196.6. Though the poem was studied in the schools I know of no reference to Ó Clumháin's case by later poets in a similar predicament, which would suggest that Ó Conchobhair probably did not respond in the way the poet wished and thus denied himself the *duan gach éigis* promised in the poem.

Many bardic poets, as we know, were both professional poets and teachers,[36] and it may be instructive at this point to return to what O'Sullevane says about the teacher's role in the schools and to examine primary evidence for the relationship between teacher and pupil. The teacher's role, according to O'Sullevane's account, involved assigning students to the appropriate classes or grades (presumably the *seacht ngráidh* to which the poets themselves refer),[37] instructing them in the intricacies of metre, giving assignments suitable to each class, assessing their work and awarding them grades or degrees. The account is skeletal but it covers all the work one might expect a teacher to be engaged in. More to the point, the evidence is, for the most part, backed up by the poets themselves, and from their works, particularly their elegies to former teachers, we can add not only meat and flesh to O'Sullevane's account but also some soul, in the form of expressions of intimacy and references to the trust and friendship which developed between teacher and pupil.

O'Sullevane's reference to the instruction given by the teachers in metre and the assignment of tasks may be corroborated by the 17th-century treatise on prosody attributed to Tadhg Óg Ó hUiginn.[38] Having listed the most commonly used metres and explained the nature of a *duan* the text states: *& asé ba cúrsa saothruighthe do chách, suím dh'áiridhe do dhuanoibh do dhēunamh ar gach aisde dhíbh sin thúas* 'and each student's course of study involved composing a certain number of poems in each of the metres above' (lines 3415-7). I understand the *cúrsa saothruighthe* of this statement to refer to 'a course of study' rather than a 'lifelong career', partly because it makes

---

[36] The usual term for teacher in bardic poetry is *oide* (frequently rhyming in verse with *oige* 'composition'), less commonly *altra*, both originally meaning 'foster-father'. The student is generally designated by the term *dalta*, also *adhbhar* 'material (of an *ollamh*), *sgolaidhe/sgoláir* 'scholar', and very infrequently, *fealmhac*. Typical examples of poets who are referred to, or who refer to themselves, as teachers are Gofraidh Fionn Ó Dálaigh (*DiD* 65.38, *oide* to his son Eoghan), Aonghus (mac Amhlaoibh) Ó Dálaigh (*oide* to Fear Feasa Ó'n Cháinte, *DiD* 73, see below), Fearghal Ruadh Ó hUiginn (*oide* to his brother Tadhg Óg, *IBP* 38), Cú Chonnacht Ó Dálaigh (*oide* to Maol Domhnaigh Ó Muirgheasáin) and Fear Feasa Ó'n Cháinte (*oide* to Gofraidh Mac an Bhaird).

[37] The seven grades of student-poets (*na seacht ngráidh ghabhaid filidh*) are referred to from time to time (see Giolla Brighde Ó hEodhasa's *A-tám ionchóra re hAodh*, *DBM*, no 4, q 5b, Gofraidh Fionn Ó Dálaigh's *Filidh Éireann go haointeach*, Knott, 1911, q 14, and *O'Reilly* 8.34) and they are listed in full in *Mór an feidhm deilbh an dána* (McKenna, 1951) q 9 as follows: *Fochlag, Mac Fuirmidh feasach / Dos, Clí na gceard neimhcheasach / fiu an dánbhoth* (*sic leg.*)*, a chara, a ccradh / Cana, Ánshruth is Ollamh* 'A Fochlog, a learned Mac Fuirmhidh, a Dos, a Clí with his deft productions, a Cana, an Ánshruth, an Ollamh - the rich productions of these (alone) are worthy of their (origin in a) composition-hut'. With the exception of *án(sh)radh/án(sh)rath* and *ollamh* these terms seldom appear in the poetry on their own.

[38] See *Graiméar Uí Maolchonaire* in Mac Aogáin, 1968.

better sense in the context, but also because the words *saothar* and *saothrughadh* are used elsewhere of a course of study in a bardic school. In the poem by Ó hEodhasa already referred to, *A-tám i gcás idir dhá chomhairle*, for example, the poet contemplates leaving Munster and returning home to Fermanagh without completing his studies, the last expressed with the words *is cuid dar saothrughadh ar nach cuirfinn críochnughadh* 'and some of my training left incomplete' (q 3d). As already pointed out, he did not contemplate this course of action for long, but decided to stay put. This decision he announces with the words *Anfad re cuma ar nduaine deiridh-ne* 'I will stay to compose my last *duan*', which in the context must surely refer to the last poem prescribed for the course, the one with which, we may assume, he might secure whatever qualification he was seeking. This I understand to be a poem of the type referred to in O'Sullevane's account, i.e. one set for examination by the *oide* of the school, and we have a very interesting reference to another one of these in Giolla Brighde Ó hEodhasa's *A-tám ionchóra re hAodh* 'I can defend myself to Aodh', composed around 1592 for Aodh Ruadh Ó Domhnaill (*DBM*, no. 4). Ó Domhnaill's refusal to pay for a poem Giolla Brighde had composed for him – on the grounds that the poet was only an *Ánroth* (second-last grade of the seven grades of poet, see fn. 37) at the time he composed it – is the subject of this interesting piece. Giolla Brighde's argument is firstly that Aodh Ó Domhnaill was not chief of his clan at the time of composition (*A-tá liomsa leithsgéal maith: / nár hoirneadh Aodh 'na ardfhlaith / re hucht a[39] adhmholta sin / ós gurt armghonta Oiligh* 'I have a good defence: that Aodh had not been inaugurated king over deadly-armed Aileach's field when he was eulogized' (q 7) and, more to the point, that the poem in question was the last he composed as an *Ánroth*, the composition which secured him the grade of *Ollamh*, and if it was good enough to do that it was good enough for the chief in waiting: *Mo fhreagra 'na aghaidh air / gurbh í ar nduan dheiridh shaothair / do dhealbhamar, más dáil dtruim (?), / do shealbhorradh chláir Chonuill* 'My answer to him is that it was my graduating poem, which, difficult as it was, I composed for the lord of Conall's plain' (q 9). Note the phrase *duan dheiridh shaothair* referring to a composition composed to secure graduation,[40] and note also that the same

---

[39] *Sic leg.* and ignore Mhág Craith's note on the fault (*DBM* vol. 2, 115)?

[40] The term *duan shaothair* appears in Tadhg Dall Ó hUiginn's request for protection addressed to Cormac Ó hEadhra, *Ag so an chomairche, a Chormaic* 'Here is the guarantee, Cormac' (*TD* no. 30) in a section of the poem in which the poet details what he will give to his protector in return: *Do-ghéan an laoidh ngréasaigh ngloin / do-ghéan duit an duain shaothoir* (q 20ab). Knott is unsure of the meaning ('the laboriously wrought(?) poem') but adds in a note that it is probably a technical term like *duan díchill*, and in this I have no doubt that she is correct. All of the terms used by

poem uses the phrase *orradh gach gráidh druim ar druim* 'the fitting subject for composition of each and every grade', probably the equivalent of O'Sullevane's assignments to each class of subjects suitable to their ability. The students' works, once completed and written down, were submitted to the teachers for examination, according to O'Sullevane's account, and there is ample testimony in bardic poetry to this aspect of the *oide*'s work, which, in the words of Fear Flatha Ó Gnímh, we may refer to as *feidhm daghoide ar dhán* (*IBP* no. 27.1c). The anonymous and nostalgic *Aonar dhamhsa eidir dhaoinibh* 'I am alone among men' (*IBP* no. 42), as we have seen, reserves a special 'house' in the bardic academy for this activity (*teach breithimh* (*sic leg.*) *gach gréasa gloin* 'the house of the critic of each fine work') and the terms *sgagadh* 'straining, sifting',[41] *glanadh* 'cleansing',[42] *gleódh* 'purifying' and *breithniughadh* 'judging, examining' appear elsewhere in the poetry in the context of this aspect of bardic training. The beautiful early seventeenth-century elegy, *Bean dá chumhadh críoch Ealla* 'Críoch Ealla is a woman of two sorrows' (*DiD* no. 73), mourns the passing of Domhnall (mac Airt) Ó Caoimh of Dúthaigh Ealla and his ollamh Aonghus (mac Amhlaoibh) Ó Dálaigh, chief professor in the local bardic school in Baile Uí Dhálaigh, Co.

---

poets in reference to their compositions need to be studied carefully. For *saothar/saothrughadh* used of the professional work of the poet, as opposed to his training, see: *AiD* 19.10b: *mo dhán ar n-a shaothrughadh le fada ...* 'my poem long since finished'; *IBP* 28.7cd: *monuar gan aoibh na moghadh / 'gan chaoir shuadh ar shaothrughadh* 'alas that the generality of poets cannot secure from their labours (even) the comforts enjoyed by serfs'; *Magauran* 6.8: *mo shaothar is riot caithfear* 'For thee I will labour'.

[41] Both the composition and the poet may undergo the process of *sgagadh*. Cú Chonnacht Mág Uidhir (†1589), for example, can be referred to metaphorically as a *grés oide d'éis a sgagtha* 'polished poem of a teacher' (*Maguire* 2.45a; or 'poem of a polished teacher') and in the same volume Ó hEodhasa tells us that Brian Ruadh mac Meic Con Midhe refused to compose poetry for Énrí Ó Néill († 1489) *co raibhe sgagtha* 'until he was purified' (i.e. fully trained). Again, in his fourteenth-century attack on Gofraidh Fionn Ó Dálaigh's refusal to acknowledge his training, Maolmhuire Mág Craith laments the investment of too much energy in a student's career with these opening words: *Mairg chaitheas dlús re dhalta / más fhíor, d'éis a dheaghsgagtha, / bheith dar ndaltai-ne ag dréim rinn* 'Alas that anyone should take pains with his student if it is true that, after having been well-trained [by us], our former student is now contending with us' (*DiD* no. 104). For another example of a *dalta* undergoing *sgagadh* see *IGT* ii 1826 = 2156. The verb(al noun) *fromha(i)dh* and past participle *fromhtha* can be used in the same way as *sgaga(i)dh/sgagtha*.

[42] In Mág Craith's *Mairg chaitheas dlús re dhalta* (see last fn.) the *snuadh a nglanta* 'complexion of perfection' (q 3) on Gofraidh Fionn's compositions (*gréasa*) he owes to the Mág Craith school, even if he is not prepared to admit it (*Ní rinn bheireas a bhuidhe*), while Eochaidh Ó hEodhasa, as we have seen, refers to his many teachers as the *gaibhne glanta ar gcearda* 'purifying smiths of our craft' (*Mór an t-ainm ollamh flatha*, q 14).

Cork. The poet, Fear Feasa Ó'n Cháinte, was a student of Ó Dálaigh, and the affection in which he held his former teacher is evident throughout the poem and will be discussed below. For our present purpose we may note his reference to his former teacher as *oide sgagtha na sgoile* (18) 'the teacher who sifts the [work of the] school', *fáidh glanta na Gaoidheilge* (43) 'purifying scholar of (Classical) Irish', and *ursa breithnighthe gréas ngill* (43) 'chief/master of assessment of prize-poems' and we gather from qq 31-2 that it was not only the compositions of students which were subjected to critical analysis of the kind implied by these laudatory terms. The poet tells us that if Ó Dálaigh himself had survived and composed an elegy (*gréas marbhnaidhe*, q 31) for Ó Caoimh, his patron, the poem would be of such quality (*gréas badh sgoithghile sgiamhadh*) as to come through a student/teacher analysis session unscathed: *Níor ghuais dí 'n-a dheaghaidh sain / toibhéim oide ná adhbhair; / níor bheag d'fheitheamh, a Dhé, dhi / gomadh breitheamh é uirre* 'Criticism by teacher or student would not constitute a danger for the composition; no small guarantee of its quality, O God, would be the fact that he (as its author) was its judge.' And the understandable fear of having one's shortcomings exposed in such a dissection is referred to in a seventeenth-century elegy by the Scottish poet, Maol Domhnaigh Ó Muirgheasáin (*Cia feasda as urra don eol* 'Who is guardian of learning now?', Black, 1976), to Cú Chonnacht Ó Dálaigh (†1642), head of the bardic school at Tolcha, Co. Limerick (see Breatnach, 1989, 33-4) and former teacher of the poet, when he says: *Don eagna as cuma gá conn / gan urra re a h-agra ann / ní guais locht dá leagar liom / a thocht riom gérbh eagal am* 'It makes no difference what interpretation is applied to learning when there is no expert to challenge it; I am not afraid [now] that any of the mistakes I let slip may redound against me, though I was afraid once' (q 35). In the same poem, which is an elegy to poetry in general as well as to Ó Dálaigh in particular, we are told that now that this teacher of the composition of poetry is dead there is no one left to evaluate or scrutinise the work of poets: *d'éis oide dealbhtha na nduan / ar n-oige ní fhaghbha a gleódh* (q 12ab).

Anyone who faced some of the senior professors in seminars at the Dublin Institute for Advanced Studies in the 1970s will know how frightening an experience a grilling of the kind referred to in the preceding paragraph could be, and how one prepared in great detail in advance to avoid it. The same will undoubtedly have been true for bardic poets – we shall see in a moment just how caustic bardic criticism could be – but the experience would no doubt stand the trainee poet in good stead. Ó'n Cháinte, in his poem *Mór an feidhm deilbh an dána*, to be discussed in more detail below, admits as much when, in boasting his ability, he says *a hucht a ttroide as teann sinn / na hoide dob fhearr d'Éirinn* 'I have a strong resolve, having debated with the best teachers in Ireland' (q 15), and we shall see that he needed a strong resolve to deal with a former student with whom relations were particularly sour. For the most part, however, students and teachers seemed to form a strong bond and the student's dependence on the teacher, together with his affection for him, is evident in the poetry. We get tantalising hints of this relationship in stray couplets from the grammatical tracts such as *Anois ní tráth troide rinn / ar sgáth mh'oide ní fhuilim* 'this is not a time for contending with me, I do not have my teacher's protection' (*IGT* ii ex. 1159),[43] but it is particularly prominent in the elegies composed by students for former teachers.

Few in the field of Irish studies will not be familiar, for example, with Tadhg Óg Ó hUiginn's moving elegy to his brother and teacher, Fearghal Ruadh, *Anocht sgaoilid na sgola* 'Tonight the schools disperse' (*IBP* no. 38). Here, of course, there is a family relationship involved so that the teacher's interest in his brother's studies, expressed in the words *dom ullmhugadh níor áil lais / mo bheith adhaigh 'na égmais* 'in order to prepare me he would not have me (even) one night away from him' (q 18ab), might be put down to this. Of the student body in general, however, we learn that they were loath to hear the cuckoo, as this signalled the end of the school-year (*do bhí adhbhar far fhuath libh / labhradh na gcuach do chluinsin*, 5cd = *IGT* ii 1768)[44] and that the bond they had formed with Fearghal was such that they found it easier to disperse and return to their homes[45] than to seek a new teacher, studying under a strange teacher being like captivity compared with the homeliness of the familiar (*breath bhroide, a Dhé, dá dhalta / dá mbé ag oide iasachta* q 8cd). The kindness of the teacher to his students is expressed by the phrase *ag cor chomaoineadh* in the couplet *foide iná an sgol do sgaoileadh / gan m'oide ag cor chomaoineadh* 'sadder than the break-up of the school is the fact that my teacher can no longer show kindness' (q 7cd; quoted in *IGT* iv 1028) and this brings us to a similar phrase in Fear Feasa Ó'n Cháinte's *Bean dá chumhadh críoch Ealla*, when he says *Ní bhíodh sgolaidhe don sgail / dá mbíodh i mbaile Í Dhálaigh / gan chomaoin éigin ón fhior* 'There wasn't a single student in the school at Ballydaly who was not under some compliment to the man' (*DiD* no. 73, q 16abc). Here the man in question is Domhnall Ó Caoimh, patron of the school, whom the students visited regularly (q 17)[46] but the great regard which the poet had for

---

[43] Compare the phrase *mur oide ag car sgáth sgol* 'like a teacher protecting the pupils' (*Maguire* 13.13d).

[44] O'Sullevane tells us that the school-year ran from Michaelmas to the 25th of March.

[45] 'Homes' is expressed by the word *dúthaigh*, implying, as in O'Sullevane's account, that they had travelled some distance to study with Ó hUiginn.

[46] Compare O'Sullevane's: 'Every Saturday and on the Eves of Festival Days they broke up and dispers'd themselves among the Gentlemen and rich Farmers of the Country, by

his *oide*'s skill in poetry is reflected in phrases such as *órthóir an dána dhírigh* 'gilder of *Dán Díreach*'[47] (q 41), *ceann foghloma na bhfileadh* 'chief in learning among the poets' (q 42), *altra cáigh i n-ar gceird-ne* 'teacher of all in our profession' (q 43), and in the statement that he surpassed other teachers in the quality of his compositions (*geall gach oide 'ga ucht slim / a hucht a oige n-inghill*, q 33). It is not surprising, then, that his school attracted scholars from far and wide as we read that the deaths of its patron and teacher left *sgolaidhe na gcóig gcóigeadh* 'the scholars of the five provinces' in mourning (q 14). And·what greater sign of friendship than the teacher's and the patron's tolerance in the face of arrogance on the part of the student: *Géarsam uaibhreach orra sain / mo lucht comtha, mo chomhthaigh / – teidhm as tinne do threaghd mé – / a bhfearg rinne ní raibhe* 'Though I was arrogant in my treatment of my [two] friends, my [two] companions, they never responded in anger; this is my greatest cause for remorse' (q 45).

Needless to say, relationships between the students themselves or between students and teachers could also turn sour, and the bardic temperament, in particular the bards' own well-documented arrogance,[48] undoubtedly fuelled

---

whom they were very well entertain'd and much made of, till they thought fit to take their leave, in order to re-assume their Study.' Ó'n Cháinte's poem gives beautiful expression to the bond of friendship between the *oide* (Ó Dálaigh) and the school's patron (Ó Caoimh). Consider, for example: *Suaimhneach dá gach duine dhíobh / gan marthain d'fhulang ff[h]airbríogh / i ndiaidh an chomhthaigh ro chleacht; / liaigh dá n-orchraibh a n-imtheacht* 'Soothing it was for both of them that neither survived to suffer the excessive loss of his companion; the death of each one healed [what otherwise would have been] their great anguish' (q 25).

47 *An t-Órthóir*, 'the Gilder', as a nickname for the poet Eoghan Mág Craith (see *IBP* 27.6b) has been explained by Simms (1987, 65-6) as arising from his audacious claims for the ubiquity of gold among the Leinstermen in his poem to Art Mac Murchadha Caomhánach, † 1418, *Iomdha uaisle ar iath Laighean (DiD* no. 100, qq 15-18). In our poem, however, 'the gilder' has the more complimentary sense of 'perfectionist', with which compare Ó hEodhasa's pursuit of *óradh ughdair an léighinn* 'the gilding (i.e. the best of) learned authors' as reported in the anonymous *Fogus orchra don éigsi (IBP* 48.9b), and Ó hEodhasa's own remark (already noted in fn. 7) on the consequences of his sojourn in Munster to perfect his art, *meath na healadhna a hóradh* 'perfecting art (merely) results in its decline'. For *óradh briathar* 'gilding of words', i.e. using dazzling words, see *DBM* 12.7; see also *le Gaoidheilg d'éis a hóroidh* 'with gilded Irish', *LB* 61.21d, referring to the poet's compositions. The verb *óraidh* in the sense 'endows' is used in Ó hEodhasa's *A Bhriain Mhéig Uidhir éist roinn (Irisleabhar Muighe Nuadhad*, 1929, 35ff., q 12): *A Bhriain Uisnigh óras dáin* 'O Brian of Uisneach who endows the arts'. Again Ó hEodhasa uses the verb *óraidh* in the sense of endowing poetry in *O'Reilly* 25.5c: *í Cholla Oirghíall ro-m-ór* 'The Í Cholla of Oriel, who endowed me'.

48 This is given neat expression in Ó Clumháin's *Dorn idir dán is dásacht* 'A fist is all that stands between learning and madness' in the line *do-bheir an dán an díomas* 'the profession of poetry nurtures arrogance' (*DiD* 84.3d) and in Ó hEodhasa's *Mór an t-*

many a dispute in their academies, as it did in their relationships with their patrons. Again we find hints of discord within the schools in lines like Ó hUiginn's *Guth oram budh aimhleas damh / ós íseal ris an ollamh, / beag dtaraidh don té adéradh, / dé am aghaidh ní fhuiléngadh* 'A reproach against me to my hurt, made in secret to the *ollamh* – little profit it was to anyone who should utter it; he would not endure a breath against me' (*IBP* no. 38.19), and we have several references in the poetry to disputes between poets or criticism by one of another. It may be a tribute to the bardic sense of propriety, or the result of censorship, that few of these are recorded in detail.[49] But the censor's net, if such there was, did let one exchange slip through, and this is as good a piece of academic bitching as anything our 19th- and 20th-century scholars have produced in their reviews of one another. I refer to the exchange between Fear Feasa Ó'n Cháinte (*oide*) and Gofraidh Mac an Bhaird (*dalta*), published by McKenna in 1951. Like many a personalised wrangle this probably generated more heat than light for the contemporary observer, but for us, looking in from the outside, it is highly illuminating, whether we take it in earnest or not. Indeed, with the exception of Gofraidh Fionn Ó Dálaigh's *Madh fiafraidheach budh feasach* 'If one be given to questioning one grows wise', also published by McKenna (1947), there is probably no better insight to be had in the poetry, as opposed to the grammatical tracts, into the strict academic regime of the bardic schools.

A summary will suffice for our purposes: In the opening poem of the exchange, *Mór an feidhm deilbh an dána* 'The composition of poetry is a great task', Ó'n Cháinte argues, apparently in response to some criticism of his own ability, that the composition of poetry is for the highly intelligent only, those who have succeeded in passing through all the grades from *Fochlag* up to *Ollamh* as he has done. Not all, according to the poet, have the ability to see them through this course, with the result that there are some practising the craft without the necessary qualifications (*gan seacht ngarma do ghabháil*). These he dubs *aos an ainbh[fh]is* 'ignorant folk' who not only cannot compose faultless verse in the different metres laid down, but cannot even distinguish between the metres themselves (*roinn eaturra ní fhéaduid*). For one of these to contend with Ó'n Cháinte would be the height of stupidity, like trying to stop the sea from flooding the shore (*cosg muire i dtrágh do theacht*), as he has perfected his art in the bardic forge (*A gceardcha na gceasd ndorcha / do sgiamhas sgath m'ealathna*) and studied

---

ainm ollamh flatha (see fn. 7) in which Aodh Mág Uidhir is told that one must put up with the excesses of the *ollamh fileadh* 'qualified poet': *cóir iomchor re a aindligheadh* (3b). For a brief discussion see Breatnach, 1983, 39-40.

[49] I am not referring here to the likes of *Iomarbhágh na bhfileadh* 'The contention of the poets', in which the contestants pit their wits against one another on some contentious issue, but rather to bitter *ad hominem* attacks by poets on their peers.

in many schools (*ní ar éansgoil fhuaras m'fhoghluim*). Having immersed himself in the streams of learning and purified his compositions in them he is now an *oide* and a *maighisdir* and no one who was obliged by lack of ability to remain on the shore of the sea of poetry should dare to challenge one who has explored every foot of that same sea (*Córuide gan righe riom / don lucht anas 'na himioll / ní fhuil troigh nar thomhais mé / do mhoir fhorais na héigse*).

In Gofraidh (mac Briain) Mac an Bhaird's response, *A fhir shealbhas duit an dán* 'O friend who lays claim to the art of poetry', Ó'n Cháinte is taken to task for what is seen as insufferable arrogance and his failure to learn humility from a couplet which he should have come across in his studies, namely *neach féin go mór dá mholadh / céim as lór dá lochtughadh* 'for a man to praise himself highly is a step sufficient to bring him blame' (see fn. 15). Ó'n Cháinte can boast, says Mac an Bhaird, because the schools have for the most part dried up and there is no one of authority to challenge him (*Do-chuaidh sgaoileadh fa sgolaibh, / díosg ar ndul fan ealodhain, / a-tá do theannfhacal libh, / neambacadh trá ar do thuislibh*). The truth, however, is that there is no texture in his poems (*ní d'abhras saor na seacht ngrádh / snáth t'oige*) and his self-satisfaction is a flame with nothing to feed on (*t'uaill ag adhnadh asuibh féin / lasuir gan adhbhar eiséin*). Mac an Bhaird lists a number of faults which distinguish Ó'n Cháinte's work, even if the latter is blissfully unaware of them (*Duit-se acht nach léir do lochta*), and the list is interesting in that it shows that the grammatical tracts which have survived, or something akin to them, were the handbooks of the schools attended by these gentlemen.[50] Ó'n Cháinte is accused, for example, of an inability to distinguish the 18 prepositions (*na hocht n-iairmbéarla déag*),[51] the correct use of gender and case (*Innsgne a n-ionad a chéile / ainm a n-*

---

[50] Are the grammatical tracts the 'books' referred to by Ó'n Cháinte in the lines *Ní dhéanabh cainnt seocha sain, / go bhfuilim inghill ionntaibh / na leabhair do léaghadh liom* 'I'll content myself with saying that I am well versed in the books I have read'?

[51] On which see, for example, *IGT* i §§73-4: *Náoi n-íairmbérla linn as léir / chuireas feirinnsgne a ttuilréim* 'We know of nine prepositions which put a masculine type noun into its [special] dative form' and *Naoí n-íairmbérla go cinnte / nach cuir réim ar feirinnsgne* 'There are nine prepositions which do not put *réim* on a masculine type noun' (i.e. they govern the accusative). Compare too Gofraidh Fionn Ó Dálaigh's *Naoi n-iairmbérla – áireamh ceart – do-ní ar fheirinnsgne fhoirneart; / ní fortail an fear nach tuig; / ó fhoclaibh as eadh fhásuid* 'Nine prepositions – exact number – affect a masculine noun (i.e. put it into the dative case); weak in learning is he who does not understand this; they all derive from stressed words' (*Madh fiafraidheach budh feasach*, McKenna, 1947, q 27) where *ó fhoclaibh as eadh fhásuid* is echoed in *IGT* i §73's *íairmberladha tig ó gach focal díobh* 'prepositions derive from each of these stressed words'. For citations from Ó Dálaigh's poem in *IGT* and *BST* see McManus 1997.

ionad tuilréime),[52] motion and rest after prepositions governing both accusative and dative (*A n-áitibh ar-oile soin / ciall chomhnaidhe, ciall shiobhail*)[53] and a damning number of metrical faults is identified in his work (*maoithe, maoile, caoiche, claoine, cleathrámh; neimhtheacht céille, gnás, ionannas, seirbhe ráidh*, and *gnúis gharbh*).[54] This being the case, his dogmatising gives rise only to contempt and many a wise man would question his assertion that he has successfully explored the sea of learning of the poets. Echoing the opening line of Ó'n Cháinte's poem, Mac an Bhaird finishes off in agreement with his contention that the composition of poetry is indeed a complicated task, but one Ó'n Cháinte simply isn't up to (*Mór an feidhm deilbh an dána / do dheilbh ní deilbh diongbhála*)!

Ó'n Cháinte's reply to this, *Créad dá sealbhainn damh an dán?* 'What if I do make claim to the poetic art?', takes us to a new low in the debate. Mac an Bhaird's lack of ability, he says, is not surprising, given that his father (*Brian an bhaothraidh* 'Brian of the silly speech') couldn't read a poem, never mind criticise one (*sár ar laoidhibh ní léamhadh / dán aoinfhir ní oirléaghadh*), and his son has the unenviable distinction of having learned nothing (*níor thógbhais eisdibh aiceacht*) from the *Treasfhocal*, the *Agallamh* and the *Auraiceapt*, all of which he studied, or was supposed to have studied, at school. Alas that he, Ó'n Cháinte, should have to bother replying to the likes of Mac an Bhaird (*Suaith lem meanmaa dar mó móid / nach saoi a-tá ad chuid don chuspóid; / olc linn ar malairt dá mhéid / sinn do labhairt led leithéid*), a failed student whose attempts at composition grated on his feelings when, as his teacher, he had to read them (*Fuair tú tuisleadh fad ghrádaibh / ar gcaill ar do chéaddálaibh; / bíodh gur chná h'oige m'anaim-se / do bhá am oide agaibh-se*). Thankfully, Ó'n Cháinte had other students who negotiated the course successfully and whose skill will reflect well on him as an *oide* (*Mór an sruith oidis fhoirbhthe / mór bhfealmhac bhféith bhfaobhoirthe / as fhearr iná thú ar mo thréad / as gheall rem chlú do choimhéad*). Mac an Bhaird would have been well-advised to have kept his mouth shut in these matters, but then he never listened to advice anyway (*Éagcóir nar anuis ad thost / acht nach gabhann tú teagosg*). Anyone would recognise immediately in his feeble attempts at poetry that he never had it in him; he wouldn't have the wherewithal to

---

[52] Compare *Ferindsgni do bainindsgi* and *Bainindsgi d'ferindsgi* 'masculine for feminine' and 'feminine for masculine' (*IGT* v §§29-30) as faults in poetry and *ibid* §§16-17 on *Anréim* 'the incorrect use of case'.

[53] See *IGT* i §§73-4 on *cíall chomhnaidhe* and *cíall shiobhail*.

[54] Several of these will be found in *IGT* i (§2) and in *IGT* v (see the index) and some are mentioned among the *béimeanna as cóir do sheachna san dán* 'faults which should be avoided in poetry' in Giolla Brighde Ó hEodhasa's *De arte poetica* (Mac Aogáin, 1968, 104).

challenge even Ó'n Cháinte's *bard* (*A bhaird gan an mbairdneacht féin / a abhlóir bhig, a bheigéir/ mar shruth ngarg gidh teann a-taoi / do gheall lem bard do-béarthaoi* 'You bard without *bairdneacht* itself, you petty buffoon, you beggar; bold as you are like a brawling stream, you wouldn't even be a match for my reciter'.

This is hot stuff, if in earnest. But whether in earnest or in jest, it shows just what a session of *glanadh* or *sgagadh* or *breithniughadh* might produce, and why a poet might fear it. More importantly, it shows that the material of the grammatical tracts and that of the seventeenth-century treatises on poetry were studied carefully in the schools and were a vital part of the poet's training. Careful analysis of poetry is also evident in the way each contestant repeats lines or couplets from his adversary's contribution,[55] and in the repetition by each of the couplet from Ó Dálaigh's *Créad agaibh aoidhigh i gcéin*, a poem which, like many others attributed to Muireadhach Albanach, is the source of several citations in the grammatical tracts (McManus, 1997). Ó'n Cháinte, the teacher, also echoes the sentiment and the structure of a poem which had a huge influence on the framers of the grammatical tracts[56] and must have been essential reading in the schools, viz. Gofraidh Fionn Ó Dálaigh's *Madh fiafraidheach budh feasach*, as he throws questions of the kind *Gá méad iairmbéarla re rádh?* and *Gá méad iairmbéarla uile / labhruid an t-aos eagnuidhe?* back at Mac an Bhaird.[57] One cannot but feel that question and answer sessions of this kind were an important part of the

---

[55] Ó'n Cháinte's *Do iarras go foirfe ar gceird / na trí tighe a-tá a nGaoidheilg* (q 16ab) is undoubtedly corrupt (witness the absence of alliteration in the first line and the bad grammar in the second) and can be corrected from Mac an Bhaird's echoing lines *Go rángabhar roighne a cceard / na trí tighe a dtá an Ghaoidhealg*. Again Ó'n Cháinte's *i mbéilshlighe na mbalg bhfis / ní thard éinfhile m'éislis* (q 18cd) and *mo sproigeacht riu dá ronnar / as fiu an oideacht fhuaromar* (q 21cd) are brought together in Mac an Bhaird's retort as *Adhbhar sbéise do sbroigeacht, / cúis aithis bhar n-ardoideacht, / gidh do bhéilshlighe bhalg bhfis / is dréimire ard anbhfis*.

[56] This is evident from the quotations already referred to and from the statement by the compiler of *IGT* i to the effect that Ó Dálaigh had omitted *Ó an tshloinnti ⁊ ailm na hagallmha* 'the Ó in surnames and the vocative particle *a*' from the list of words 'which put *réim*', and had been criticised by Ceann Fáolaidh Ó Cuill for doing so (*IGT* i §129). As the editor of Ó Dálaigh's poem points out, the two quatrains in which these words are referred to by Ó Dálaigh (*Iairmbéarla ann dá n-aithle / nar chuir riamh réim iollraighthe / - as mór sgol ara snaidhm soin - / is a chor ar ainm uathaidh* and *Iairmbérla ele - as é an glas - / chuireas réim fir go follas / 's gan réim mná dhó do dhéanaimh; / a-tá só 'nar soisgéalaibh*. qq 18 and 19) are missing from the oldest copy of the poem, the Book of Uí Mhaine (written before 1372). Clearly, faulty transmission was as much a problem then as it is now.

[57] Compare Ó Dálaigh's *Cá méad iairmbéarla d'fhoclaibh / chuireas réim, rian comhachtaidh?* (q 7ab) *etc.*

training of the aspiring bardic poet, and that, as Ó Dálaigh puts it, 'questioning' was 'the door to wisdom' (*doras feasa fiafruighe*, q 1d).

In this short survey, then, we have seen that much of O'Sullevane's account is supported by the evidence of the poetry. Poets travelling long distances to study at particular schools, being assigned to class according to their ability; reading, writing and a good memory as essential parts of the training, composition in the dark, submission of work for examination etc. are all referred to directly or indirectly in the poetry itself. We have seen grudging acknowledgment of the 'gift of the muse' but priority given to the acquirement of skills by hard work and training. In particular, we have seen the emphasis put on a study of the master-poets of the genre as a feature of that training. It might be argued that much of the evidence used in this paper comes from the latter part of the bardic era, but given that this was the period in which the grammatical tracts took the form in which they have come down to us,[58] it does not seem far-fetched to suggest that the school environment we have been examining provides the perfect conditions for the compilation of tracts of this kind. Careful and minute analysis of the works of master craftsmen is the hallmark of the grammatical tracts and this is precisely the activity we have seen students and teachers alike engaged in. The purpose of that activity was to mould the trainee student into a master-poet, the spin-off was the guarantee of 'immortal fame' for the patrons whose generoslty financed it, and its legacy is the wonderfully illustrated analysis of Classical Modern Irish which today's scholar can enjoy.

BIBLIOGRAPHY

Armstrong, J. (1981): 'Vowel equivalences in Classical Modern Irish rime: Modern and Medieval analyses compared', *Indo-European Studies* 4 (ed. C. Watkins), 613-724.

Bergin, O. (1916-55): *Irish Grammatical Tracts* (I *Ériu* 8 (1916), II §1-§11 *Ériu* 8 (1916), §12-§87 *Ériu* 9 (1921-23), §88-§207 *Ériu* 10 (1926-28), III, IV *Ériu* 14 (1946), V *Ériu* 17 (1955).

Black, R. (1976): 'Poems by Maol Domhnaigh Ó Muirgheasáin' (I)', *Scottish Gaelic Studies* 12, 195-208.

Breatnach, P. A. (1983): 'The chief's poet', *Proceedings of the Royal Irish Academy*, 83, C, no. 3, 37-79.

---

[58] Witness the fact that the poets whose works have so far been identified in the tracts (McManus 1997, 2000b and de Brún 1998) flourished in the period from the 13th to the 15th centuries. Breatnach (2000, 14) identifies an elegy to Aodh Ó Domhnaill († 1505), viz. *Cionnus tig Éire gan Aodh* 'How will Ireland fare without Aodh?' (*Book of O'Conor Don*, fol. 168a) as the latest datable composition cited in the tracts.

(1989): 'Cú Chonnacht Ó Dálaigh's poem before leaving Aodh Ruadh', *Sages, saints and storytellers; Celtic Studies in honour of Professor James Carney* (ed. D. Ó Corráin *et al.*), Maynooth, 32-42.

(1993): 'A covenant between Eochaidh Ó hEodhasa and Aodh Mág Uidhir', *Éigse* 27, 59-66.

(1997): *Téamaí taighde Nua-Ghaeilge*, Maynooth.

(2000): 'The metres of citations in the Irish Grammatical tracts', *Éigse* 32, 7-22.

Breatnach, R.A. (1942): 'Marbhna Fhearchoir Í Mháoil Chíaráin', *Éigse* 3, 165-85.

Carney, J. (1955): *Studies in Irish literature and history*, Dublin.

(1967): *The Irish bardic poet*, Dublin.

de Brún, P. (1998): 'Varia iv: *IGT* citations – some additional identifications' *Ériu* 49, 175-6.

Flower, R. (1953): *Catalogue of Irish manuscripts in the British Museum*, vol. 3, London.

Knott, E. (1911): 'Filidh Éireann go haointeach: William Ó Ceallaigh's Christmas feast to the poets of Ireland, A.D. 1351', *Ériu* 5, 50-69.

Mac Aogáin, P. (1968): *Graiméir Ghaeilge na mBráthar Mionúr*, Dublin.

McKenna, L. (1947): A poem by Gofraidh Fionn Ó Dálaigh', *Féilscríbhinn Torna* (ed. S. Pender), Cork, 66-76.

(1951): 'Some Irish bardic poems': xcvii (*Mór an feidhm deilbh an dána*), xcviii (*A fhir shealbhas duit an dán*) and xcix (*Créad dá sealbhainn damh an dán*), *Studies* 40, 93-96, 217-222, 352-364.

McManus, D. (1996): 'Classical Modern Irish', *Progress in medieval Irish studies*, ed. K. McCone and K. Simms, Maynooth, 165-87.

(1997): 'The Irish Grammatical and Syntactical tracts: a concordance of duplicated and identified citations', *Ériu* 48, 83-101.

(2000a) 'An elegy on the death of Aodh Ó Conchobhair († 1309)', *Ériu* 51, 69-91.

(2000b) 'VARIA IV, *IGT* citations and duplicate entries; some additional identifications', *Ériu* 51, 193-4.

Murphy, G. (1953): *Duanaire Finn* vol. 3, *Irish Texts Society* 43, Dublin.

Ó Cuív, B. (1968): 'A Colam Cille dialogue', *Éigse* 12, 165-72.

(1971): 'An appeal on behalf of the profession of poetry', *Éigse* 14, 87-106.

(1980): 'A mediaeval exercise in language planning', *Progress in linguistic historiography* (*Amsterdam studies in the theory and history of linguistic science* 3), (ed. K. Koerner), Amsterdam, 23-34.

Ó Foghlú, S. (1992): *Four bardic poems from Leabhar Chlainne Suibhne*, unpublished M. Litt. thesis, TCD.

Ó Háinle, C. (2000): ' Teora dréachta adhmholta do chuinghidh shíodha"', *Saoi na hÉigse: Aistí in ómós do Sheán Ó Tuama* (ed. P. Riggs *et al.*), Dublin, 1-22.

O'Rahilly, T. F. (1942): 'A poem by Piaras Feiritéar', *Ériu* 13, 113-18.

Quiggin, E. C. (1913): 'O'Conor's house at Cloonfree', *Essays and studies presented to William Ridgeway* (ed. E. C. Quiggin), Cambridge, 333-52.

Simms, K. (1987): 'Bardic poetry as a historical source', *The writer as witness: literature as historical evidence* (ed. T. Dunne), (*Historical Studies* 16), Cork, 58-75.

ABBREVIATIONS:

AiD: *Aithdioghluim Dána*, L. McKenna, 2 vols., *Irish Texts Society* 37 (1939), 40 (1940), Dublin.

BST: *Bardic syntactical tracts*, L. McKenna, 1944, Dublin.

DBM: *Dán na mBráthar Mionúr*, 2 vols. (1967, 1980), ed. C. Mhág Craith O.F.M., Dublin.

DiD: *Dioghluim Dána*, L. Mac Cionnaith, 1938, Dublin.

GBMC: *The poems of Giolla Brighde Mac Con Midhe* (ed. N.J.A. Williams), *Irish Texts Society* vol. 51, 1980, Dublin.

IBP: *Irish bardic poetry*, O. Bergin, 1970, Dublin.

IGT: see Bergin (1916-55).

ISP: *Irish syllabic poetry 1200-1600*, E. Knott, 1928, Cork and Dublin.

LB: *Leabhar Branach, The book of the O'Byrnes* (ed. S. Mac Airt), 1944, Dublin.

LCAB: *Leabhar Cloinne Aodha Buidhe*, (ed. T Ó Donnchadha), 1931, Dublin.

Magauran: *The book of Magauran*, (ed. L. McKenna), 1947, Dublin.

Maguire: *Duanaire Mhéig Uidhir*, (ed. D. Greene), 1972, Dublin.

O'Reilly: *Poems on the O'Reillys*, (ed. J. Carney), 1950, Dublin.

SGS: *Scottish Gaelic Studies.*

TD: *The Bardic poems of Tadhg Dall Ó hUiginn*, E. Knott, 2 vols., *Irish Texts Society* 22-23 (1922, 1926).

THE NOVEL FRUSTRATED:
SEVENTEENTH- TO NINETEENTH-CENTURY FICTION IN IRISH[1]

Cathal G. Ó Háinle

When the movement to restore the fortunes of the Irish language was begun in the last quarter of the nineteenth century, what was undertaken was, not only the revival of the language and its re-establishment as the common tongue of Ireland, but, by that means, the preservation of the Irish identity also. This was done under the influence of ethnocultural, apolitical nationalism and not of political nationism (the terminology is that of Joshua Fishman[2]), though it is true that it was the movement for the revival of Irish that generated much of the energy of the demand for political independence at the beginning of the twentieth century. A language serves as a basis for nationality because it is a powerful means of uniting a people and of distinguishing them from other peoples, though, of course, it can hinder the fulfilment of another need that a people has, namely, the need for contact and communication with other peoples. The two eighteenth-century German philosophers, Johann Gottfried Herder (1744-1803) and Johann Gottlieb Fichte (1762-1814), developed the theory of the bond between nationalism and language, and it is quite clear that it was the influence of their philosophy which led the nineteenth-century political leader of the Young Irelanders, Thomas Davis, to formulate, with reference to Irish, such catch-cries as 'A people without a language of its own is only half a nation'. National languages are always symbols and badges of identity as well as means of communication, a fact which was well understood by the writer who remarked in the first number of *Irisleabhar na Gaeilge* (*The Gaelic Journal*) (1882): 'A language is a most distinctive mark of the intellectual independence of any nation, and the best guarantee of its continuance'; while David Comyn, one of the founders of the language revival movement, believed that Irish was 'the one indelible and unmistakable mark of Irishmen'.[3] Indeed, if the revival of Irish involved nothing more than communication, it is clear that it would have been a waste of effort, since the English language was available to Irish people

---

[1] Translation from Irish to English of extracts quoted in the course of this essay is my own. I wish to acknowledge, however, that translations by the editors of some texts were found useful.

[2] Fishman, Joshua A., *Language and nationalism*, Rowley, Mass. 1972, 3-5.

[3] Comyn, David, 'To the readers of *The Gaelic Journal*', *The Gaelic Journal*, vol 1, no 17 (1882), 17.

as a potent means of communication among themselves and with the two large population groups to the east and to the west of Ireland.

In order that Irish would serve as a proper basis for nationality and as a symbol and badge of identity, however, it was necessary that it could be seen to be a language which had real status. Most sophisticated people in western Europe at that time would not have believed that a language which was not being used for literary purposes was a truly developed language; rather would they have regarded it as a mere *patois*.[4] But this was the situation of Irish: it had ceased to be used for any purpose that deserved the name 'literary'. Irish language revivalists believed from the beginning, then, that it would not be enough to get Irish spoken widely again, but that it would be necessary, too, to get it written and read, and to have it used again as a literary medium. In 1877 the founders of *The Society for the Preservation of the Irish Language* announced that one of their aims was 'to encourage the production of a Modern Irish Literature – original or translated' and that it was their intention to found a journal 'for the cultivation of the language and literature of Ireland'.[5] Thomas O'Neill Russell expressed a simplified version of this understanding of the need for a literature in Irish when he wrote:

> ... If we are to save Irish from death we need books and literature. Even if everyone in Ireland knew Irish, it could only survive for a short time unless many books of every kind of literature are written in it.[6]

But how had it come to pass that Irish, which had such a remarkable literary heritage, had stopped being used as a medium of prose literature by the middle of the nineteenth century?

The general circumstances of the Irish-speaking population in the nineteenth century were not such as would lead one to expect a great flowering of literature in Irish in that period. Irish had ceased to be used in any high social domain (apart from some preaching in church) and so had suffered a massive fall in status; it was no longer the language of the upper, nor of the middle classes, and, by the second half of the century, was confined, not only socially to the most deprived in society, but also

---

[4] The words 'literary' and 'literature' here and in the following sentences are used in the narrow sense as referring to written literature. Of course, there existed in Irish a vibrant oral literature which survived as a living tradition well into the twentieth century.

[5] Ní Mhuiríosa, Máirín, *Réamhchonraitheoirí*, Baile Átha Cliath 1968, 6.

[6] Russell, Thomas O'Neill, *Teanga thíoramhuil na hÉireann*, Baile Átha Cliath 1897, 11.

geographically to an ever-shrinking portion of the poorest areas of the west of Ireland; education, even of the most basic kind, was not available in Irish, and so literacy in Irish had become virtually non-existent. Verse continued to be produced, often by non-lettered poets; but most of it was doggerel about local events and concerns, and was quite ephemeral. In prose the first half of the century saw the production of a meagre amount of factual literature and a tiny quantity of fiction – I shall return to this later – but nothing at all that might approximate to the novel as it had developed in other European languages. The second half of the century, up to the time that the revival movement began to have some success, is a complete blank, in terms of prose writing of any kind. As I have said, the general circumstances of Irish in the nineteenth century do not make this surprising. But why had Irish failed to produce a modern prose literature in the seventeenth and eighteenth centuries, when the spread of Irish had not become so restricted, and when literary activity had continued in the language? It is to offering some answer to this question that I now want to address myself. It is not enough, in any case, simply to say that Irish literary men would have clung to the traditional and resisted the introduction of novelty. Previous ages had seen the borrowing into Irish literature of European themes and genres; the seventeenth century had seen the same happen in the important area of political verse; and eighteenth-century Irish prose shows some awareness of contemporary trends. Irish writers may have been slow to borrow, but they did not refuse to do so.

Perhaps I may be allowed to give an outline of what I understand to be an acceptable view of what was happening elsewhere. We may describe the classical novel as an extended prose narrative which purports to give a true account of the experience of an individual or of individuals, which is realistic in that it is the product of 'a mind with a true grasp of human reality, never deceived or deceiving about [the author] himself, his characters or the human lot in general',[7] and which, in concerning itself with the character of the protagonists, provides for the investigation of their motives and for the development of their characters in the course of the narrative. The serious novel has, of course, a moral purpose.

It is interest in character and concern for realism that mark the classical novel as a radically new departure in the long tradition of fictional narrative forms, and indeed allow us to claim that Cervantes' *Don Quixote* stands as the prototype of the new form and as its inspiration. The claim to represent a historically real experience is not unique to the novel. Shorter narratives of the kind referred to in Irish as

---

[7] Watt, Ian, *The Rise of the novel*, Harmondsworth (1957) 1968, 301.

seanchas did claim to be historically true and were frequently introduced in oral delivery by the formula 'Ní scéal scéil atá agam air, nó bhí mé i láthair' (My report is no second-hand one as I was present [when these events happened]). However, longer narratives, of the kind that the novel might have been expected to grow out of, were, in general, pure fiction (*cumadóireacht* in Irish) with no basis in reality, were accepted by their audience as such and were introduced by a formula of the 'Bhí fear ann fadó agus is fadó bhí' (There was a man once upon a time and a long time ago it was) variety and concluded with the words 'Sin é mo scéal. Má tá bréag ann bíodh, nó ní mise a chum ná a cheap' (That's my story. If there is a lie in it, let there be, since I did not compose nor invent it). The moral purpose of the serious novel is not necessarily unique either, for, as Dr Caoimhín Breatnach has demonstrated, modern versions of some earlier Irish tales were made for political and other didactic purposes.[8]

The late medieval and early modern tradition of Irish story was to a large extent parallel to, and to some extent indeed part of, the European tradition. Stories were narrated orally, either delivered from memory or read from a manuscript to a largely illiterate audience; and this situation was responsible for the style and form and for much of the content of the stories. The style tended to be inflated and florid, dotted with synonymous pairs and alliterative strings of words to please the ear and marked by stereotypical phrases or 'runs' which provided both teller and audience with periodic resting places; the narrative structure tended to be uncomplicated so as not to make undue demands on the ability of the teller and audience to cope; while the content consisted entirely of recitation of events and actions, with little or no interest being taken in motive, nor hence in character, so that the protagonists were merely what held the sequence of episodes together. Lack of interest in character also reflected the dominant philosophical tendency of the time, interest being focussed on the nature of Man (what was common, unchanging) rather than on personality (what was individual, subject to change). The escapist imperative almost required that the demands of realism and of verisimilitude be ignored. The *roman d'aventure* was the classic realisation of this kind of literature in the late middle ages. In the fifteenth century, stories of this kind were produced in great numbers in Spain and Portugal. They were much in demand in those two countries and throughout Europe in the sixteenth and seventeenth centuries, and were translated into French, Italian, German, Dutch, English and Irish. In the seventeenth century, however, they were to some extent displaced by the French style of romances which were written by Honoré d'Urfé,

---

[8] Breatnach, Caoimhín, *Patronage, politics and prose*, Maynooth 1996, 1-39.

Madeleine de Scudéry and La Calprenède and imitated in English by such as Roger Boyle, and which were in turn 'thrust out' as the contemporary English publisher and romancer, Francis Kirkman, wrote in 1672, 'by the present slighting and neglect of all books in general, by the particular esteem of our late *English stage Plays*'.[9]

Though romances continued to be written, translated and widely read throughout Europe in the seventeenth century,[10] the coming together of a constellation of factors in the seventeenth and eighteenth centuries created the opportunity for more subtle change and enabled the emergence of the novel in European literature. These included the development of more efficient methods of printing, the spread of literacy, the emergence of a comfortably-off middle class, and the growth of interest in the individual, due on the one hand to the philosophic work of René Decartes and John Locke, followed by David Hume in the eighteenth century, and on the other to social developments such as the Reformation, a new economic order and the rapid growth of towns and cities. None of these on its own would have effected the change. Very many *romans d'aventure* were published in the sixteenth and seventeenth centuries: the recognition that the redundant style, simple traditional plots and concentration on events and actions were unsatisfactory came only when the habit of reading became widespread due to the spread of literacy and a degree of leisure, and books came to be widely bought by a reasonably well-off middle class; while change in characterisation could not have taken place without the philosophy to fire and sustain it. The philosophy of individualism, on the other hand, could not have generated change, if the public performance of literature were not replaced by private reading, which was facilitated by the printing press and the spread of literacy, and which could accomodate the greater complexity of plot and treatment required by a more sophisticated characterisation which public performance would have made it impossible to sustain.

It is hardly surprising that the Spanish *romans d'aventure* should have provided a butt for parody; but it certainly is strange that it should have been Cervantes who composed that parody in *Don Quixote*, for he had a much higher regard for his own two *romans*, *Galatea* which he published in 1584 and *Persiles y Sigismunda* which was published posthumously in 1617, than he had for *Don Quixote*. Nevertheless parody it certainly is, though it seems to have a satirical intent also. The style of the romances, so beloved of the Don, is mocked:

---

[9] Hollo, Kaarina, 'Eachtra Ridire na Leomhan ina comhthéacs Eorpach' in Ní Dhonnchadha, Máirín (ed), Nua-léamha, Baile Átha Cliath 1996, 57-63.

[10] Hollo, 'Eachtra', 68.

> Above all [the Don] preferred [the romances] written by the famous Feliciano de Silva on account of the clarity of his writing and his intricate style, which made him value those books more than pearls; especially when he read of those courtships and letters of challenge that knights sent to ladies, often containing expressions such as 'the reason for your unreasonable treatment of my reason, so enfeebles my reason that I have reason to complain of your beauty'. And again: 'the high heavens which, with your divinity, divinely fortify you with the stars and make you the deserver of the desert that is deserved by your greatness.' These and similar rhapsodies bewildered the poor gentleman's understanding, for he racked his brains day and night to unbowel their meaning, which not even Aristotle himself could have done, if he had been raised from the dead for that purpose.[11]

In undertaking his first knightly expedition, the Don sees himself as acting in accordance with, and imagines himself being described in terms of, his beloved romances. Indeed it is precisely those romances which have addled his brains and turned him into a mock-hero as the narrator explains at the beginning of his account:

> [Don Quixote] so immersed himself in those romances that he spent whole days and nights over his books; and thus with little sleeping and much reading his brains dried up to such a degree that he lost the use of his reason. His imagination became filled with a host of fancies he had read in his books – enchantments, quarrels, battles, challenges, wounds, courtships, loves, tortures and many other absurdities. So true did all this phantasmagoria from books appear to him that in his mind he accounted no history in the world more authentic ...
>
> At last, having lost his wits completely, he stumbled upon the oddest fancy that ever entered a madman's brain. He believed that it was necessary, both for his own honour and for the service of the state, that he should become knight-errant and roam through the world with his horse and armour in quest of adventures, and practice all that had been performed by the knights-errant of whom he had read.[12]

The satiric intent seems clear: Cervantes points up the pernicious influence of the romances and writes a parody of them in order to

---

[11] Starkie, Walter (ed), *Don Quixote of la Mancha by Miguel Cervantes Saavedra*, London 1954, 4.

[12] Starkie, *Don Quixote*, 5, 6.

debunk them. But his imaginative ability as a writer carried him beyond that intent and enabled him to portray the opposition between the ideal and the real. Don Quixote inhabits an ideal, romantic world; Sancho and the rest live in the real world, though paradoxically it is not possible to say that Sancho's view of life is the correct one and that the Don's is mistaken. Indeed, as Dorothy Van Ghent has said, 'the visionary is placed in the perspective of the rational, the rational in the perspective of the visionary ... [so that] the reader cannot eliminate either one from his own view'.[13] This underlying opposition finds detailed expression in many facets of the work and is reinforced by a series of oppositions between features of the first part which was published in 1605 and of the second which was published in 1615. Thus the perspective of the work is realist rather than romantic or idealist: the characters are essentially ordinary people whose personalities are investigated and whose lives and actions in the ordinary world are placed under scrutiny. That the principal character is deranged and that his view of the world is bizarre does not make him extraordinary, nor his story unrealistic. It is in this sense then that I have suggested that *Don Quixote* deserves the label of 'novel' or at least 'proto-novel'.

The first part of *Don Quixote* was a resounding success, as was reported by Cervantes himself at the beginning of the second part:

> I believe there are to-day in print more than 12,000 volumes of the said history. For proof you have only to ask Portugal, Barcelona and Valencia, where they have been printed, and it is rumoured that it is being printed at Antwerp, and I am convinced that there is not a country or language in the world in which it will not be translated. And, mark you, it does not need a commentary to explain it, for it is so clear that there is nought in it to puzzle anyone. Children turn its leaves, young people read it, grown-ups understand it, and old folks commend it.[14]

It certainly aroused great interest almost immediately in England. Thomas Shelton published an English version of the first part in 1612, and an English version of the second part appeared in 1620. Between 1602 and 1676 twenty-five plays were published by thirteen different authors in which the Spanish romances and their readers were held up to ridicule. Though it is clear that the earliest of these could not have been influenced by *Don Quixote*, they reveal a community of antipathy with it which must have provided fertile ground for Cervantes's influence, and

---

[13] Van Ghent, Dorothy, *The English novel: form and function*, New York (1953) 1967, 29, 22.

[14] Starkie, *Don Quixote*, 284.

certainly Beaumont's and Fletcher's play of 1613, *The knight of the burning pestle*, shows clear traces of that influence, as does Butler's satiric poem *Hudibras* which was published much later in the century (1663). *Don Quixote* also had a strong influence on the form and structure of the English novel as it came into existence in the eighteenth century in the work of Defoe, Richardson, Fielding, Sterne and Smollett; indeed Defoe's *Robinson Crusoe* (1719) has close parallels with *Don Quixote*, while Fielding stated that in writing *Joseph Andrews* (1742) he was imitating Cervantes.

To group the eighteenth-century English novelists together in that way is not to suggest that they constituted some kind of school of new writers, or that their work shows linear development, one to the next. Nevertheless they are all heirs of Cervantes in that they concerned themselves with the individual man rather than with Man, a fact which the titles of their works proclaim, *Don Quixote, Robinson Crusoe, Moll Flanders, Pamela, Clarissa, Joseph Andrews, Tom Jones, Tristram Shandy, Roderick Random*, as does also their increasing tendency in their novels to eschew characteristic names which suggest a type of person and to use ordinary names whose function is to symbolise the fact that the character is to be regarded as though he were a particular person.[15] Thus they all rejected the literary theory of the neo-Platonists who demanded that literature should concern itself with 'the typical aspects of human conduct rather than those which are unique'.[16] However, the English writers took the novel a stage further than Cervantes in seeking to portray the development of character in the course of the story; in other words, as we read, our understanding of, and insight into the character of the protagonists increases.

A parallel development did not take place in eighteenth-century Irish. Why?

There would seem to have been some awareness in Ireland of the emergence of the new fictional form in English. We know that English novels, including Defoe's *Moll Flanders*, were read in hedge-schools in Ireland in the early nineteenth century,[17] and it is likely that they were also being read in the eighteenth, though there is little direct evidence to sustain this supposition. However, *The gentleman's magazine* was an influential force in moulding the taste for the kind of reading which

---

[15] Watt, *Rise of the novel*, 19-20.

[16] Forcione, Alban K., *Cervantes' christian romance*, Princeton 1972, 6.

[17] Dowling, Patrick J., *The hedge schools of Ireland*, Cork (London 1935) 1968, 65. While this demonstrates that such books were available and were being read in Ireland, Dowling makes the point that they were never used as class books, but that 'each child read his lesson from the book he happened to possess at the time', 69.

found an appropriate fictional form in the novel. Its editor and publisher, Edward Cave stated in 1741 that it was 'read as far as the English language extends, and ... reprinted from several presses in Great Britain, Ireland, and the Plantations'.[18] In 1778 Fanny Burney, herself a novelist, resonated with other commentators of her time in criticising the contribution of the circulating libraries to the debasement of literary taste. These libraries which were availed of by 'every butcher and baker, cobbler and tinker, throughout the three kingdoms' stocked all types of literature, but novels were widely regarded as their main attraction.[19]

The Irish language was spoken throughout the century by the greater part of the country's population, and though its geographic spread had begun to shrink, absolute numbers of Irish speakers rose sharply in the latter part of the eighteenth century as the population increased dramatically. Literary activity in Irish in both prose and verse continued unabated also.

Much historical and religious prose was written in Irish in the early seventeenth century, and later the well-known and influential social satire *Pairlimint Clainne Tomáis* (The parliament of Clan Thomas) appeared. Prose romances were popular and stories with a native framework, based, for instance, on the Fenian cycle, and also ones with a foreign setting continued to be composed in the period [20] A number of early seventeenth-century examples appear to have been directly influenced by French or Italian romances. Brian Ó Corcráin, the author of *Eachtra Mhacaoimh an Iolair* (The story of Eagle-boy), tells us in his preface that he had heard an outline of the story from a nobleman who said he had heard it told in French.[21] If this is true, he certainly expanded what he heard to a substantial degree. *Eachtra Mhelóra agus Orlando* (The story of Melora and Orlando)[22] is based on an episode from Ariosto's *Orlando Furioso*, an English version of which was known and appreciated in Ireland in the later years of the previous century, having been presented by its translator, Sir John Harrington, to the Earl of Tír Eoghain.[23] A further possible case of influence by, or borrowing from,

---

[18] Watt, *Rise of the novel*, 53.

[19] Watt, *Rise of the novel*, 44.

[20] Some at least of the Fenian tales were composed in the sixteenth century. It is significant that the earliest (seventeenth-century) manuscripts of a number of Fenian tales, which were clearly composed in Ireland, are Scottish: see Bruford, Alan, *Gaelic folk-tales and mediaeval romances*, Dublin 1966, 47.

[21] de Teiltiún, Ioraird & Seosamh Laoide (eds), *Eachtra Mhacaoimh an Iolair*, Baile Átha Cliath 1912, xix.

[22] Mhac an tSaoi, Máire (ed), *Dhá scéal artúraíochta*, Dublin 1946, 1-41.

[23] See Flower, Robin, *Catalogue of the Irish manuscripts in the British Museum* 2, London 1926, 339. Harrington had obtained the copy of his translation in Dublin; he also found it being read by a lady in Galway.

an Italian original is the seventeenth-century romance *Eachtra Ridire na Leomhan* (The story of the Knight of the Lions)[24] which shows interesting similarities to *The honour of chivalrie: the history of Don Bellianis* which had been 'Englished out of Italian' in 1598 and made extremely popular by Francis Kirkman's later seventeenth-century revision of it, which was presumably the version of it which was on sale in Dublin in 1668.[25] Direct translations into Irish were also made, for example the three made by Fr Maghnus Ó Domhnaill at the end of the seventeenth century from the Spanish of Juan Perez de Montalvan (+1638), *Eachtra an pháláis dhraíochtúil* (The story of the enchanted palace), *Eachtra an cheithearnaigh choille chompáisigh* (The story of the compassionate outlaw) and *Eachtra Risteaird agus Liosarda* (The story of Richard and Lisarda).[26]

Towards the end of the century there appears to have been a minor explosion of creativity in the south-east Ulster area, to which we owe a sizeable collection of romantic tales which, naturally enough because of their provenance, revive the old Ulster heroes and introduce them into the standard romantic setting where they seem to be as much at home as any of the Arthurians. They behave in accordance with the highest standards of Spanish, French and Italian chivalry; travel the known world, overcoming impossible odds and doing battle in defence of kingdoms; protect the honour of defenceless maidens; and eventually return home, having won honour, renown, a noble spouse and a kingdom.

Thus in the course of the seventeenth century no fundamental change had taken place in Irish fiction. The themes of the stories are the standard ones of romantic literature and their treatment is as unrealistic as ever. Yet, though a radically new approach could not be accomodated, there is some evidence, however slight, of an awareness that change was needed, though it would be foolhardy to presume that this was due to the influence of developments in English literature rather than to the democratisation of Irish literature effected by the collapse of the old order which deprived literary men of patrician patronage and forced them, from the middle of the seventeenth century on, to seek to find an audience among the ordinary people.

---

[24] Ní Chróinín, Áine (ed), *Eachtra Ridire na Leomhan*, Baile Átha Cliath 1952.

[25] Hollo, '*Eachtra*', 64-67, 57, 60.

[26] Murphy, Gerard, *The ossianic lore and romantic tales of medieval Ireland*, Dublin 1955, 36; Ó Maonaigh, Cainneach, 'Scríbhneoirí Gaeilge an seachtú haois déag', *Studia Hibernica* 2 (1962), [182-208], 199. The first two of those stories are in Royal Irish Academy ms 331 (23M3) and the third is in RIA ms 335 (23M10), both of which were written by Maghnus Ó Domhnaill himself.

Firstly the style of the later stories is less florid than that of the earlier ones. Secondly there are occasional instances of a somewhat more complex structure. The form of Irish stories, unlike their European counterparts, was a simple linear one for the most part with little diversion or interruption. In one of the south-east Ulster group, *Eachtra na gcuradh* (The story of the heroes),[27] however, the main narrative consists of a brief introduction which describes a feast at which a number of the Ulster heroes were present, followed by the narration by three of them, Conall Cearnach, Cú Chulainn and Oilill Fionn, of accounts of their adventures to date; Cú Chulainn's story is punctuated by a series of anecdotes within anecdotes. Thirdly there is a single straw in the breeze of verisimilitude. In the romantic stories, travel to distant lands presents no language barriers or difficulties of communication. At the beginning of the earlier *Story of Eagle-boy*, in what is nothing more than an unusual addition to the standard description of suitable royal accomplishments, the king of the foreign country, Sorcha, is described as being 'fluent in many languages of lands and peoples' and his son receives an education which confers a similar fluency on him, but the implication of the motif is not further considered or developed. In a later story, again one of the south-east Ulster group, *Tóraíocht Gruaidhe Griansholas* (The pursuit of Gruaidh Ghrianoholao), however, the language barrier is confronted and the ability of heroes from different language backgrounds to converse is explained by the existence of a common Esperanto-like language:

> If you wonder, dear reader, at how those strangers and foreigners understood each other's language, know that there was a language in existence at that time which was common to peoples and which was not proper to any one people, which was called *Béarla Teibhidhe*, just as Latin is now used; and without doubt that was the language in which these two spoke to each other on that occasion.[28]

---

[27] Ní Chléirigh, Meadhbh (ed), *Eachtra na gcuradh*, Baile Átha Cliath 1941.

[28] O'Rahilly, Cecile (ed), *Tóruigheacht Gruaidhe Griansholus*, Irish Texts Society 24, London 1924, 68-9. The phrase *Béarla Teibhidhe* (recte *Teibidhe*) means 'selected language' (see RIA *Dictionary of the Irish Language*, s.v. *teipide*) based on the understanding recorded by Séathrún Céitinn 'that there are words from every language as loan-words in ... *Béarla Teibhidhe* ... And thus as there are words from French in it, so there are words in it from Spanish, Italian, Greek, Hebrew, Latin, and from every other chief language.' (Dineen, Patrick S. (ed) *Foras feasa ar Éirinn* 2, Irish Texts Society 8, London 1908, 62-3.)

Such hopeful indicators of the possibility of change were insufficient to assuage the dissatisfaction of the anonymous author of *Siabhradh Mhac na Míchomhairle* (The enchantment of Scapegrace), who late in the seventeenth century,[29] took it upon himself to parody the romances of which he clearly had had his fill. I take it that, as in the case of *Don Quixote*, this parody is a plea for, and a stimulus to change, and as such is another indicator of the possibility of change.

In this tale the opportunity to demonstrate his valour and thereby to win a noble bride is presented to Scapegrace. The typical hero would have accepted both invitations with alacrity and zest: Scapegrace is torn between his terror at having to go into battle and his desire for the lady. His cowardice is, of course, the antithesis of what is expected of the hero of romance; and his behaviour towards the lady is anything but chivalrous, being nothing but undisguised lust. Three times he attempts nocturnal forays into the lady's bed; each time he fails, being frustrated by his own imagination which creates dreadful experiences for him. Three times he yells in panic when threatened by monstrous spirits and beasts and has to be rescued by the young lady and her father. The spirits turn out to be only screeching cats; and the beasts nothing more dreadful than a pet pig and a pup. When rescued, Scapegrace is found the first time in a vat of beer, the second in a trough of pig-swill, the third in a candelabra. Thus, whereas the romantic hero overcomes almost insuperable odds, Scapegrace cannot even defeat his own imagination. The typical Irish story was embellished with poetry, and so too are many of the seventeenth-century romances in Irish (e.g. *The story of Eagle-boy, The pursuit of Taise Taobhgheal,[30] The pursuit of Gruaidh Ghriansholas*). *The enchantment of Scapegrace* is also embroidered with verse, but, instead of the delicate speech-poems of the romances, this has a fair amount of sexual innuendo, especially in the first poem, which uses the fact that Scapegrace has just played backgammon with his prospective father-in-law, to provide the *lingua franca* for the expression of Scapegrace's libidinous fantasy.

This is quite successful as parody. However, whereas Cervantes' imaginative strength carried him beyond the mere parodic into the realm of proto-novel, as has been mentioned, the author of *The enchantment of Scapegrace* proved more limited in vision and his work remains at the level of parody. Neverthless, like Cervantes', his work did have a significant influence in that it probably provided the inspiration for a series of further works which employ the sexual motif to good broad

---

[29] Watson, Seosamh (ed), *Mac na Míchomhairle*, Baile Átha Cliath 1979, 110-111 (date), 115-26 (author).

[30] Ní Mhuirgheasa, Máire (ed), *Imtheacht an dá nónbhar agus tóraigheacht Taise Taoibhghile*, Baile Átha Cliath 1944.

comic effect and many of which use the evolving pattern of language shift from Irish to English in eighteenth-century Ireland to produce inter-language puns and misunderstandings to add to the humorous content. But just as *Don Quixote* failed to kill off the appetite for romantic tales and to give rise to a new genre in the seventeenth century, so too *The enchantment of Scapegrace* failed to trigger the production of a new kind of fiction in Irish in the eighteenth.

In the first quarter of the eighteenth century, Seán Ó Neachtain, who was originally from the Athlone area of Roscommon but settled in Dublin's Liberties, composed three long romances: *An Gleacaí Géaglonnach* (Valiant Fighter) which is in the Spanish style and is replete with long letters addressed by the various characters to one another and with character switches which make the action difficult enough to follow; *Imeacht an chúigir* (The travels of the five), a pseudo-Ossianic tale which turns five Fenian heroes, including Fionn mac Cumhaill and Goll mac Morna, into medieval European knights and presents the odd spectacle of Goll and his companions taking part in jousts and masked balls; and *Scéal Jacobides agus Carina* (The story of Jacobides and Carina), a semi-historical narrative based on the life of James Fitzjames, Duke of Berwick.[31] About the middle of the century Mícheál Coimín composed two further romances, *Eachtra Thoroilbh mhic Stairn* (The story of Torolbh son of Starn),[32] which introduces a new arena of activity into Irish romance by taking the protagonist to Africa, and a sequel, *Eachtra chloinne Thoroilbh* (The story of the family of Torolbh). A romantic tale of a different kidney is a late revision of 'the narrative which has become popularly known as the Modern Irish version of the so-called "Deirdre story"',[33] *Oidheadh Chloinne Uisneach* (The violent death of the sons of Uisneach). This late revision, *Imeacht Dheirdre le Naoise agus oidhe Chloinne Uisneach* (The departure of Deirdre with Naoise and the tragic fate of the children of Uisneach),[34] which is of East Ulster provenance and unknown authorship, appears in a manuscript written by Samuel Bryson of Belfast between 1805 and 1809. Its date of composition cannot be established, but may well have been not much anterior to the date of Bryson's

---

[31] None of those three romances by Ó Neachtain has been published, though *The story of Jacobides and Carina* has twice been edited in unpublished masters' theses. For information on these and on the manuscript sources of the other two tales see Ó Háinle, Cathal, 'Ar bhás Sheáin Uí Neachtain', *Éigse* vol 19 (1983), [384-94], 391-3.

[32] Ó Neachtain, Eoghan (ed), *Torolbh mac Stairn*, Baile Átha Cliath n.d.

[33] Breatnach, *Patronage, politics and prose*, 6.

[34] Ó Buachalla, Breandán (ed), 'Imthiacht Dheirdre la Naoise & oidhe Chloinne Uisneach', *Zeitschrift für Celtische Philologie* 29 (1962-64), 114-54.

manuscript copy. Instead of the typical 'happy ever after' ending of romance, this ends with the tragic deaths of the hero and heroine.

During the eighteenth century, then, on the one hand some traditional romances were written in Irish, and on the other the novel failed to emerge. It may very well be that conservatism may have played a rôle in this failure, but that cannot be the full explanation. As I have already said, Irish men of letters, while undoubtedly conservative, had historically adopted and adapted foreign models, and this occurred in verse in the seventeenth and eighteenth centuries when political themes from earlier French prose and verse were subsumed into Irish verse together with the *aisling* in which they achieved classical expression. As we shall see later there were indeed in the prose work of the eighteenth and early nineteenth centuries significant hints of a tendency to seek to introduce modern features into prose writing in Irish. Why did Irish literature fail to continue in this line of development? Why did not the novel or something akin to it emerge? The answer I gave to these questions more than twenty years ago[35] was that Irish fiction was denied the use of the printing press and so lacked the stimulus to change. From the end of the sixteenth century books had indeed been printed in Irish: Elizabeth I had provided a press and a set of type which was used to print Seán Ó Cearnaigh's *Aibidil Gaoidheilge & Caiticiosma* (An Irish ABC and Catechism, 1571) and Uilliam Ó Domhnaill's *An Tiomna Nuadh* (The New Testament, 1602-3) and *Leabhar na nUrnaightheadh gComhchoidchiond* (The Book of Common Prayer, 1608) and further works in Irish in the interest of the reformed faith, including Uilliam Bedell's Old Testament (1685), were published during the seventeenth century. Religious works in the Roman Catholic interest were printed on the Continent and smuggled into Ireland. But printing was an expensive business in the seventeenth century and continued to be so in the eighteenth, and publication of books had to be funded by patrons who had the means to do so, for example, the State or the Churches. It is clear that none of those institutions would have had any great interest in funding the printing of works of Irish fiction; nor is there any evidence that any other patron considered doing so, even though the funding in the second quarter of the seventeenth century of Mícheál Ó Cléirigh's researches in Irish history might have provided a model. Thus no work of Irish fiction was published in print during the seventeenth and eighteenth centuries, and so Irish fiction was not subjected on a large scale to the test of private reading which was greatly facilitated by the production on the printing press of multiple copies of texts.

---

[35] Ó Háinle, Cathal, 'An t-úrscéal nár tháinig', *Promhadh pinn*, Má Nuad 1978, 74-98.

All of that is true; but it is at best an incomplete answer. As I have suggested already, a number of interrelated factors contributed to the emergence of the novel in European languages. The development of printing techniques which eventually made posssible the relatively cheap book was one of those; but on its own it would not have led, and did not lead to the kind of change that produced the novel. Very many romances of the traditional kind were published and read avidly in the languages of Europe and printed romances in English were still being used as school readers in Ireland in the nineteenth century. The fact of the matter is that none of the other factors existed in the world of the Irish language either. A large reading public only becomes possible where literacy is common in the population. In the case of Irish, even basic literacy was never widely available, and the irony is that as basic literacy did begin to be widely taught, in the hedge schools, for example, in the eighteenth century and in the primary schools of the Board of Education in the nineteenth, it was almost universally literacy in English which was imparted, literacy in Irish being generally neglected. Thus there was no readership and no market for books in Irish. In those circumstances the price of books is largely irrelevant; nevertheless it is worth mentioning that as the status of Irish became more and more reduced, and it was spoken only by the more deprived, the cost of books would have been prohibitive for the only possible readership. Some school textbooks in English cost as much as six shillings at the end of the eighteenth century; but a more average price of two shillings would have represented a week's wages for a labourer in the poorer parts of Ireland.[36]

The stimulus of higher education and an exposure to newer philosophies was also denied to Irish-speakers in the eighteenth century, by law, of course, and also by economic circumstances. The upper classes, the well-to-do farmers in rural areas and the growing number of merchants in the large towns and cities had turned their backs on Irish, were English-speaking and were receiving education in English. But the part of the population from which writers of fiction in Irish were drawn had little opportunity to be exposed to the kinds of ideas that would suggest the need for change in literature from traditional types to individual characters.

Finally the novel, being concerned with the experience of the common man, is based on the premises that 'society [values] every individual highly enough to consider him the proper subject of its serious literature; and [that] there [is] enough variety of belief and action among ordinary people for a detailed account of them to be of interest to

---

[36] Dowling, *Hedge schools*, 62.

other ordinary people, the readers of novels.'[37] These circumstance were created by the industrial revolution which led to the growth of large towns and cities which lacked the strong sense of communal life of rural communities and produced a diversity of individual experience, and by changes in religious belief and practice. Again these conditions failed to emerge in Irish-speaking Ireland which was completely rural and remained almost universally Roman Catholic.

So, in fact, none of the interrelated factors which were necessary to the independent emergence of the novel in Irish were present in the eighteenth century; and the absence of three of those factors, printing, literacy and a reading public interested in the individual, would have made imitation of the emerging novel in English highly improbable. Nevertheless, Irish writers who were literate in English must have read some of the creative literature then available in English and may have felt the urge to imitate some features of what they read. As a result, just as had been the case in the seventeenth century, there were in eighteenth-century Irish writing, also, hints of an awareness of the requirements of realism, and in a few instances even more than mere hints.

Not only did Mícheál Coimín (1688-1760) extend the theatre of Irish romance by having his hero visit Africa, but he provided this picture of African women who were present at victory celebrations in honour of the hero, Torolbh mac Stairn, and his lady, Fionnabharthach:

> The womenfolk of the king were there, namely, fifty yellow and brown, black and blue women who were half naked, [wearing] only a strip of silk or of cotton wound around their bodies. The twisted, jet-black fur which was their hair was only a inch long, like the wool of a black, month-old lamb. There were four loops of a chain of red gold twisted around the breast and arms of every one of them, and four loops of it up to their elbows, and each woman had a large gold ring hanging from her nose and reaching to her chin. Thus were the womenfolk of the king of Iorruaidhe apparelled and dressed at that time. They were not allowed to sit on the ground, but had to stand and serve the king; and only the king himself and Torolbh and Fionnabharthach were sitting. Indeed those unattractive women did little attending or serving, for they were so amazed and astonished at the woman who was sitting that they could not take their eyes off her, since they had never before seen

---

[37] Watt, *Rise of the novel*, 62.

anything so astounding as the whiteness of her skin, the redness of her cheek, and the length and fairness of her hair.[38]

Clearly Ó Coimín had been reading some novels or travel literature or some of the many geography text-books which were available in English in the eighteenth century, and was anxious to parade his information. Risible though the passage may appear to the modern reader, it clearly represents an attempt to enable the reader to visualise a group of servants in the house of an African prince.

I would want to claim, however, that another prose fiction by Seán Ó Neachtain, *Stair Éamainn Uí Chléirigh* (The history of Éamann Ó Cléirigh),[39] though written in the first quarter of the eighteenth century, is more surely than any other eighteenth-century fiction in Irish inspired by a realism of the kind that was so important in the emerging novel in English. Ó Neachtain, who, as I have mentioned, wrote three romances, died in 1729, and there is evidence that at least two of his three romances were in existence ten years before that, so that I think that we can take it that *The history of Éamann Ó Cléirigh*, was also composed before 1719. One of his romances is an allegory, and so too is the *The history of Éamann Ó Cléirigh*. In it the eponymous hero struggles with the demons of drink and gambling, and descends to the bottom of the pit of depravity before eventually being rescued and restored.

It has been suggested that *The history of Éamann Ó Cléirigh* is autobiographical: this seems quite unlikely to me, and in any case is not particularly relevant to this discussion. It is true, however, that the work is anchored in Ó Neachtain's own experience in various ways. The wizard who cures the hero's alcoholism is Ó Neachtain's clerical friend, Fr. Pól Mac Aogáin, and an individual mentioned in passing in the story is Feardorcha Ó Dálaigh, another of the author's contemporaries. Ó Neachtain was a school-teacher; so is Éamann Ó Cléirigh. Ó Neachtain came from Co. Roscommon and settled in Dublin's Liberties; Éamann Ó Cléirigh's first encounter with Alcohol is in Thomas Street in the Liberties, where a Mr Rainsford had a porter brewery at James' Gate before the famous Arthur Guinness established his there in 1759, and Éamann is pursued by Alcohol across Ireland into Connacht. More important to an assessment of this fiction are the elements of realism involved and the portrayal of the hero's character.

Other eighteenth-century works had, as I have mentioned, used the emerging language shift from Irish to English to sustain an element of humour. Seán Ó Neachtain was seen by the nineteenth-century scholar,

---

[38] Ó Neachtain, *Torolbh mac Stairn*, 20.
[39] Ó Neachtain, Eoghan (ed), *Stair Éamuinn Uí Chléire,* [Baile Átha Cliath] 1918.

James Hardiman, to have had the same intention and the early twentieth-century editor of the work, Eoghan Ó Neachtain, seems to have concurred in that he quotes Hardiman's comments without demur: 'It would appear as if written for the purpose of turning into ridicule persons learning the English language. It abounds with genuine humour.'[40] I would disagree with this assessment. The language element of the content only emerges in the latter pages of the body of the text, and only gains prominence in a long addendum to the tale, which forms no integral part of the allegory. Furthermore I would argue that Ó Neachtain, though quite capable of using language problems to comic effect, as is clear from other works by him, in this case is more concerned to give a true portrayal of the behaviour of many of his contemporaries who were abandoning a good command of rich Irish and acquiring in its stead an unsure competence in threadbare and inaccurate, baboo English. To Ó Neachtain this was tragic rather than funny, and he does not seek to ridicule; therein lies the realism of his projection of the situation. And this realism is only one small part of the overall realism of his fiction in this work. For here, rather than romantically portraying the heroic behaviour of a noble character, he confronts the squalid reality of the life of his protagonist, Éamann, who is anyman or everyman. Éamann literally does descend into the pit: after one severe bout of drinking he loses consciousness and crawls off on all fours into a pig-sty, where his tormentor fails to recognise him, his snoring is so like the grunting of a pig; on another occasion, having no money, he gambles his clothes, loses all and is ejected naked from the house, and slinks off covered only by a stinking horse-blanket. Thus, portrayal of the principal character in *The history of Éamann Ó Cléirigh* is realistic, both in the older sense of being, like Daniel Defoe's *Moll Flanders*, for instance, a portrayal of low life, and in the more recent sense of offering a true grasp of the reality of human life. The realism of the work, it must be admitted, is limited by the incomplete realisation of the character of Éamann Ó Cléirigh. He does indeed come alive much more than do the stock-characters of the romances, but certainly not as fully as do the characters in a successful novel. In this sense, and allowing for its allegorical nature, *The history of Éamann Ó Cléirigh* might with justice be categorised as another proto-novel. The fact that Ó Neachtain wrote it around the time that Defoe wrote *Robinson Crusoe* (1719), *Moll Flanders* (1722) and *Roxana* (1724), or perhaps even earlier, underlines how suggestive *The history of Éamann Ó Cléirigh* is of what could have emerged in eighteenth-century Irish prose if circumstances had been favourable. Unfortunately they were not. Indeed

---

[40] Ó Neachtain, *Stair*, ii.

The history of Éamann Ó Cléirigh was only published in print at the beginning of the twentieth century; and the few other prose works that were produced were romances, as we have seen.

If my suggestion that *The departure of Deirdre* was produced late in the eighteenth century is correct, there is a very large gap between it and Seán Ó Neachtain's *The history of Éamann Ó Cléirigh*; and whereas Ó Neachtain's tale is entirely original, *The departure of Deirdre* is a re-working of the Deirdre story, as I have mentioned. In its own way, however, *The departure of Deirdre* is almost as fascinating as Ó Neachtain's tale for the evidence it contains of its author's awareness of trends in modern literature.[41]

The brief descriptions in the early part of the narrative of the mansion to which Deirdre is consigned by king Conchobhar are rather gothic, which may be due to the anonymous author's awareness of the gothic novel in English.[42] Another development has to do with the care taken by the author with the portrayal of Deirdre's character, part of which is the somewhat bizarre series of incidents in which Deirdre's desire for Naoise is first portrayed. In earlier versions of the legend, Deirdre, having seen a raven drink the blood of a slain calf which has fallen on the snow, expresses her desire for a lover who would have black hair, red cheeks and white skin. Naoise fits the description. Here, however, the motif is developed as follows:

> Cailcín, Deirdre's foster-father went to kill a calf to prepare a meal for her; and after the blood of the calf had been spilled on the snow a raven began to drink it, and when Deirdre noticed this as she was looking out through a window of the fortress, she groaned loudly so that Cailcín heard her.
> 'Why are you sad?' said he.
> 'Alas,' said she, 'that I did not have what I see.'
> 'You shall have that, if possible,' said he; and raising his hand he threw his knife unerringly at the raven, cut off one of its legs, caught the bird and threw it down beside Deirdre. She started immediately and fainted. When Leabharcham [her foster-mother] came to help her she said:

---

41 About 1820 an unknown Scottish writer produced 'a sort of attempt at a Gaelic novel' which is based on a folk version of the story of '*An t-amadán mór*' but reflects contemporary trends in novel-writing: see Bruford, Alan, *Gaelic folktales and mediaeval romances*, 149.

42 Ó Buachalla, 'Imthiacht Dheirdre', 122 (§3), 124 (§6). If this feature is in fact derived from the gothic novel, it would confirm that *Imeacht Dheirdre* is indeed, at the earliest, a late eighteenth-century work, for the gothic novel was inaugurated by Horace Walpole's *Castle of Otranto* in 1764.

'Why are you as I see you, dear girl? For you have been looking sad since yesterday.'

'I have conceived a wish,' said Deirdre.

'What is that wish?' asked Leabharcham.

'[My wish is for] three colours which I have seen,' said Deirdre, 'namely, the blackness of the raven, the redness of blood and the whiteness of the snow.'

'It's easy to get that for you now,' said Leabharcham, and she went out immediately and collected a vesselful of snow and a half beakerful of the blood of the calf, and she plucked three feathers from the wing of the raven, and she laid them on a table before the girl. Deirdre began as if lazily to eat the snow and to taste the blood from the tip of a feather of the raven while her foster-mother observed her closely, until Deirdre asked Leabharcham to leave her alone for a while. Leabharcham did so, and when she returned she found Deirdre making the shape of a man's head from a lump of snow, using the tip of a feather of the raven to paint it with the blood of the calf and putting fine black down on it as hair. Deirdre did not notice her foster-mother watching her until she was finished.[43]

Leabharcham questions her as to the identity of the man and Deirdre insists that she has seen him in a dream and that her desire for him is so great that she will not live without him. The word 'mian' [desire] is repeated three times for emphasis, and this triple emphatic repetition is a feature of this section of the tale. Subsequently Deirdre admits to Leabharcham that she had already met the man she so desires a long time before when he was a youth playing on the green of Eamhain Mhacha and had again seen him the previous day, and she exclaims that '[as a youth] he was beautiful in appearance and was most pleasing yesterday'.

'My girl,' said Leabharcham, 'you have not seen the youths nor the green of Eamhain [Mhacha] since you were seven years old, and that is seven years ago.'

'Seven bitter years,' said Deirdre, 'since I saw the pleasant green and the play of the youths when Naoise surpassed all the other youths of Eamhain [Mhacha].'

'Naoise mac Uisneach,' said Leabharcham.

'Naoise is his name as he told me,' said Deirdre ...

'As he told you?' said Leabharcham.

---

[43] Ó Buachalla, 'Imthiacht Dheirdre', 123 (§4).

'As he told me,' said Deirdre, 'when he threw a wild cast of the ball which veered off over the heads of the group of girls who were standing on the edge of the playing-field, and I got up from among them all and took the ball and handed it to him and he squeezed my hand with delight.'

'He squeezed your hand?' said Leabharcham.

'He squeezed it lovingly and said that he would see me again. But that was difficult for him and I did not see him again until yesterday. And so, dear mother, if you wish me to live, take a message from me to him and ask him to come to visit me and to talk to me in secret to-night ....'

Labharcham protests and mentions the great danger involved, but eventually relents and agrees to arrange the tryst,[44] and the story moves forward.

Those two excerpts deserve a close reading. It must suffice to say here that the proto-Jungian undertones of the first and the concern in the second to provide a reasonable basis for Deirdre's present emotional state represent important advances on the simple attempts at characterisation of the traditional romances and of the earlier versions of the Deirdre saga.

In the early nineteenth century, Amhlaoibh Ó Súilleabháin (1780-1838), also seems, in his *Tóraíocht Chalmfhir* (The pursuit of Brave Man)[45] which he wrote in 1826, to be attempting to push Irish romance in a new direction. This tale consists of a limited number of the common themes of romance which are presented in the purple prose typical of the genre and are embellished with two speech-poems. The narrative consists of short series of events which are imagined as having happened early in the nineteenth century: in a description of Callan, Co. Kilkenny, as the hero found it, there is a reference to the fact that Fr John Rice began the building of the new church in the village in 1811, and there are references to late eighteenth-century historical events and persons in Ireland, Europe and America. Brave Man is, in fact, one of the O'Tooles of Wicklow and represents the noble Irishman who strives against English oppression and meets his death as a result. Thus, while failing in this tale to break with the typical elements of traditional romance, Amhlaoibh Ó Súilleabháin introduced into it quite untraditional matter.

---

[44] Ó Buachalla, 'Imthiacht Dheirdre', 125-126 (§8).

[45] McGrath, Michael (ed), *Cinnlae Amhlaoibh Uí Shúileabháin* 4, Irish Texts Society 33, Dublin 1937, 114-50; Mághnus Ó Domhnaill (ed), *Tóruidheacht Chalmair Mhic Mhearchuradh*, Baile Átha Cliath 1939. There is a lacuna in this brief text, see McGrath, *Cinnlae*, x

Dáibhí de Barra (1757/8-1851), in' *Cath na deachún* (The tithe battle)[46] which he wrote in 1833, gives an account of an affray which took place in Co. Cork in June of the same year, and which was an incident in the Roman Catholic resistence to the payment of tithes to the Church of Ireland clergy. This short piece is another interesting experiment in a kind of prose writing that could have been fruitful in creative terms. In it the historical basis for the conflict which gave rise to the battle is first sketched and then an account of the battle itself is given, including the names of cómbatants on both sides and reasonably accurate details of features of the confrontation. The author's sympathy with his Catholic neighbours is clearly conveyed, as is his antipathy towards their oppressors and in particular his contempt for the process-server and for the police. However, there is a fictional element involved in the attribution of snatches of speech to various individuals and possibly in the arrangement of the action of the *dénouement*. The combination of factual reporting with elements of fictionality could have provided de Barra with a template for the writing of, say, a historical novel. Unfortunately the style and linguistic register of the piece remain to a large extent those of the romances, and it contains no serious attempt at characterisation. In fact, de Barra, as far as is known, produced no further work of this kind.

Amhlaoibh Ó Súilleabháin had the kind of interest in the written word, in social affairs and in human psychology which could well have formed the basis for writing a novel had he been able to make the break with the kind of writing that *The pursuit of Brave Man* represents. His *Cín Lae* (Diary)[47] which he wrote in the years 1827 to 1835 gives many clues to his concerns and thought patterns and clearly demonstrates his interest in, and involvement with social issues, while the following entry is extremely important in showing the response of his enquiring mind to what seems like an instance of psychosomatic trauma:

---

[46] Ó Cuív, Brian (ed), 'A contemporary account in Irish of a nineteenth-century tithe affray', *Proceedings of the Royal Irish Academy*, 61 C (1960), 1-21.

[47] Edited in McGrath, *Cinnlae* 1-4, Irish Texts Society 30-33, London & Dublin 1936-37; edited excerpts in de Bhaldraithe, Tomás, *Cín lae Amhlaoibh*, Baile Átha Cliath 1970. It would seem to have been through his friendship with local medical people, particularly Pádraig Céitinn whom he describes as a professor of surgery, that Amhlaoibh came to take an interest in science, particularly natural philosophy or botany. This inspired him to begin writing a nature journal in English, but almost immediately he turned to writing it in Irish and gradually extended its scope to that of the normal diary, including, not only his observation of nature, but all kinds of matters in which he took an interest and wished to record.

There is a remarkable story going around hereabouts just now. Elineora Ní Dhorchaí, the daughter of Séamas Ó Dorchaí from Baile Laighean, was coming home from Cill Bhaoithín, having heard Mass, on the second day of the present month, i.e. on Sunday, in the company of Nioclás Tóibín and other people, when she saw the Fairy Host around Machaire Mór. A dark person came out from the Host and sought to injure her. She was running around Nioclás Tóibín to avoid being injured, but it was little help to her, for the [fairy person] would have injured and indeed destroyed her if her mother, who had died six years before that, had not come to save her. Her mother looked sad.

Then the Fairy Host left her, and Nioclás Tóibín and the others brought her home. She was without speech until the cock crew after midnight, when she recovered her speech, and then she lost the power of her leg which was as cold as ice. She remained so for thirteen days, viz. until Saturday the fifteenth of this month, crying and weeping and being sad until her mother came to her and asked her if she would like to be cured. She said she would.

[Her mother said,] 'I would have come to you sooner but I could not while anyone was with you. And now that I find you alone, I shall cure you. Come out with me to the roadside.'

They both went out, though not by the same route, and her mother showed her an herb and told her to pull it, for no-one else should pull it. She pulled it, and it had neither skin nor leaf nor flower. And her mother told her to cook it in boiling water and to rub it on her leg six times in the name of the Father and the Son and the Holy Spirit. And her mother left her then, and she did as she had been told. And the first time that she made the Sign of the Cross on her leg it became straight and she has been in full health since then.

This is a remarkable story, unless she was in a delirium like a person in a fever, or unless it was a story of her own invention. But some of the neighbours say that her leg was as cold as ice. Her own father told me the story from beginning to end and Donnchadh Ó Briain from Droichead Bhaile Laighean [told it to me] in the same way. But indeed, he suspects that it was an invention, and that she pretended to be dumb and lame; but he admits that respectable people told him that her leg was cold as I have already said. I wash my hands of it.[48]

---

[48] de Bhaldraithe, *Cín lae*, 15-16.

In this carefully crafted piece Amhlaoibh's concern to present an accurate report based on the clear evidence of reliable, named witnesses is obvious; on the other hand he reports the doubts of one witness and his own misgivings. The folk mentality is perfectly at ease with an aetiology of illness which is based on preternatural intervention and with a cure effected by similar intervention and by the use of a charm. As a modern man professing an interest in science, Amhlaoibh must be sceptical of such an explanation; nevertheless contemporary psychological science provided no alternative one, so that his only valid stance is to admit that a satisfactory explanation is not available to him: 'I wash my hands of it!'

Amhlaoibh's account is given as a normal diary report of an actual event and there is no suggestion that it is fictional. There is, however, evidence that he was prone to use fictional devices to embellish anecdotes in his diary; and in this case there exists a parallel account (without any commentary, of course) preserved in the folklore of South-west Kerry collected by Séamas Ó Duilearga from the narration of the great Seán Ó Conaill.[49] This may not be significant, as such occurrences of trauma were scarcely uncommon; however, the similarities between the two accounts are striking and it is entirely possible that Amhlaoibh Ó Súilleabháin's anecdote is an attempt to use fiction for the purpose of psychological study.

The anecdote is also an example of Amhlaoibh's tendency in all his writing, despite his active involvement in efforts to alleviate the deprivations of the poor, to treat the common people with near contempt, in this case by portraying their gullible belief in fairies, the return of people from the dead and herbal healing. This attitude to the lower order in society runs right through a series of sketches[50] which Amhlaoibh composed and in which the folk belief in preternatural intervention is a significant element. In one sketch he describes the accidental death of a farmer, Páidín an Óir, who on a night of abominable weather fell into a deep ravine and was smothered by snow. Subsequently the rabble who gather at his wake express their belief that he met his death at the hands of a ghost, the King of the Rath, or of the fairies for whom Páidín had not had due respect.[51] On the other hand,

---

[49] Ó Duilearga, Séamus, *Leabhar Sheáin Uí Chonaill*, Baile Átha Cliath (1948) 1964, 294-5. de Bhaldraithe points out, *Cín lae*, 16, n. 1, that Amhlaoibh's story consists of common folk themes.

[50] McGrath, *Cinnlae* 4, 170-296; Mac Craith, Mícheál (ed), *Fiadhach is tóir is scéalta eile*, Baile Átha Cliath 1954.

[51] McGrath, *Cinnlae* 4, 192, 204-8. In another sketch a further reference is made to Páidín's death in the context of a discussion of mainly preternatural matters, Mac Craith, *Fiadhach is tóir*, 30; while in yet another sketch in the latter book the

Amhlaoibh gives a very sympathetic account of middle- and upper-class people. Thus when the principal character of the sketches, Calmar mac Tréinfhir [Brave Man son of Strong Man], is confronted by a ghostly spectre, he reacts with perfect composure, unlike Páidín an Óir who is terrified.[52]

It has been suggested by their editor, Michael McGrath/ Mícheál Mac Craith SJ, that this fairly extensive series of sketches was intended by Ó Súilleabháin to form 'sections or chapters of a novel, the action of which was to centre round Calmar, his sister Béal Binn [Sweet Mouth], Óigear Álainn [Beautiful Young Man] ... and his sister Ainnir Álainn [Beautiful Maiden]'. The first two of these belong to the remnant of the old Catholic Gaelic aristocracy who still retained some part of their estates and former social status, while the latter two 'ancestrally perhaps no less noble, represent a class ... who through successive confiscations had been reduced to·the rank of substantial farmers'. The background is the eighteenth century: the Penal Laws are shown to be making life difficult for Catholics, particularly in matters of education and land tenure, and two further characters, a Protestant minister, and a lawyer who is the son of a former Catholic who had conformed to Protestantism, seem set to complicate and perhaps defeat the romantic intentions of the first four.[53] There is much social realism in the sketches, including descriptions of work practices, customs, entertainment (singing, music, storytelling) and sport (hunting, hurling). There is, however, insufficient information to enable one to do more than guess at what the plot might have entailed.

Fr McGrath's regret that Ó Súilleabháin failed to weave this material into a complete novel[54] is scarcely warranted, for there are a number of features of the existing material which justify one in thinking that, had the project been completed, it was doomed to be unsatisfactory as a novel. As was the case with the author of *The departure of Deirdre*, several of Amhlaoibh Ó Súilleabháin's sketches show that he had a high regard for the gothic novel, the influence of which is apparent in his penchant for descriptions of ruined buildings, apparitions of ghosts and angels[55] and nights of ferocious weather. On the other hand, remaining

---

death of a farmer with a similar name, Eoinín an Óir, is attributed to the fairies by a *seanchaí*, 47-9.

[52] McGrath, *Cinnlae* 4, 172-82.

[53] McGrath, *Cinnlae* 4, xi.

[54] McGrath, *Cinnlae* 4, xx.

[55] To be fair to Ó Súilleabháin, however, in a revealing note he seeks to provide a rational explanation for these apparitions: 'The fact is that I have read a lot about images in the air in frosty weather. They are [seen] on frosty mountains in the western world [and] on frosty islands in the north sea, and why should they not be

trapped in the earlier tradition of the romances, he used type-names for his protagonists in a manner that is symptomatic of his inability to project individuals with any depth of character, and this problem is compounded by his use of the inflated style of the romance tradition, so that, in terms of a realisation of normal personalities, the language of the sketches was unhelpful in the narrative, and was particularly disabling in the dialogue which is utterly stilted.

Even if Amhlaoibh Ó Súilleabháin had completed a novel based on those sketches, it would have remained unpublished. None of the prose works of the seventeenth, eighteenth and nineteenth centuries which I have mentioned were published in print until scholarly editions of many of them appeared in the twentieth century; and indeed until John O'Donovan began to publish his editions in the eighteen-forties and the volumes of the *Transactions* of the Ossianic Society began to appear in the eighteen-fifties, the only examples of creative prose in Irish to have been published were the two early versions of the Deirdre legend which Theophilus O'Flanagan edited for the Gaelic Society of Dublin in 1808.[56] An extensive readership, literate in Irish, simply did not exist, and so there was no market for published creative Irish literature. Indeed in terms of the manuscript market, *The departure of Deirdre* and the work of Dáibhí de Barra and Amhlaoibh Ó Súilleabháin made no impact, for each of them exists in only one or two manuscript copies.[57]

Though a significant amount of interesting Irish verse continued to be written throughout the eighteenth century and even well into the nineteenth, only a relatively small amount of creative prose was produced over the same period. The work of Dáibhí de Barra and Amhlaoibh Ó Súilleabháin might have seemed to herald a new dawn,

---

[seen] on the frost-bound mountains of Ireland? The whole thing is only a mirage.' (McGrath, *Cinnlae* 4, 242-4).

[56] O'Flanagan, Theophilus (ed), *Transactions of the Gaelic society of Dublin*, [Dublin] 1808. For some account of the work of Charles Wilson (c. 1782), Charlotte Brooke (1789, 1816), Theophilus O'Flanagan (1808) and James Hardiman (1831) in publishing Irish poetry, including a tiny amount of recent verse, see my forthcoming essay 'An Ghaeilge agus an Béarla faoi chló a chéile sa naoú haois déag' in Denvir, Gearóid (ed), *Oidhreacht na Gaeilge*. The texts in all of those publications were accompanied by English translations or versions, and such bilingual publications were aimed principally at an English readership. The publication, from 1802 onwards, of the verse of Tadhg Gaelach Ó Súilleabháin (?1715-1795) and, in 1829, of that of Pádraig Denn, served a pious rather than a literary readership.

[57] This can be compared with eighteenth-century texts such as *The enchantment of Scapegrace* of which at least seventy-seven manuscript copies of the eighteenth and nineteenth centuries exist, Seán Ó Neachtain's *The history of Éamann Ó Cléirigh* of which at least eight manuscript copies have survived and Mícheál Coimín's two stories of which there are very many copies.

and, in view of the linguistic strengths of their writing it is unfortunate that this did not prove to be the case. Writing of the song tradition, George Petrie, in the preface to *The ancient music of Ireland*, referred to the 'awful, unwonted silence' in which the country was enveloped as a result of the Great Famine of 1845-48, a silence which he feared would swallow the music, language and traditions of the Irish.[58] It is impossible to imagine that in those circumstances the effort to sustain a creative literature in Irish could have been maintained. There were no successors to Dáibhí de Barra and Amhlaoibh Ó Súilleabháin and the silence remained unbroken until, with remarkable vision and courage, the revivalists of the late nineteenth century set about creating the conditions in which creative literature in Irish could again begin to flourish.

---

[58] Petrie, George, *The Petrie collection of the ancient music of Ireland* 1, Dublin 1855, xii.

152

ANDREW SALL (1624-82)
Textual Editor and Facilitator of the Irish Translation of the Old Testament

Terence P. McCaughey

In a letter from London at the end of April 1682 to the Protestant Bishop of Meath, the Hon. Robert Boyle writes as follows:

> Worthy Sir,
> I received with a great deal of regret, the sad and surprising news your letter brings me of the decease of so worthy and useful a person as doctor Sall, whose death I look upon, especially at this juncture of time as a great loss, not only to those who knew him, but to the church of Ireland in general.[1]

What made Dr Sall's death such a loss to Boyle was his involvement in the latter's project of printing the Irish translation of the Old Testament which had been made earlier in the century under the aegis of William Bedell, Bishop of Kilmore. In the same letter Boyle gives notice that the first trial sheet of that translation is on its way to Dublin from the printer in London. Of course, Dr Sall had earlier assisted Robert Boyle in the reprinting of the Irish New Testament of 1602 and of the Book of Common Prayer of 1608. Indeed, he had provided a preface to the new edition of the New Testament.

Irish scholars have never forgotten Andrew Sall's involvement in this project, a contribution cut short by his sudden death on 5 April 1682 at the age of fifty-eight. Even people who know nothing about the subject of this paper are familiar with the title of Dr Nicholas French's book attacking him, entitled *The doleful fall of Andrew Sall*.[2] Sall's doleful fall, in the view of Nicholas French, exiled Catholic Bishop of Ferns, consisted in his forsaking of the Society of Jesus and the Roman Catholic Church, after a public declaration to that effect, made in the presence of Thomas Price, Archbishop of Cashel, and Hugh Gore, Bishop of Waterford, in St John's church, Cashel, on 17 May 1674.

Sall's declaration provoked the publication of four ripostes, one of them by a fellow Jesuit, Fr Ignatius Brown, who had been a student of his in Salamanca.[3]

---

[1] Boyle, Robert, *The correspondence of Robert Boyle*, ed. Hunter, Michael, Antonio Clericuzio and Lawrence M. Principe, London and Vermont 2001, vol 5, 291-2.

[2] *The doleful fall of Andrew Sall, a Jesuit of the fourth vow, from the Roman Catholick apostolic faith, lamented by his constant friend, Nicholas French*, Douai 1674.

[3] *The unerring and unerrable Church; or An answer to a sermon preached by Mr Andrew Sall, formerly a Jesuit and now a minister of the Protestant Church, written by I.S.*, 1675.

At first sight it may seem strange that Andrew Sall's defection did not provoke an even greater spate of hostile publications. Criticism may have been inhibited by the then General of the Society of Jesus who almost immediately directed that while members of the Society might answer Sall's doctrinal errors, no word should be used against him likely to confirm him in his obduracy. 'Do all you can', he wrote to the Superior of the Society in Ireland, Fr Stephen Rice, in July 1674, 'that may in any way conduce to bring back the wretched man.'[4] In the end nothing would serve to bring him back, though a rumour recorded by Dr Brennan, Roman Catholic Bishop of Cashel, did circulate to the effect that on his death bed, Sall had sought in vain to have a Catholic priest attend him.[5] Oral tradition links Sall's name with that of another former priest, Pól Ó hUiginn, who was employed by Provost Narcissus Marsh in Trinity College to give lessons in Irish:

> ['S iad] Pól is Sál [móráil] a bhí gan chéill,
> [ná go gcuala sé guth Dé 's a chionn sa spéir].
> Ní le pógadh mná a gráitear croí Mhic Dé
> ach le deora cráidh 's a dtáirt in íoc ár gcréacht.[6]

In Protestant circles he has been remembered rather differently – as a spectacular convert, even something of a trophy. Richard Cox, Recorder of Kinsale, cites a letter recalling the excitement in Munster at the time. With undisguised satisfaction, the author of the letter writes:

> Sometime before this, there was a great blow given to Popery by the Conversion of Dr Andrew Sall, a learned and pious man. He had been a Jesuit of the Fourth Vow, and in great esteem amongst that Party. He was

---

Brown appears as no. 27 in the *Catalogus Patrum Societatis Iesu qui sunt in Hibernia... 1665-6* (Mac Erlean transcript in the Jesuit Archive, Leeson St., Dublin, of *Archivium Coll. Hib. Rom. xx*) where the following account is given of him: 'P. Ignatius Brunus; Waterfordiensis; natus ao. 1630; ... admissus in Hispania, 27 Junii 1651 ...'

[4] Ó Fionagáin, Proinsias, typescript history of the Jesuit 'Third Mission' in the Jesuit Archive, 35 Leeson St., Dublin, p. 344.

[5] For information on John Brennan see Power, Canon P., *A bishop of the penal times, being letters and reports of John Brennan, Bishop of Waterford (1671-93) and Archbishop of Cashel (1677-93)*, Cork 1932.

[6] Cited in Ó Moghráin, Pádraig, 'Pól Ó hUiginn', *Béaloideas* 15 (1945), [87-101], 101. The text is corrupt, ''S iad' and 'móráil' are editorial emendations, while line 2 is doubtful. In line 4 'dtáirt' is taken to stand for 'dtabhairt' and 'ár gcréacht' probably means 'our sins'. For another version of the verse see *Béaloideas* 16 (1946), 233. For further information on Pól Ó hUiginn see Ó Fiaich, Tomás, 'Pól Ó hUiginn', *The Maynooth Review* 2.1 (June 1976), 42-51.

afterwards made one of the King's Chaplains, and continued a good Protestant till his death.[7]

Almost one hundred and forty years later, in 1832 the Rev. Caesar Otway wrote an article on Andrew Sall, in which he claims that the real significance of the man lies in the fact that his conversion gives the lie to the widespread conviction in Catholic circles that no Roman Catholic of real intellectual distinction ever became a protestant.[8] In 1840 two of Sall's publications were again made available to the public by the Rev. Josiah Allport.[9] It is clear, however, that the reissue was itself a part of a more general nineteenth-century Protestant endeavour to 'dissuade from popery'.

The three categories of person who have from time to time remembered Andrew Sall have tended to recall one aspect only of the man – the Jesuit father, the Protestant polemicist or the collaborator of Robert Boyle – each without more than necessary reference to the other two. Yet the minister of the Church of Ireland can be better understood by reference to his time as a Jesuit and the learned scholar who died in the midst of his efforts to bring Bedell's Old Testament to the printers can certainly be discussed more fairly when we pay attention to his own account of his earlier life and conflicts. As in the case of John Henry Newman, with whom in this respect he may be compared, it is a mistake to concentrate on the abrupt change of confessional allegiance at the expense of the development and the continuum of the man's faith.

I: IN SPAIN

Andrew Sall was born in 1624 into a family of Sean-Ghaill (Old English) in the city of Cashel, Co. Tipperary. According to Patrick Woulfe, the name is probably de la Salle.[10] Besides holding grants of land in Aherlow, Co. Tipperary, they were merchants and professional people in the city itself. One of them, a lawyer, was hanged at the Rock of Cashel when it was besieged by Lord Inchiquin. A certain John Sall is mentioned as Mayor of Cashel in James II's charter granted to Cashel in 1687. Five burghers referred to in the same document bear the surname Sall (one a merchant and two apothecaries). But particularly interesting to us is the close association of the family with the Society of Jesus. In the seventeenth century no less than five Jesuits including another Andrew, who became Superior, bore the surname Sall. Two other

---

[7] *Hibernia Anglicana, or The history of Ireland from the conquest thereof by the English to this present time*, London 1689, 1690, vol. 2, 15-16. The reference to Sall appears after entries for the years 1678 and 1679.
[8] In *The Christian Examiner*, 41.7 (November 1828), 341-5.
[9] *True Catholic and apostolic faith, maintained in the Church of England ...*, London 1840.
[10] *Sloinnte Gaedheal is Gall, Irish names and surnames*, Dublin 1923, 276. See also McLysaght, Edward, *The surnames of Ireland* (6th ed), Blackrock 1985, 265.

priests, whose mothers were members of the Sall family, appear in the records. A cousin was rector of the Irish College in Santiago (1631-46) and the Bishop of Compostela's examiner of ordinands. With such a background it is hardly surprising to find the young Andrew FitzJohn Sall setting off to study in Spain in 1638. He was to stay there for the next twenty-six years. After two years, which he describes as being given over to the exercise of devotion, he began his three years of philosophy and four of theology. During the remaining seventeen, spent teaching in various institutions in Castile and Navarra, he claims that he 'never took so much liberty as to view Madrid or the famous Escurial not far from him when others made long voyages to see them'.[11]

The pattern of his teaching career itself followed the conventional order. Appointments to teach Latin, together with rhetoric, cosmography and history at the junior colleges of Numacia and Villagarcia were followed by a transfer to Pamplona, Palencia and Tudela and finally Salamanca to teach philosophy and divinity – scholastic, moral, polemic and controversial. He speaks also of 'frequent preaching' during those years, but also of his 'chief delight', the study of 'Holy Scripture, Councils, Fathers and History Ecclesiastic', mildly complaining of how often this was interrupted during those years by 'duty and employments enjoined upon me!'[12]

His period on the staff of Numacia and Villagarcia was probably routine and unremarkable. Almost certainly his life became a lot more interesting when he was promoted to be 'Reader in Divinity' at Pamplona. Pamplona was the seat of government for Navarra and it was not long before the young Jesuit became adviser and probably confessor of El Conde De San Stephano, who was subsequently Captain-General of Galicia and was eventually to become Captain-General of Peru. After Sall had left Pamplona for Salamanca the Count published a book in Lyons (in 1660) which includes a Latin eulogy on Andrew Sall.[13] A copy of this book was presented personally by the Count's son to the Pope. Already the young Andrew Sall, only in his mid-twenties, was highly thought of by Spaniards certainly and by at least one exiled Irish bishop, Dr Nicholas French of Ferns who in 1652 thought so highly of him that he wrote a letter to the then Provincial of the Society in Castile, Fr Martin Lezaun, begging the Provincial not to transfer Fr Sall from Pamplona or 'to deprive the Scholes of Pamplona of so famous a Master, the people of a preacher, the Princes and

---

[11] Sall, Andrew, *True Catholic and apostolic faith, maintained in the Church of England* ... , Oxford 1676, part I, 179.

[12] Sall, *True Catholic and apostolic faith*, 180.

[13] The book was entitled *Horae succesivae Didaci Benavidii, comitis Sti Stephani, Proregis Navarrae*, Lyons 1660. The eulogy on Andrew Sall appears on p. 278. See Sall, *True Catholic and apostolic faith*, 23.

Peers of the Kingdom of a Counsellor in matters of conscience, and me, an afflicted and sad Prelate groaning in banishment, of my only comfort.'[14]

Despite Nicholas French's plea, Sall was moved to Salamanca. Here he was to be given positions of greater influence and authority than he had held up to now, and almost certainly more prestigious than any he was to hold again during the remainder of his time as a member of the Society, whether in Spain or in Ireland. We know from correspondence that he was Rector of the Irish College in Salamanca by February 1652. It was a small institution, of course, established in 1592, the same year as Trinity College, Dublin. After Sall's conversion to protestantism his former pupil from those days at Salamanca, Fr Ignatius Brown, anxious to play down the significance of the responsibilities Sall had been given while he was a Jesuit and the prestige of his position as rector, wrote years later:

> Rector of the Irish College he was; an employment that requires no more than a mediocrity of discretion, to govern half a dozen lads peaceably ...[15]

Brown was exaggerating the smallness of the student numbers a little. During its first two decades there were probably never more than ten or eleven students resident in the college at a time, but two hundred and eight passed through it during its first nineteen years. Nobody at the time would have dismissed the significance of those students for the future of the Church in Ireland. Certainly the students, their leaders and patrons did not underestimate themselves socially: the proper title of the college was El Collegio de San Patricio de Nobles Irlandeses. Since 1616 the students had gained permission to cast aside 'the plain black soutane worn by "ordinary" students, in favour of red and white crossed with a front of green, the symbol of a patrician, and emblematic of the Irish nation.'[16] Any rector was likely to have problems, not least from Irish bishops who complained that the best of the students were being creamed off for service as Jesuits and lost to the secular priesthood. Then there were complaints from people of influence that the college accepted and favoured Munster and Leinster ordinands in preference to those who hailed from Connacht or Ulster. And, of course, there were constant worries about money. Father Francis Finegan's words about the college of Seville at this period, almost certainly applied equally to Salamanca:

---

[14] Sall, *True Catholic and apostolic faith*, Preface, 14. For French's attitude after Sall's conversion to protestantism, see above n. 2.

[15] Brown, *The unerring and unerrable Church*, Preface, 14.

[16] O'Boyle, James, *The Irish colleges on the continent*, Dublin & Belfast, 1935, 168.

> Throughout the [seventeenth] century Spain in her decline was growing poorer ... [W]ith the passing of the years ... in spite of undertakings from the Kings of Spain to pay his *viaticum* for every Irish priest returning fresh from his studies to his homeland, the administrators of an exhausted royal treasury were dilatory in paying up.'[17]

In fact the only extant letter to Bilbao from Andrew Sall (in Spanish) during his time as rector requests the viatica of Walter Henry ('Gualtero Henri') and others who were ready to go back to Ireland. All the letters to him in that capacity are from just such administrators of the treasury, most of them disappointing him in his requests.[18]

Fr Ignatius Brown later claimed that Sall had been cast out of the rectorship after only one year, before the end of 1652. All we know for sure is that by late 1654, 'el Padre Andres Salo' had been replaced by a Spanish Jesuit, possibly reflecting tension between Irish and Spanish members of the Society, but perhaps indicating no more than a growing convention of strict alternation. Fr Sall's impatience with administration may well, more than anything else, have contributed to his giving up the rectorship. In fact he did not leave Salamanca in 1652. For two years more, he held the professorship of controversial theology in the university itself, and had auditors, Spanish, French and Irish. This post he held by direct licence from the Bishop of Palencia, the Inquisitor-general of Spain. It was being renewed annually, and entitled him to 'keep and read prohibited books'. It enjoined upon him the duty of reporting 'any censurable proposition' he found in his reading to 'his Grace or the Council'. Years later, he recalled that, although he had this permission, he 'could never find one book of a protestant to read'.[19] The arguments he deployed in his own publications post-1674 are formulated in dialogue with Bellarmine, Suarez and

---

[17] Finegan, Francis, 'Irish rectors at Seville, 1619-1687', *Irish ecclesiastical record* (5th series) 106 (July-December 1966), [45-63], 48.

[18] Fr Sall's letter is dated 28 May, 1652, and signed 'el P. Andres Salo de la Compagna de Jhs Ror. del Colegio de los Irlandeses de esta Universidad de Salamanca'. See *Archivium Hibernicum* 3 (1914), 104. The Salamanca archive in the Russell Library, St Patrick's College, Maynooth, contains (i) three letters from El Conde de Ayala, Madrid, addressed to 'Andres Salo', Rector of the Irish College in Salamanca, and dated 17.02.52, 03.07.52 and 19.02.53, and another addressed to Pe Rector, without proper name, dated 17.02.52; (ii) a letter, catalogued XV/D/I/14 from Francisco Diaz, Madrid, addressed to Andres Salo as Rector, as is a second letter from the same, dated 03.08.52 and catalogued XV/D/I/15. The next letter in the collection, catalogued XV/D/I/16, is from the same correspondent and is dated 11.08?.55 and addressed to Pe Andres Mendo without the designation 'Rector'. However, a letter dated 13.12.54 is addressed to Fr Mendo 'Ror de Colegio Seminario Yrlandes. Comp. de Jhs Salamanca'. This indicates that by that date Fr Mendo had succeeded Fr Sall as Rector.

[19] Sall, *True Catholic and apostolic faith*, Preface, 14-17.

others, with whose arguments against the Protestant reformers he was familiar. He never cites Calvin or Luther directly, though there is evidence that he read Jeremy Taylor after his return to Ireland in 1665.[20]

After 1655, when his time at Salamanca was over, he was 'operarius' at Oviedo, and in 1658 he was back in Pamplona teaching. He eventually returned to Palencia, the see of his patron, the Inquisitor-general, and there he took the Fourth Vow and was solemnly professed. In 1661 he was still in Palencia when a Dominican friar preached 'on the feast day of one of their saints' (almost certainly Thomas Aquinas). Sall took such exception to the preacher's claim that the doctrine of the saint in question was incapable of error and of equal authority with the Bible, that he wrote a paper in protest. It was not the only protest he made in those years. He also wrote to the Inquisitor-general to report certain 'exhorbitancies' associated with the cult of saints '... exhorbitancies' of which he later said that to 'spite Jews and seem good Christians they will eat more pork than their stomachs can bear.'[21]

More substantial, more public and more dangerous than this protest was the paper he wrote against those, particularly though not exclusively Franciscans, who over-energetically promoted the doctrine of the Immaculate Conception. He claimed that persons who promoted that doctrine tended to be appointed to posts or promoted, while others who laid less stress upon it were passed over.[22] The complexion of Andrew Sall is said in the Roman catalogue of Jesuits in Ireland in 1665-6 to be 'sanguineo-cholerica', appropriate enough for one who never shunned controversy.[23]

II: BACK TO THE IRISH MISSION

Fr Sall returned to Ireland not later than 1665. Perhaps his return is to be associated with that of his older namesake and cousin, also a Jesuit, who returned to Ireland in 1662 and in the following year was made Superior of the

---

[20] Jeremy Taylor's book, *Dissuasive from popery, to the people of Ireland*, was published in Dublin in 1664, immediately before Andrew Sall's return to Ireland.

[21] Sall, Andrew, *A sermon preached at Christ-Church in Dublin before the Lord Lieutenant and Council, July 5, 1674*, Dublin 1674, 75.

[22] The doctrine of the 'immaculate conception' of the Virgin Mary did not become a dogma of the Church until it was declared to be so by Pope Pius IX in 1854. However, a feast in honour of her conception had been observed in the Church for a good seven hundred years before that, even though its precise significance was hotly disputed during most of that time. In the thirteenth century Aquinas took the view that it was proper to venerate Mary as the mother of Christ, but did not go so far as to say, as the Franciscans were doing, that she had been miraculously conceived. The Franciscans were from the beginning the great promoters of this doctrine in the western Church, and received strong support from a number of Popes, including Alexander VI and Sixtus IV, the latter being himself a former General of the Franciscans.

[23] *Catalogus Patrum Societatis Jesu qui sunt in Hibernia ... 1665-6*, f.268 (see n. 3 above).

Irish mission. Certainly he was one of a substantial number of priests who returned to the Irish mission in the early years of the reign of Charles II, encouraged by Charles' accession to hope that things were going to get better now for Roman Catholics and for their Church in Ireland.

Even though it was going to prove impossible for the new government to satisfy the claims and counter-claims to land as between the Irish, Old English, 'old' Protestant and 'new' English, it appears to have been the case that the Old English families, like that of Andrew Sall and indeed most Jesuit fathers of the time, had succeeded in recovering a good proportion of their former property. By 1665 there were twenty-seven Jesuit fathers in Ireland.[24] Most seem to have expected to find accommodation with some reasonably substantial Catholic family for whom they then acted as chaplain and confessor. It is not surprising then that Andrew Sall on his return appears to have made for his native Cashel and to have resided in Tipperary for the next ten years, latterly at the house of a Catholic nobleman, possibly Butler at Kilcash.[25] From a letter of the General of the Society of Jesus, written in 1678, it may be inferred that some of his brethren felt a twinge of jealousy, accusing him of despising the profession of poverty and of being 'resentful of hardship.' As late as 12 October, 1669, the General in a letter to Fr Francis White, Superior of the Society in Ireland, says: 'Keep Andrew Sall junior to his duty, and make him follow the example of Father Sall senior' i.e. his cousin.[26] Nevertheless, the Roman catalogue of the Jesuits in Ireland in 1665-6 describes him as 'in confutandis Jansenistis et hetherodoxis potens.'

The Ireland to which he returned was riven with controversy as to how exactly allegiance to a potentially, if not consistently, sympathetic king was to be sustained at the same time as obedience to the Pope. A contemporary describes Andrew Sall's cousin, Andrew Fitzbenet Sall, Superior of the Irish Mission, as 'very active in defending the rights of the Holy See against the loyal Remonstrance of the Franciscan, Fr Peter Walsh'. Fr Walsh and others had drawn up and promoted a 'loyal formulary or Irish remonstrance' in the mid-sixties which would make it clear to all that loyalty to the Pope did not involve disloyalty to the King. It represents its signatories as 'loyal subjects notwithstanding any power or pretension of the pope ... or any authority spiritual or temporal, proceeding or deriving from him or his see against your

---

[24] According to *Arch. Coll. Hib. Rom. xx,* f. 273r there were twenty-three Jesuits in Ireland in 1662, and twenty-seven by 1665/6 (*ibid.* f. 268).

[25] Sall, *Sermon* (1674), Preface, 21, and *True Catholic and apostolic faith*, Preface, 83.

[26] Citations from Fr Proinsias Ó Fionagáin's typescript history of the Jesuit 'Third Mission' (see n. 4 above), 344, 174.

majesty'. It goes on to disclaim the Pope's pretension to absolve Catholics from the King's authority and asserts the divine ordination of princes.[27]

A majority of the Irish clergy and the Vatican itself opposed Walsh. His Remonstrance was rejected at a national congress of clergy in June 1661, though they accepted a compromise formulation put forward by Edmund O'Reilly, archbishop of Armagh, which said almost the same things in more pacific terms. Fr Andrew Sall senior also opposed the Remonstrance. However, there is at least some indication, in what he wrote later, that Fr Andrew Sall junior was not in agreement with his older cousin, the Superior of the Jesuits, and this may have been a factor in the increasing restiveness of the younger man. Fr Sall felt obliged to write a treatise, prudently produced in Latin, wherein, as he says himself he 'demonstrated by evident testimonies of Scripture, Councils, Fathers, Authority of Divines, and Declarations of Popes, that the Doctrine I delivered, was Catholic Faith, and the Contrary of it was heresy and blasphemy.' He circulated copies of the treatise 'to them of more authority and learning in the Kingdom', stating 'that Protestants may be saved, and that many called Hereticks, are not such indeed.'[28] No copies of the treatise have survived: it may, however, be dated 1670 or 1671 and, since four archbishops were by that time installed, one of them in Cashel, we may assume that they may be the 'persons of authority' to whom he sent it. Fr Ignatius Brown had certainly read it and gave as his opinion that

> ... it was not that doctrine [of Sall's] that was censured; it was his indiscretion that was censured ... for if a preacher was sent to convert Pagans to Christianity, would it be a discretion to teach them, 'Sirs, the Christian Religion is the best, but you may very well be saved in that you hold, if you be invincibly ignorant' ... This is Mr. Sall's case, that was sent into Ireland to convert Protestants who thought themselves perhaps to be invincibly ignorant.[29]

It was another paper in manuscript form, and not intended for circulation, however, which precipitated the most dramatic change in his life. His association with Archbishop Thomas Price had aroused in him further misgivings about aspects of Roman Catholic doctrine and practice. Later he acknowledges that he entertained the thought of separation from the Roman Catholic Church, but had decided earnestly to spend the remnant of his days 'retired and unknown, to prepare better for the long day of Eternity'. 'To doubt a doctrine is not to deny it', he wrote. During the time that he thought of a

---

[27] Fitzpatrick, Brendan, *Seventeenth-century Ireland, the war of the religions* (*New Gill history of Ireland* 3), Dublin 1988, 229, 236, 242.

[28] Sall, *Sermon* (1674), 114.

[29] Brown, *The unerring and unerrable Church*, 140f.

return to Spain, he prepared what he called 'a soliloquie with God', a paper in which he set down as a framework for prayer and meditation 'the reasons for his dissatisfaction with the Roman Church'. This paper, he says, 'dropped from me and fell into the hands of some ... who so incensed my former friends and relations against me by a report that I was already become a Protestant minister as made them, out of a zeal, threaten to destroy me ...'[30]

The situation became so dangerous by 1674 that 'the Lord Archbishop, the Mayor and other English gentlemen of the City of Cashel' set out in search of him and conveyed him safely to a place of asylum in the Archbishop's house. It appears that when they found him he was not at home but on a visit. Before setting off for Cashel with them, he took the opportunity to write a quick letter to the nobleman at whose house he had been staying prior to this. In it he explained what was happening and assured him that he would never declare against the Roman Church whilst any hope was left of being satisfied in the doubts he had and which he had delivered in writing. He begged the nobleman to communicate the contents of this letter to others of his friends and relations. On arrival at Cashel, Sall immediately sent notice to the Vicar-General begging for meetings with bishops or other clergy if they were disposed to give him satisfaction on the points contained in his letter. Looking back at those days later, he claimed to have done everything he could conducible for quieting his mind and setting him in his former profession. He wrote:

> No tree after many years' growth and deep rooting in a kind soil, was plucked up with more violence than I was wrought from my natural inclination and sensible comfort to forsake the society and communion of my former friends and brethren.'[31]

But another factor had in fact intervened from outside, which must have served to concentrate the mind of Andrew Sall wonderfully. The Earl of Essex, on arrival in Ireland in 1672 as Viceroy, had implemented the plans of King Charles II for the readmission of Catholics to the corporate towns, including Cashel. The New English, who felt threatened by this leniency, immediately used their contacts in the English House of Commons, and in March 1673 they presented an address to the king asking for the banishment of all priests, whether regular or secular. Charles responded with a decree proposing to expel all regular clergy from the kingdom of Ireland.

The exchange of letters which took place between Fr Sall and the Superior of the Society of Jesus, Fr Stephen Rice in Dundalk, after Sall's declaration for the Church of Ireland of 17 May, is a sad one, but unmarked by rancour on the part of either man. It ends with Fr Rice, ever a gentle man, writing and offering to

---

[30] Sall, *True Catholic and apostolic faith*, Preface, 2-4
[31] Sall, *True Catholic and apostolic faith*, Preface, 4.

make amends for any offence Sall may have received from himself or any other member of the Society, 'so that union at least of Christianity if not of religion, may be entire among us'.[32]

Sall responded to this charitable letter in a like spirit, ending with a request that Fr Rice should 'prevail with some able men of his fraternity' to reply to the points made by Sall in his declaration of 17 May. The reply should be 'with the gravity and modesty which becometh learned and worthy men; that on both sides we might concur with our studies to the glory of God and the manifestation of the Truth, setting aside all wonted acerbities'. He adds that since the separation between himself and the Society of Jesus did not arise from personal grievance, but on weightier considerations, it would now be better to handle the difference in public, 'the matter going through a more exact trial that way.'[33]

Sometime in the course of the summer of 1674, Andrew Sall took up residence, 'in Trinity College near [Dublin]', then an institution of some two hundred and ninety or three hundred students. He set to work at once on a thesis with two conclusions for the degree of D.D. The conclusions were:

> That out of the Roman Church there is a safe way for Salvation;
> That the way of the Church of England is safer to Salvation than that of the Church of Rome.[34]

Andrew Sall has left an account of the public defence of his thesis made in November of the same year. Having secured permission for Catholic opponents of the thesis to come to the College and argue the points against it, he wrote to an unidentified 'honoured Doctor', inviting him and any others to come 'next Thursday to the chapel of the College' – which did not leave the doctor much time to prepare. He goes on:

> As Suarez, Belarmine and others, the ablest defenders of the Roman cause, are read here with due regard to their learning, so any learned man will be welcome to our dispute, and in his good behaviour will have a sure indemnity for what he shall say against us by scripture and reason'.[35]

Interestingly enough, this invitation was accepted by the 'honoured Doctor' and some others who came to the chapel but 'resolved not to oppose in that

---

[32] This correspondence is transmitted and discussed by Andrew Sall in *True Catholic and apostolic faith*, Preface, 4-7, 28.

[33] Sall, *True Catholic and apostolic faith*, Preface, 16.

[34] Sall, *True Catholic and apostolic faith*, Preface, 7.

[35] Sall, *True Catholic and apostolic faith*, Preface, 8-9.

public manner', perhaps not trusting the indemnity too far. However, opposition to the thesis was forthcoming, in that some Doctors of Divinity of Trinity College and Masters of Arts, 'well furnished with skill in controversies and the best arguments our adversaries have, did propose them vigorously.' Andrew Sall never ceased to believe in the value of rational debate, even to the extent of wishful thinking or naiveté, as when in *True Catholic and apostolic faith* (1676), he called for a Council, 'truly ecumenical and free, wherein the Roman bishop and faction, as others, may sit with like freedom and indifference to judge and be judged by the word of God.'[36]

Some, at any rate, of the theological points which the Catholic disputants refrained from making that Thursday in the chapel of Trinity College, were no doubt committed to print later by Fr Ignatius Brown in his book which came out in 1675 (see note 3 above). His book, like Sall's reply to it of 1676, was dedicated to the Lord Lieutenant, Lord Essex. Brown's criticism of Sall was severe enough. Less restrained were Fr John Egan's *A counter-poison prepared by a faithful hand* (Louvain 1674), and Nicholas French's *The doleful fall of Andrew Sall* (Douai 1675). This latter work alternately cajoles Andrew Sall and attacks him. Later Sall answered Nicholas French in print, but remarkably mildly, speaking of him as a 'grave and ancient prelate of my acquaintance ... whom I will endeavour to satisfy in sober, serious and sincere terms.'[37]

The last vain attempt to recall Andrew Sall was ecclesiastically more high powered. It was a Bull of Clement X, sealed and signed by his *protonotarius apostolicus*, Claudius Agrete, and received in September 1675. It offered 'an entire and absolute remission of all that is past and a favourable reception to [his] former condition and privileges if [he] would return to them'. A covering letter which is unsigned, warned him of evil designed against him. So far as we know, Sall made no reply.[38]

Andrew Sall's objections to Catholic doctrine are predictable enough. What is not predictable is the spirit in which he made them and defended them. In a century of robust religious and theological controversy, Sall is remarkable for his restraint. At a time when to doubt credal articles was often, if not usually, deemed to be the same thing as to deny them, he maintained the contrary. In his writings he is consistent in his commitment to rational discussion. In the century of religious wars he condemns those who, as he says, 'follow the rules of Mahomet to "defend with the sword when words will not do."'[39]

No objective reader can doubt, I think, the sincerity of Andrew Sall's belief that he never left the Catholic faith, but rather, as he says, 'fastened' himself to it by the change he made in 1674. 'It shall be my constant and inflexible

---

[36] Sall, *True Catholic and apostolic faith*, Epistle Dedicatory, f. 3b-4a.
[37] Sall, *True Catholic and apostolic faith*, Preface, 12.
[38] Sall, *True Catholic and apostolic faith*, Preface, 28.
[39] Sall, *True Catholic and apostolic faith*, Preface, 26.

resolution to hold that faith to the end of my life, wheresoever it be uncorruptly professed, whether in Rome, Jerusalem or elsewhere; I know it is not tied to places.' To those who objected that he was the first of his family to become a Protestant he replied: 'So was Paul the first of his to become a Christian'.[40] That is no more than a ready debating answer, but again and again he shows deep sensitivity to the pain he had caused to family and friends, and the degree to which he shared it. In the sermon of 1674 he determined not 'to speak in prejudice' of the party he was forsaking, and he stuck to that resolution, with the proviso that he must be allowed to justify his departure from the Roman Communion when taxed on the question. He wrote:

> I refuse to scold or insult upon my former brethren in the Roman Communion. I may not hate them without hating myself ... I could not in pity abandon the Mother at whose breast I sucked the Belief of a Christian, if with tears or sweat I could hope to wash away the stains which corruption of time has cast upon her face, once fair or glorious.'[41]

The contact he seems to have managed to keep with family and friends, even after his departure, argues that some, at least, may have accepted the good faith of his declaration, however bitterly disappointed they were by it.

III: OXFORD

Towards the end of July 1675, Andrew Sall D.D. set off for Oxford, and armed with letters of commendation, was first received into Wadham College. Shortly after he had moved into a house in Holywell, he became ill and was rescued by Dr John Fell who had recently been elevated from being Dean of Christ Church to be Bishop of Oxford. Fell installed Sall in 'convenient lodgings in the recently restored cloister of the college near the chaplains' quadrangle of Christ Church, where he appears to have stayed for most of his time in Oxford.[42] The

---

[40] *Sermon* (1674), Preface, 6.

[41] *Sermon* (1674), Preface, 10.

[42] See Wood, Anthony, *Athenae Oxoniensis* 2 (*Fasti Oxonienses*) col. 875, London 1692. Dr John Fell (1625-86) is credited with improving the style of printing at the University Press. He co-operated with Robert Boyle in the publication of the Gospels and of the Acts of the Apostles in Malay, both of which Boyle paid for. Boyle also assisted William Seaman, the Turkish scholar, in his translation of the New Testament and the Catechism into Turkish and contributed substantially to the publication of the Turkish New Testament in 1666. For an account of his support for mission and translation, see Madden, R.E.W., *The life of the Hon. Robert Boyle, F.R.S.*, London 1969, 111-2, 141. Of interest also is the fact that the Malay translation of the four Gospels and the Acts of the Apostles, entitled *Jang Ampat Evangelia* (1677), is dedicated to Robert Boyle. The Preface, 'For the English Reader', particularly mentions the Jesuits and the desirability of following their example 'who daily compass Sea and Land to make proselytes' but who, the author notes, for all their

relative comfort and security of college life freed him for teaching and writing. The university press published three books by Andrew Sall between 1676 and 1680. A book on philosophy was at an advanced stage of preparation but never reached the press.[43]

The Franciscan, Fr Peter Walsh, saw Andrew Sall in London in the last week of July 1675, immediately after his first arrival in England. In a letter to Bishop Nicholas French, he describes Sall as 'much caressed by several persons of quality' and even introduced to the King and the Duke of York. The following month Peter Walsh called on Sall and they discussed his change of allegiance. Afterwards, Walsh expressed to French his belief that Sall had made that change conscientiously and out of conviction.[44]

The Bishop of Oxford, Dr Fell, had more or less saved Sall's life by installing him in Christ Church. But neither he nor the Bishop of Winchester, to whom he looked, came up with the preferments in England which Dr Sall was angling for. It seems that by 1680 he felt sure that he would be as well to return to Ireland and to the preferments he had already acquired there.[45]

---

converts, have not as far as he knows, translated ' one entire book of Holy Scripture'. This preface was written by Thomas Marshall of Lincoln College, Oxford. He had served as a chaplain in the Netherlands during the Commonwealth. In 1681 and 1684, he was one of the delegates for the Chancellor of the University, the Duke of Ormonde, who was in Ireland. He assisted Parr in his life of James Ussher.

[43] The books which were published were: (i) *True catholic and apostolic faith maintained in the Church of England, being a reply to several books published under the names of JE, NN and JS against his Declaration for the Church of England and against the motives for his separation from the Roman Church declared in a printed sermon which he preached in Dublin*, Oxford 1676. (ii) *Votum pro pace Christiana, quo exponuntur et amoventur praecipua obstacula pacis per Romanae ecclesiae ministros objecta, et ostenditur quam immerito pacem respuant cum reliquis Christianis ecclesiis, praecipue vero cum Anglicana*, Oxon. 1678. (iii) *Ethica, sive moralis philosophia ex veterum et recentiorum sententiis concinnata*, Oxon 1680. The work on philosophy was in hand in 1679, according to a letter addressed to Robert Boyle on 29.06.79. See Boyle, Robert, *Correspondence 5*, 161.

[44] *Four letters on several subjects to Persons of Quality. The fourth being an answer to the Lord Bishop of Lincoln's Book, entitled Popery etc. by Peter Walsh, of St Francis' Order, Professor of Divinity*, 1686. Letter II, which is Walsh's first letter to Nicholas French, Bishop of Ferns, is dated August 1, 1675, and letter III, his second to him, is dated 13 March, 1676. Peter Walsh had read French's *The bleeding Iphigenia by N.N.* [i.e. Nicholas French], dated 23 December, 1674, and had been sent by the author a copy of French's other much longer book *The doleful fall of Andrew Sall*. In these letters, Peter Walsh takes up a number of the points made by Nicholas French in the above-mentioned books. According to his own account (p. 122), Walsh found out Andrew Sall's lodging and spent the greater part of three days in his company discussing the circumstances of, and the reason for, his 'change'.

[45] Letters to Robert Boyle refer to his felt need for further livings, e.g. Boyle, Robert, *Correspondence 5*, 160-1, 274, 279, 289.

IV: BACK IN IRELAND (1680-82)

Courtesy of Archbishop Price, Sall had one living in the diocese of Cashel, the chancellorship of the cathedral, which was worth one hundred and eighty pounds, another in Meath worth eighty pounds and the prebend of Swords, worth seventy pounds. He may also have held the chantership of St David's in Wales and a further living near Cashel. The Bishop of Derry at the time, thought he had been catered for adequately. He wrote quite sourly about his desire for further preferments.[46]

Sall's return to Ireland was also prompted by a desire to assist Robert Boyle and his sister Lady Ranelagh in the project of reprinting the Irish versions of the Book of Common Prayer and the New Testament and later, the printing of Bedell's translation of the Old Testament. Sall may first have met Boyle independently in London or in Oxford, or he may have met him through Dr Fell, who shared an enthusiasm with Boyle for the dissemination of the scriptures in as many languages as possible, through the agency of his rejuvenated university press in Oxford. Boyle and his circle were now anxious in their pious undertakings to emulate the missionary activities of the Jesuits in every part of the world.[47] Certainly Sall was in correspondence from Oxford with Boyle as early as 1678 about the reissue of the Irish New Testament (1602) and the Book of Common Prayer (1608). In a letter to Boyle in 1678, he advised that the Roman print be employed, thus following the good example of Stapleton's Catechism of 1639. Unfortunately, his advice was not taken.[48] By May 1680, we find him charged to write a preface to the New Testament. Boyle had originally felt that the preface to the French Jansenist translation would serve. 'Being a work of great learning and piety', he suggested it would 'recommend the introduction of the Irish testament to the better sort of Papists themselves, for whose benefit it was chiefly made'. Aodh Ó Raghallaigh, a scribe employed by Robert Boyle in London, was asked to translate the original

---

[46] The letter of the bishop of Derry, which is addressed to Archbishop Sancroft and dated 13 August 1680, is printed in *The Tanner Letters, extracted from the collection in the Bodleian Library, Oxford*, IMC, Dublin, 1943, 426-7. The relevant passage reads as follows: 'I had sooner obeyed your grace's commands if I could sooner have got any certainty of the provision this poor Church of Ireland hath made for Dr. S. [superscript in hand of Sancroft, 'Andr. Sall']. By this day's post I received an account from Dublin (and I do not believe it to be very exact) that he hath one living in the diocese of Cashel worth 180 l., another in Meath worth 80 l., a third which is the prebend of Swords near Dublin worth 70 l. and which if out of lease were worth 200 l.; but that advantage the Dr. is not likely to see. Besides I have been told (as I informed your grace) that he was Chanter of St. David's, which he held by royal dispensation; which if he still hold with the rest make up the sum I mentioned, and afford him a competency that he need not complain of neglect, nor seek any other charity, unless it be to pardon his accepting it.'

[47] See note 42 above.

[48] Boyle, Robert, *Correspondence* 5, 135.

French into English and send it as soon as possible to Henry Jones, Bishop of Meath, and to Dr Sall.

However, when Henry Jones actually saw the Jansenist preface, he was perturbed on two grounds: (1) its attacks on the Protestant reformers, and (2) the long disquisitions on the difficulty of translating satisfactorily. The Provost of Trinity College, Dublin, Narcissus Marsh, agreed, adding that in any case it was imprudent to advertise the fact that there are serious problems, not to say uncertainties, in the translation of the sacred text from time to time. It was agreed that Sall would produce a preface in English avoiding these offences, but which would make some use of the Jansenist preface. The text was approved by all, and in due course was translated into Irish by Aodh Ó Raghallaigh in London, Sall demurring that he would not be sufficiently 'magisterial' in Irish himself.[49]

One last project which he had to leave unfinished, indeed had hardly more than begun, was the publication of the great translation of the Old Testament into Irish made by Séamus de Nógla (James Nangle) and Muircheartach Ó Cionga under the aegis of William Bedell, Bishop of Kilmore, in the 1630's. The manuscript had been rescued and preserved by Donnchadh Ó Sioradáin, a protégé and friend of Bedell, and had in due course been given by him to Henry Jones, Bishop of Meath, who for years had desired to have it printed.

The availability of a scholar like Sall and of a patron like Robert Boyle encouraged Bishop Jones to send the Bedell manuscript to Andrew Sall in the first days of December 1681. Sall had already seen the text at Dr Jones' house and had expressed the opinion that 'the Irish version of the Old Testament manuscript should be first revised before it was exposed to public view.'[50] With reference to the New Testament and the Book of Common Prayer two or three years earlier, he had discussed a number of the methodological questions involved. On the question of 'register', for instance, he had this to say:

> This much in general I shall insinuate, that if I were fit to be a translator, of two ends men may aim at in such a work, the one of getting the credit of skill in the primitive ancient Irish, the other of benefiting common readers by expressions now in use, I would choose the latter...[51]

He goes on to condemn the use of 'obsolete, antiquated words, alien from common perception,' and, with reference to discussions he had had with

---

[49] Boyle, Robert, *Correspondence* 5, 134. On the preface to the second edition of the New Testament, see also vol. 5, 220, 250, 252, 263, 265-9, 272-3, 275, 278n. Also vol. 3, 349-50.

[50] Boyle, Robert, *Correspondence* 5, 264.

[51] Boyle, Robert, *Correspondence* 5, 135.

'eminent speakers of Irish', 'to defend the use of words derived into Irish from Latin when speaking philosophically or theologically.'[52]

When he first came actually to examine the Bedell manuscript, he discovered it to be

> ... a confused heap, pitifully defaced and broken. It was a work of very great labour to bring it into some order. I sent for a book binder to bind up what I could gather, of which and another uncouth bulk, sent to me from [Trinity College, Dublin], I hope to make up a complete Old Testament by the help of God and of Mr Higgin [i.e. Pól Ó hUiginn], the Irish lecturer ...

He goes on to speak of what a labour it 'will be to draw up a clear copy of the whole, purged from errors and foolish additions or alterations, interlaced by some unlucky corrector, pretending to criticism in Irish'.[53] He might have hesitated to speak this way if had recognised that the 'unlucky corrector' was possibly none other than Bishop Bedell himself. It appears that Sall and his assistant filled lacunae in this text of various lengths with their own translation, modelled no doubt on the style of the original translators.

Sall worked at the text of Bedell's Old Testament during the early months of 1682, and by February seventh, he reported that eight chapters of Genesis had been written out from the manuscript, 'in very fair letter as clear as any print'.[54] The scribe, Mr Mullan, a bachelor of physic, had agreed to the rate of 11 pence per sheet, with the acquiescence of Dr Marsh, Provost of Trinity College, and Pól Ó hUiginn, the lecturer in Irish there. Mullan supplied first transcriptions under Sall's supervision. He also stayed at Sall's house, and Dr Sall says of himself that he would lay aside other studies so as to attend to this work. Actually he had just over two months left; he never returned to his other work, nor did he finish this task either. But for the time that was left he threw himself into it, both the work on the text and the administration of a subscription list. By June some one hundred and forty sheets had been copied, but by that time Andrew Sall was two months dead. He passed away on the evening of the fifth of April, and the project of copying the corrected and revised text and sending it to London was taken up and brought to completion under the direction of Provost Marsh.

In the course of all this, Andrew Sall discovered, rather to his surprise at first it would seem, that the project of making the scriptures available in Irish and the scheme of proselytisation of which it was an essential instrument, was

---

[52] Boyle, Robert, *Correspondence* 5, 135.

[53] Boyle, Robert, *Correspondence* 5, 279.

[54] Boyle, Robert, *Correspondence* 5, 287.

actually opposed by some within the Protestant camp, while others remained at least ambivalent.

Andrew Sall from the first found the Lord Lieutenant, Bishop Jones of Meath, and Provost Marsh of Trinity College enthusiastic, and the Provost 'willing to contrive the reading of New Testament and the Irish prayers in the college'. But by the autumn of 1680, Dr Sall was contrasting the enthusiastic support of 'the best and greatest men of this kingdom' who commend Robert Boyle's pious zeal on the one hand with

> [1] the private opposition of the Roman clergy who would have had themselves to be the only teachers, [and 2] a more public and bolder opposition by some of our apparent but really false brethren, who are not ashamed to profess a dislike of our endeavours to convert the natives of this country, upon maxims like those of the American planters, in hindering the conversion of their slaves to the Christian religion. One of them had the gallantry to tell me in my face, and at my own table, that while I went about to gain the Irish (to God, I mean), I should lose the English. Our good Archbishop [i.e. Thomas Price of Cashel] has continual battles with me on this subject.[55]

By November of the next year he was even more disillusioned by Protestant opposition or indifference to the project, and wrote to Boyle that he was waiting impatiently to get to work on the manuscript,

> to contribute my small endeavour, while those few live who have any of the zeal of the conversion of the natives here; how few they be I bemoaned sadly and seriously with our lord lieutenant this afternoon, admiring how few they were that followed your heroick example, even of those whose calling did strictly oblige them to it, and from whom I am to expect little thanks for my endeavours to co-operate herein.[56]

In spite of the set-back occasioned by the sudden death of Andrew Sall at the beginning of April, 1682, the Duke of Ormonde and Dr Marsh in Ireland, financially supported by Robert Boyle and his sister in London, saw Bedell's Old Testament into the hands of the printer and had it distributed in Ireland and in Scotland in 1685/6 and in the following years, despite the 'new English' opposition.[57] However, as the seventeenth century wore into the eighteenth, it was obvious even to some persons like William King, Archbishop of Dublin and previously Bishop of Derry, who had been involved in endeavours at

---

[55] Boyle, Robert, *Correspondence* 5, 220.
[56] Boyle, Robert, *Correspondence* 5, 273-4.
[57] Boyle, Robert, *Correspondence* 5, 291-2.

proselytising, that whole-hearted support for it was not likely to be forthcoming from people who held their land and other privileges on no other ground of claim than that they were Protestant.

But Andrew Sall, the polyglot Irish speaker from Cashel, whose Anglo-Norman family had put down very deep roots in Ireland over four hundred years, had arrived at a Reformed position by the route described. He had no inhibition in endeavouring to share his new perceptions and to do so through the medium of the language he had spoken since he was a child.[58]

[58] This paper, in a somewhat different form, was delivered as an O'Donnell Lecture in Trinity College, Dublin, in 1995. The author is much obliged to Dr Muriel McCarthy, keeper of Marsh's Library, Dublin, for hospitality and assistance during the preparation of this paper. He also acknowledges the hospitality and assistance of Ms Penny Wood of the Russell Library, St Patrick's College, Maynooth, and of Fr Stephen Redmond S.J. at the Jesuit Archive, 35 Leeson St., Dublin.

RELIGION, RIOT AND ROMANCE
SCOTTISH GAELIC PERCEPTIONS OF IRELAND
IN THE NINETEENTH CENTURY

Donald E. Meek

Scottish Gaelic perceptions of Ireland in the nineteenth century are a fascinating field of reflection, particularly for those of us on both sides of the North Channel who are aware of the Gaelic continuum which has linked Gaelic Scotland and Gaelic Ireland across the centuries and which was at its strongest in the period before 1700. The question which perhaps arises naturally from some of the earlier essays in this collection is how long, beyond 1700, that relationship lasted, and how perceptions changed, and under what circumstances. My contention in this paper is that the nineteenth century was perhaps the last century in which there was any strong natural awareness of Ireland on the part of Scottish Gaels, to the extent that Ireland was referred to fairly regularly in the poetry and prose of Gaelic Scotland. I have chosen the three Rs of 'Religion, Riot and Romance' to summarise, in broad terms, the most prominent of the themes which appear in the surviving record.

The importance of the nineteenth century in preserving an intuitive, rather than a reconstructed, awareness of Ireland from the Scottish Gaelic side can be seen if we compare the nineteenth century briefly with the twentieth. In the twentieth century, the significance of Ireland diminished to the point of being comparatively small in Scottish Gaelic eyes. Only the academic sector tended to cherish the older links, and these were maintained very largely on the basis of linguistic awareness. This led gradually to the reconnecting of Ireland and Scotland, often through a desire to compare the dialects of Gaelic and Irish, or to compare aspects of the common cultural heritage of the sea-divided Gaels. For example, a vitally important reconnection with Ireland was made in the middle of twentieth century, through the collecting of folklore, and supremely through the person and work of Calum MacLean, who was employed first by the Irish Folklore Commission and then, from 1951, by the School of Scottish Studies. We could add to that a small but important list of initiatives of various kinds which came to birth in the second half of the twentieth century, among them the Irish-Scottish Academic Initiative.

However, my concern is with the nineteenth century, and with how Scottish Gaels viewed Ireland in that period. We have to be wary of generalising too easily, and assuming that there was a completely uniform set of perceptions of Ireland among Scottish Gaels. The Scottish Gaelic community of the nineteenth century was by no means homogeneous. It was socially and culturally stratified, with its poets, its politicians, its academics, its doctors, lawyers, ministers and clergy, and its many other groups, including its communities of crofters, who had been facing challenges to their existence which were shared with Ireland, and in which Irish politicians participated. Parts of the Scottish Gaelic community had moved overseas, as a consequence of clearing and emigration; other parts had moved to the Lowland south, where new Gaelic communities were created in the cities.[1] Perceptions of Ireland varied depending on where one was placed – how near or how far one was from Ireland, in body or in spirit or in both. It could function as the land of religious difference, or the land of political riot, or the home of a romantic freedom now being lost in Gaelic Scotland, but also (paradoxically) being lost in Ireland itself. So let us begin with romance, and end with religion.

Romance

For some native Scottish Gaels living at home, Ireland occasionally preserved something of the romance of the otherworld land of bliss and happiness and escapism. It appears to have been helpful in allowing them to come to terms with the wider sweep of change. Perhaps such perceptions harbour echoes of tales and stories of the Fianna, as well as a more mystical and magical perception created by nineteenth-century romanticism. It is this thumb-nail sketch of a romantic Ireland that we meet in a song composed by Dr John MacLachlan (1804-74) of Rahoy, the medical practitioner in Mull and Morvern in the first half of the nineteenth century. MacLachlan composed a number of songs on the clearances in his area, and also a considerable number of rather sad love songs, in which he frequently bids farewell to his many sweethearts. On this occasion, he is standing on Lochaline pier in Morvern, and puts his sweetheart on board a paddle-steamer, probably the 'Maid of Morvern', bound for Glasgow. The steamship is a recurrent symbol of separation in the Gaelic songs of the nineteenth century, and here MacLachlan uses it splendidly to depict the relentless nature of physical parting:

---

[1]   Devine, T.M., *Clanship to crofters' war: the social transformation of the Scottish Highlands*, Manchester 1994, provides the best available overview, but lacks a Gaelic perspective, as it does not engage with the Gaelic evidence. Much of the material in this paper is derived from Meek, Donald E. (ed), *Caran an t-saoghail: the wiles of the world: an anthology of nineteenth-century Gaelic verse*, Edinburgh (forthcoming).

'S ann Di-màirt bho cheadha Loch Alainn
A dh'fhalbh mo ghràdh-sa le bàt' na smùid;
Bu luath a ceum dol gu tìr na Beurla,
'S tha mi fo èislean air bheagan sunnd.

'S gur ann air bàta nan roithean làidir,
'S nan cuibhlean pràis 's iad a-ghnàth cur strì;
Fear ga stiùireadh gu làidir, lùthmhor,
'S e dèanamh iùil dhi gu Diùraidh shìos.

Gur h-iomadh peucag a chì thu 'n Glaschu
Len èideadh maiseach 's lem fasan ùr;
'S ann bhios tu, eudail, mar reult na maidne,
Cur neul le airtneul air dreach an gnùis.

'S truagh nach robh mi leat thall an Eirinn,
Is m' aitreabh fhèin an taobh thall don chuan –
Dh'aithnichinn m' eudail am measg nan ceudan,
Is i mar Bhènus ag èirigh suas.[2]

It was on Tuesday from Lochaline pierhead
that my sweetheart left, on the ship of steam:
swift was her step going to the land of English,
and I am dejected with little cheer.

It was on the ship of the powerful paddles,
and the wheels of brass that forever strive:
a man steering her with strength and vigour,
guiding her down towards Jura's isle.

Many a peacock you will see in Glasgow
with their fine attire and fashions new;
but you, my darling, will be like the star of morning,
shadowing their face with a cloud of gloom.

Would that I were with you over in Ireland,
and that my dwelling were on the sea's far side;
I would recognise my loved one among the hundreds,
and she like Venus, as she would rise.

---

[2] Gillies, H.C. (ed), *The Gaelic songs of the late Dr MacLachlan, Rahoy*, Glasgow 1880, 43-45.

MacLachlan's view of Ireland lacks details of any kind, and it is highly likely that he had never visited it. This cannot be said of William Livingston (1808-70) of Islay, who composed 'Eirinn a' gul' ('Ireland weeping'), surely one of the finest poems composed in Gaelic. In Islay, connections with Northern Ireland were still very strong in Livingston's day, and remained so into the twentieth century, as Islaymen made regular visits to Ballycastle at times of fairs and markets. That helped to maintain a sense of cultural continuity, and it seems highly likely that Livingston would have visited the north of Ireland at some point. His remarkable poem is found in his collected works, published in 1882, but another text is contained in a manuscript account of Islay, 'The Queen of the Hebrides', written by the land reformer, John Murdoch (1818-1903), who was brought up in the island.[3] The copy of the poem in the manuscript was probably gifted by Livingston to Murdoch, and is dated 1861 in Livingston's hand. It is written in Gaelic script, and contains two quatrains not found in the published text, as well as a small number of variant readings.[4] The metre is an imitation of a syllabic metre, probably a form of *rannaigheacht*. The presentation and the metre both reflect the sense of a shared Gaelic culture which Livingston develops in the poem. When the additional quatrains are inserted in the text, it becomes evident that it falls into two parts and that it changes gear exactly at the mid-point. The first half of the poem (ll. 1-28) presents a splendid picture of Ireland, rejoicing in its natural beauty and celebrating the old cultural connections with a warmly romantic glow. The second half (ll. 29-56) provides a commentary on the various 'troubles' in Ireland since the Great Famine, including eviction and emigration, and there may be a passing reference to the Young Ireland rebellion of 1848 (l. 37). (John Murdoch, however, commented that the poem was inspired by the wrecking of the Irish emigrant vessel, the *Exmouth*, on Islay in 1847 with the loss of all 240 passengers, and there may be some substance in that, though there is no direct reference to the event in the poem.[5]) The grim picture of burnings, poverty and oppression in the second half of the poem stands quite deliberately in sharp contrast to the romanticism of the first, and it seems to me that the poet is making a comment not only on

---

[3] Hunter, James, *For the people's cause: from the writings of John Murdoch, Highland and Irish land reformer*, Edinburgh 1986, provides an introduction to Murdoch and a selection of his writings, including material from 'The Queen of the Hebrides'.

[4] National Library of Scotland, MS 14986 f. 81 (d).

[5] NLS MS 14986 f. 81 (d).

the troubled state of Ireland, but also on the dangers of confusing the
romantic image of any country with the political reality:

Eilein iomallaich na h-Eòrp',
A thìr as bòidhch' fo cheann-bhrat speur,
Bu tric a chunnaic mi do chòrs'
A-nunn thar linne mhòr nam beuc.   4

Nuair a shèideadh gaoth chiùin on iar-dheas,
'S an iarmailt gun cheathach, gun neul,
Bhiodh na Gàidheil san Roinn Ilich
Ag innse da chèile do sgèimh: 8

Do chòmhnardan feurach, maiseach,
Lag an Rotha rèidh 's Magh Aoidh,
'S do dhoireachan geugach a' toirt fialtais
Do cheòlairean sgiathach nan craobh;   12

D' fhuarain ghlan' a' boillsgeadh fior-uisg'
Do threudan lìonmhor feadh do ghleann,
Do choilltean, do thulaichean 's do chluaintean,
'S tu uaine bho cheann gu ceann.   16

Am madainn neochiontachd na h-òige
Fhuair mi sgeòil nan linn a dh'fhalbh,
Aig cagailtean Ile Chlann Dòmhnaill
Mun d' fhògradh na Gàidheil on sealbh;   20

A' chòisridh fhuranach lem b' èibhinn
Aithris sgeulachd Innis Fàil,
Uirsgeulan nan aoidhean còir
An sèisdean ceòlmhor nam bàrd.   24

Shaoileadh na macain gum b' fhìor,
Na dh' innseadh dhaibh o bheul nan sean,
'S gu robh thus' a ghnàth mar chualas,
Luathghaireach, sona mar sin.   28

Tha mi 'n-diugh mar a b' àbhaist,
A' faicinn d' fhàire thar an lear,
O chladach tonnach deas-thìr Ile,
'S is dubhach ri innse do chor.   32

Sgeula mulaid, cuing is fògraidh,
Gort is bròn is ana-cheart,
'S gun dòigh air d' fhurtachd od phèin,
On a bhrist thu fhèin do neart.   36

[Do thallachan nan caoirean dearg,
'S gun tèarmann dhut o fhearg do nàmh;
Do chloinn gu iomall gach tìr,
Sgarte gun dìon, gun tàmh.][6]   40

Càit a bheil gaisge[7] nan trì Aodh,
Ò Dòmhnaill laochail 's Ò Nèill,
'S Mac Guidhir gun athadh ri nàmh,
A sheas gu bàs mun do ghèill?   44

[Aig Beul Ath Buidhe na cruaidh spàirn,
Sgath sibh feòil is cnàmhan Ghall;
Le deannal nam faobhar nochd
Thug sibh buaidh air lochd mar gheall.][8]   48

Càit a bheil sliochd nan treun,
Aig Dùn a' Bhèire[9] nach d' eur gleachd,
Nuair a dh'aom iad mar thuil nan sliabh
Fo bhilibh nan sgiath breac?   52

Na creagan a' freagairt le co-fhuaim
Dan iolach bhuadhach air a' bhlàr –
Na bolgairean sìnte gun deò,
'S am fuil a' crònanaich air làr.[10]   56

Distant island on Europe's edge,
loveliest country under canopy of skies,
often did I see your coast
across the great channel of the cries.   4

---

[6] Inserted from the MS.
[7] *subhailc* ('virtue') MS.
[8] Inserted from the MS.
[9] *Dùn-a-bheire* in 1882 edn (see Footnote 10).
[10] The text is based on Blair, Robert (ed), *Duain agus orain le Uilleam MacDhunlèibhe*, Glasgow 1882, 205-6, with alternative readings and two further verses derived from NLS MS 14986.

When a gentle, south-west wind would blow
and the sky was cloudless and clean,
the Gaels in the Rhinns of Islay
would tell each other of your sheen: 8

Your level plains, grassy and splendid,
smooth Lag an Rotha[11] and Aodh's Field,[12]
and your branching thickets giving protection
to the winged musicians of the trees;   12

Your clear springs shining with pure water,
your plentiful herds throughout your glens,
your woods, your hillocks and your fields,
and you green-clad from end to end.   16

In the morning of youth's innocence
I heard the tales of ages gone,
at the hearths of Islay of Clan Donald
before the Gaels were exiled from their lot –   20

The welcoming company who delighted
to recount the tale of the Isle of Fàl,
the stories narrated by the kind hosts
in the melodious tunes of bards.   24

The young lads would regard as true
what was told to them in old men's chat,
and think you were always as was heard –
triumphant and happy, like that.   28

Today, as was once my custom,
I see your horizon across the strait
from the wave-tossed shore of southern Islay,
but your condition is gloomy to state.   32

Tidings of sadness, yoke and exile,
famine, grief and injustice,
with no means of relieving your pain
since you yourself have breached your strength.   36

---

[11] The Roe valley, near Limavady.
[12] Magh Aoidh, Connacht.

Your halls reduced to red embers,
with no sanctuary from your enemy's wrath;
your children thrust to each land's edge,
separated, without protection or rest.　　　　　40

Where now is the valour of the three Aodhs,
Heroic Ò Dòmhnaill and Ò Neill,
and Maguire, unflinching before a foe,
who stood to the death before he'd yield?　　　　　44

At Béal an Átha Bhuidhe[13] *of hard strife,*
you chopped the Foreigners' flesh and bones;
through an onslaught with naked blades
you triumphed, as you pledged, over wrong.　　　　　48

Where are the sons of the brave men
who, at Dùn a' Bhèire,[14] *refused not to fight,*
when they descended like the flood of slopes,
under the rims of the speckled shields?　　　　　52

The rocks replying with an echo
to their victorious shout upon the plain –
their fat-bellied foes lying without breath,
and their blood purring on the ground.　　　　　56

Livingston offers a warmly sympathetic picture of Ireland. He laments the loss of the older native leadership, and wishes that the Gaelic earls – and particularly the 'three Hughs' – were still there to lead the country against its present-day oppressors.

Livingston evidently found much in the history of Ireland to stimulate and expand his mind. He was also inspired by the example of contemporary Irish scholars who made the past accessible in editions of

---

[13] The Yellow Ford, Armagh, where a battle was fought between Ó Néill and the English on 14 August 1598: see Hill, James Michael, *Celtic warfare 1595-1763*, Edinburgh 1986, 27-30.

[14] The Moyry Pass, *Bealach an Mhaighre*, where Ó Néill and Mountjoy fought in 1600; see Hill, *Celtic warfare*, 30-34. Livingston's Scottish Gaelic form seems to be derived from *Dún an Mhaighre*, the Fort of Moyry, built by Mountjoy in 1601 to guard the Moyry Pass, 'gateway to the Fews', north of Warrenpoint. See Lord Killanin & Michael V. Duignan, *The Shell guide to Ireland*, Dublin 1989, 260.

key texts and in published lectures. In particular, he expressed his indebtedness to the pioneering editor, Eugene O'Curry (1796-1862). O'Curry's achievement in publishing his *Lectures on the manuscript materials of ancient Irish history* in 1861 apparently prompted Livingston's salutation, 'Rann do Eòghann MacCuirrich, fear-teagaisg Gàidhlig ann am Baile Atha Cliath' ('A poem to Eugene O'Curry [lit. Ewen MacCurrie], Gaelic teacher in Dublin'). According to the opening verse of the poem, O'Curry was responsible for awakening the poet's dormant muse:

A dhuin' uasail fhòghlaimt', mhùirnich,
Ged tha mo cheòlraidh san smùraich
Còrr is fichead bliadhna, dhùisg i,
Nuair chual' i ainm an fhir chliùitich,
      Eòghann gu buaidh.

Eirinn uaine tog do cheann,
'S na bi nas mò fo ghlasaibh teann,
Do chainnt òirdheirc oil do d' chlann,
A thogas cliù le glòir neo-fhann
      Air Eòghann gu buaidh....

Tha tìr nam beann 's nan tuil an gaol ort,
Seann Albainn chruaidh na mòrachd aosda,
Toirt furain duit le làmhan sgaoilte,
A dh'aindeoin cò their nach faod i,
      Eoghainn gu buaidh.

Cha chrois-tàra no rosg-catha,
Cha ghaoir bàis an gàbhadh chlaidhean,
Ach còmhradh solais nam flaithean
A tha an Innis Fàil 'nan laighe
      Th' aig Eòghann gu buaidh.

Tha laoich nam breacan a' cur fàilt' ort,
Le fuaim stuic 's le caithream clàrsaich,
A' labhairt riut a-nunn thar sàile
Le seirc fuil uaibhreach nan Gàidheal,
      Eòghainn gu buaidh.

'S eòl daibh seanchas na h-Eireann
Anns na linnibh cian a thrèig sinn,
'S nì iad gu deònach a leughadh
Nuair thig i o mheòir a' chlèirich,
     Eòghann gu buaidh ...[15]

Erudite, beloved gentleman,
although my muse has been in the dust
for more than twenty years, she wakened
when she heard the name of the famous man,
    Eugene of victory.

Green Ireland, raise your head,
and be no longer in tight shackles;
teach your glorious language to your children,
who, with no weak talk, will sing the praise
    of Eugene of victory

The land of the bens and torrents loves you,
old, hardy Scotland of ancient majesty,
welcoming you with open arms
despite those who say she cannot,
    Eugene of victory,

It is not a fiery cross or battle incitement,
nor the cry of death in the swords' encounter,
but the radiant converse of the nobles
who, in Inis Fàil, are resting
    that victorious Eugene uses.

The heroes of the plaids bid you welcome
with the trumpet's sound and the harp's melody,
addressing you over the ocean
with the affection of the proud blood of Gaels,
    Eugene of victory.

They are familiar with the lore of Ireland
in the distant ages that have left us,

---

[15] Blair, *Duain agus orain*, 199-200.

and they will read it with gladness
when it comes from the fingers of the scribe,
Eugene of victory ...

Riot

The intellectual view of Ireland offered by Livingston – a view which emphasised the *continua* of language and culture, and encouraged an active awareness of a shared Gaelic history – contrasts with that of another poet, John MacFadyen (1850-1935), who was also resident in Glasgow, but hailed from the island of Mull, which did not have any direct link with Ireland. In Glasgow and elsewhere in the Lowlands, Scottish Gaels found themselves competing for jobs with the Irish from Donegal, as social and economic change transformed both countries, and both Irish and Scottish Gaels had to take to the urban treadmills.[16] The Irish thus became rivals to the Scottish Gaels, and such rivalry was not accommodated easily within the cultural perspectives of the displaced Scots. The Mull poet perceived, not the old and noble Gaels with common ancestral roots, but the degenerate, music-hall Irishry consisting of boozers and brawlers. Here is John MacFadyen's song, 'Oran Margadh an t-Salainn' ('Song on the Saltmarket):

O 'n cual', an cuala sibh 'n caithream ud,
E 'n cual', an cuala sibh 'n sadadh ud,
On cual', an cuala sibh 'n tabaid,
Bha 'm Margadh an t-Salainn an-dè?   4

Nuair chruinnich iad còmhla san tigh-òsd' aig McKennie,
'S ann ann a bha bhòilich mun dòigh bh' aig an seanair,
Mar bhuaileadh e dhòrn is mar dh' òladh e searrag,
'S ann bha e 's an tabaid ro thrèin.   8

Bha pìobaire 'n aona phuirt a' bronnagail le faram,
Gun ghaoithe na phluic, ach mar chluicheadh e achlais,
Fidheall dà theud air ghleus na deannaibh,
A' togail làn aighear nan treun.   12

---

[16] A detailed demographic study of Highland migration to the Lowland cities can be found in Withers, Charles W.J., *Urban Highlanders: Highland-Lowland migration and urban Gaelic culture*, Phantassie 1998. Despite the title, it has little to say about Gaelic culture, as defined in terms of Gaelic literature and song.

Bha Bridget air cabhsair 's i dannsadh ri Brolligan,
Ceann-rùisgte, cas-rùisgte, 's chnacadh i corragan,
Spreadadh i 'm poll a-nall mu na h-oisinnean,
'S ghlaodh i le sodan, ho-rè.   16

Bha Michael MaGinty 's e seatadh ma coinneamh,
Bha toll aig an uilinn 's bha 'm mullach tro bhoineid
Bha bhriogais na stròicean 's a bhròg air a h-oir aige,
Is leth-shlat de chotan na dhèidh.   20

Ach thòisich an iorghail nuair chruinnich na fineachan
A Ulster, à Munster, à Antrim, 's Leitrim,
Connaught, 's Tralee, 's O' Shees à Limerick,
'S thàinig na fir à Kildare.   24

Na O'Rorks 's na M'Gorks 's iad a' mort nan O'Branigans,
Bh' aig Kelley shillelah 's e 'g èirigh air Flannigan,
Micheal Mulhoul gun 'n dhall e O'Rafferty,
'S leag iad M'Cafferty fhèin.   28

Nuair thòisich an tuasaid bu chruaidh a bha 'n sadadh,
Bha slaodadh air cluasan is struaiceadh air claiginn,
Gach fear air a bhualadh is spuaic air a mhalaidh,
'S e glaodhaich air caraid gu streup.   32

O'Brian, 's O'Ryan, O'Reilly, 's O'Ligerim,
O'Brearie, 's O'Learie, O'Sheaie, 's O'Sigerim,
O'Hara, M'Ara, O'Larra, 's O'Liderim,
Barney M'Fiddie, 's M'Dade.   36

Nuair shèid iad na fìdeagan chìte nan cabhaig iad,
A' crùban gan deòin 's gach fròig am falach;
Gun tug iad an cinn 's na tuill fo thalamh,
Mar radan is abhag nan dèidh.[17]   40

O did you hear, did you hear that commotion,
E did you hear, did you hear that walloping,
O did you hear, did you hear of the fighting
in the Market of Salt yesterday?   4

---

[17] MacFadyen, John, *An t-Eileanach*, Glasgow 1890, 93-94.

When they gathered together in MacKennie's hostelry
great was their boasting about their grandfather's actions,
how he would strike with his fist and drink from a bottle –
he was a really brave man in the fray. 8

The single-tune piper was making music with clamour,
no wind in his cheek, but playing under his armpit,
a two-stringed fiddle was being tuned with vigour,
raising the high spirits of the brave. 12

Bridget was on the pavement, dancing with Brolligan,
bare-headed, with no shoes, and cracking her fingertips;
she would make the mud splash around the street corners,
and cry, in glad humour, 'Hurray'. 16

Michael McGinty was stepping in front of her,
a hole in his elbow, and his bonnet was topless,
his trousers were ragged, and his shoe at an angle,
a half-yard of cotton in his wake. 20

But the stramash began when the kindreds foregathered,
from Ulster, from Munster, from Antrim and Leitrim,
Connaught, Tralee and O'Shees from Limerick,
and there came the men of Kildare. 24

The O'Rourkes and McGorks battering the O'Branigans,
Kelley had a shilleley, and was hammering Flannigan,
Michael Mulhoul blinded O'Rafferty,
and even M'Cafferty was laid. 28

When the struggle began, the whacking was mighty,
ears being pulled, and skulls a-splintering,
each man had been hit and had a wound on his forehead,
and was calling a friend to the fray. 32

O'Brian, O'Ryan, O'Reilly, and O'Ligerim,
O'Brearie, O'Learie, O'Sheahy and O'Sigerim,
O'Hara, McAra, O'Larra and O'Liderim,
Barney McFiddie and MacDade. 36

When the whistles were blown you would see them scampering,
crouching in each nook to hide so willingly,

thrusting their heads in holes under the surface,
like rats with a terrier at tail.   40

By contrast with that unseemly lot, the Scottish Gaels liked to regard themselves as restrained, chaste and politically correct. Rather than the deep mutual understanding which Livingston's verse encourages, MacFadyen's mocking roll-calls of Irish names and places reveal an innocent form of racial stereotyping, with the one group defining itself in terms of the 'unacceptable Other'. Thus perceptions of the Irish varied considerably with place and social context, but, in the case of the 'fighting Irishmen', the picture was conditioned largely by the caricature created and expected by a dominant Lowland and non-Gaelic audience. In MacFadyen's song, it is very telling that he makes no attempt to provide the Irish/Gaelic forms of surnames or placenames, but uses the anglicised forms instead. The poet sees no obvious Gaelic kinship between the two sets of Gaels.

Yet there were parallels between the two groups of Gaels which could be observed readily by those with eyes to see them. As Livingston's 'Eirinn a' gul' indicates, the nineteenth century was one of great turmoil in Irish society, as it was in Gaelic Scotland, and it was possible for Gaels on both sides of the North Channel to find common ground in such matters as famine, clearance and rebellion. Land reformers like John Murdoch did precisely that, and Murdoch, like Livingston, drew a direct parallel between the condition of Islay and that of Ireland:

> ... Islay also has experienced the curse of depopulation which has passed over Ireland. Remnants of fences there are where there is nothing to be guarded but heather. Rushes and heather have overrun the land which was evidently at one time under cultivation. Snipe and sheep now hold almost undisputed possession of what at no very distant period supported whole tribes of men. Here, too, the rage for large farms has done its work. The natives have been turned out.[18]

Murdoch had, of course, worked in Ireland before moving latterly to Inverness and establishing the *Highlander* newspaper. Anti-landlordism was a powerful sentiment in both countries, and at least one Gaelic poet envisaged the possibility that Fenians would come across from Ireland to decapitate the sheep which were displacing people from Highland estates. The estate in question in this song (composed in the 1860s) belongs to Kenneth MacLeod of Gesto in Skye:

---

[18] Hunter, *For the people's cause*, 108.

Chunnaic mise 's mi 'nam chadal
Aisling dhen do ghabh mi ioghnadh,
Na *Fenians* a' tighinn a-nall
A thoirt nan ceann bho na caoraich;
Cha bhi claigeann dhiubh ri colainn,
Thèid an sgaradh bho gach aon dhiubh;
Thèid an sgrios bho thràigh gu monadh;
An sin thig sonas air an t-saoghal.[19]

I saw while I was sleeping
a dream that caused me to marvel,
the Fenians coming over the sea
to take the heads off the sheep;
not one skull will be left attached to a body;
they will be lopped from each one;
they will be exterminated from shore to hillside;
then joy will come upon the world.

That, however, is a fairly isolated reference, which casts the Fenians in much the same role as the French, namely that of 'useful external enemy', whose anti-landlord intervention was similarly anticipated and prayed for by certain Gaelic poets in the Napoleonic period and again at the time of the revolutions of 1848.[20]

In truth, Gaelic poets have remarkably little to say about the common suffering of the Gaels of Ireland and Scotland. The reason for this is probably that there were very considerable differences in the political fortunes of both areas, but more particularly in the ways in which these fortunes were perceived and interpreted. It is fair to say that perceptions of Ireland by Scotttish Gaels were determined by a British inclusivist and integrationist agenda which had exerted a formative influence on the Highlands and Islands across the centuries. In Ireland, the mix of politics and religion produced an explosive volatility which erupted in the Fenian riots of the mid-century and the strongly nationalist movements of the later nineteenth century. In Gaelic Scotland, by contrast, the course of political history encouraged an increasing loyalty to the British crown. The two regions were travelling in opposite directions. That difference was shown clearly by the end of the nineteenth century, when Irish Home Rule became a major issue for Gladstone's government. Irish Home Rule

---

[19] Meek, Donald E. (ed), *Tuath is tighearna: tenants and landlords*, Edinburgh 1995, 64.

[20] Cf. Meek, *Tuath is tighearna*, 61-63.

intermingled with the Scottish campaign for crofters' rights. In Scotland, the Gaelic people had been gradually absorbed into the wider British state, and most would have been of a Unionist persuasion. They were thus disinclined to see Parnell and the Irish Home Rule movement in a sympathetic light. Threats to the British *status quo* and to the British crown were not well received by the majority of Scottish Gaels; rebellion had to take place within the limits set by loyalty to the Union Jack. The Irish Home Rule issue ebbed and flowed between 1880 and the end of the century, but on the whole Scottish Gaels were inclined to play the Unionist card.[21]

The few Scottish Gaels who supported Irish Home Rule were usually to be found in cities such as Glasgow, where differences of faith and easy caricatures could be set aside in times of political difficulty and at critical junctures in the course of the land agitation. Among the most prominent of these Gaels were the brothers Henry and John Whyte from Easdale, Argyll, who had journalistic interests (Henry in his spare time, and John professionally), and who used their pens to promote Highland radicalism.[22] In 1881, following the attempts of Captain William Fraser to raise the rents of his estate in Kilmuir, Skye, concerned Highlanders and Irishmen in Glasgow joined forces at the Irish Land League demonstration on Easter Monday. They were addressed by two very prominent Irishmen, Charles Stewart Parnell and T. P. O'Connor, and also by John Gunn MacKay, a shop assistant in Glasgow and later (from 1885) a shopkeeper in Portree, Skye. As a result, the Skye Vigilance Committee was formed in the city, with Henry Whyte as its secretary.[23]

From time to time during the land agitation, radical Irish leaders also visited the Highlands and Islands, but this did not mean that they exerted much influence on the long-term political affiliations of Scottish Gaels. Their impact was temporary. General elections demonstrated that disaffection to Irish Home Rule was hard to displace. Parliamentary candidates representing the crofting cause sometimes found that their electability rested not on whether they were meeting the demands of the crofting community, but on whether they were, or were not, in favour of

---

[21] Cameron, Ewen A., *The life and times of Fraser Mackintosh, crofter MP*, Aberdeen 2000; Meek, Donald E., 'The Catholic knight of crofting: Donald Horne MacFarlane, MP for Argyll, 1885-86, 1892-5', *Transactions of the Gaelic society of Inverness* 58 (1992-4), 70-122.

[22] Meek, Donald E., 'Radical romantics: Glasgow Gaels and the Highland land agitation, 1870-90', in Kidd, Sheila (ed), *Glasgow: city of the Gaels / Glaschu: Baile Mòr nan Gaidheal* (forthcoming).

[23] MacPhail, I.M.M., *The crofters' war*, Stornoway 1989, 98-9.

Irish Home Rule. The most conspicuous example of the way in which Irish Home Rule sealed the fate of a Highland pro-crofter MP is furnished by the story of Donald Horne MacFarlane, who was a native of Caithness. MacFarlane became a Parnellite MP for Co. Carlow in 1880, before moving to contest the Argyll constituency in December 1885. He was elected on that occasion, with the warm endorsement of many Gaelic poets, but less than a year later in 1886 he lost the seat because of his support for Irish Home Rule.[24] His exit from Argyll was gleefully celebrated by one of the supporters of the successful candidate, Malcolm of Poltalloch. Here are the relevant verses of 'Oran na h-election' ('Song on the election'), in which MacFarlane's Irish connections are ridiculed:

Dòmnall Adharc MacPhàrlain,
Siud an t-àrmann bha spòrsail;
Fhuair e bean ann an Eirinn
'S thug e spèis airson òir dhì;
Chuir e buileach a chùl ri
Dòigh a dhùthcha o phòs e;
B' fheàrr leis tionndadh 'na Phadaidh
Gu bhith tabaid 's a' dòrnadh
Aig Donnybrook.

Nuair bha Dòmhnall 'na òigfhear,
Siud an t-òlach bha cràbhach;
Bhiodh e an cuideachd nan 'daoine',
'S b' i an Eaglais Shaor bu lag-tàimh dha;
Ach b' fheàrr le Dòmhnallan diadhaidh
A bhith fo sgiathan a' Phàpa;
Dh'fhàg e uaidhe na 'daoine'
'S an Eaglais Shaor, 's lean e Pàrnell,
'S chan ann gu rath.[25]

Donald 'of the Horn' MacFarlane
is the brave lad who likes some fun;
he found a wife in Ireland;
and he esteemed her for her gold;
he has wholly rejected
the custom of his country since he married;
he preferred to become a Paddy

---

[24] Meek, 'Catholic knight', 80-106.
[25] Meek, 'Catholic knight', 100-5.

*so that he could go fighting and boxing
at Donnybrook.*[26]

*When Donald was a young man,
he was a character of great piety;
he would be in the company of the 'men',
and the Free Church was his place of rest;
but godly Donny liked better
to be under the wings of the Pope;
he left the 'men' in the lurch
and the Free Church, and he followed Parnell –
and it was not advantageous.*

Religion

The Free Church 'kick' in these verses is very evident, and it is highly likely that the song was composed by a Free Church minister. MacFarlane's marriage to an Irish lady is seen as the first step in his spiritual declension to the status of a Paddy and a Papist. The 'men' were, of course, the lay spiritual leaders of the northern Highlands and Islands, and it was another sign of MacFarlane's apostasy that he had rejected their company. MacFarlane was re-elected to Argyll in 1892, and held the seat until 1895.[27]

Religion undoubtedly played a major part in aligning the Scottish Gaels with the British crown. During the nineteenth century, the Scottish Highlands and Islands were deeply influenced by Protestant evangelicalism. Home missionary movements thrust their way into the Highlands, using various methods – travelling preachers, commonly of Independent and Baptist persuasion, but including prominent ministers of the Established Church of Scotland; Gaelic schools which were aimed at teaching the Gaelic people to read the Gaelic Bible (completed in 1801); and a drive towards the provision of basic texts which those who had

---

[26] The reference is to the notorious Donnybrook fair, held at Donnybrook, near Dublin. It was established in 1204. It gained a reputation for brawling and excess, 'frantic indulgence, singing and dancing', and after many attempts to suppress it, it was allowed to lapse after 1855. See Ó Maitiú, Séamas, 'Changing images of Donnybrook fair', in Cronin, Denis A., Jim Gilligan & Karina Holton (eds), *Irish fairs and markets*, Dublin 2001, 164-79. When the present paper was being delivered at Trinity College, the author recollects that the 'second half' was accompanied by sounds of student revelry in the adjacent corridor, which the chairman for the occasion, Professor Cathal Ó Háinle, compared appropriately to the Donnybrook Fair.

[27] Meek, 'Catholic knight', 106-112.

come through the Gaelic schools could read.[28] The result was the creation of a strongly evangelical profile in the Highlands, with intense movements of religious revival which tended to repeat themselves on a cyclical pattern. This evangelical profile was strengthened greatly by the emergence of the Free Church of Scotland in 1843, which the majority of Highlanders chose to follow.[29] In the Highlands and Islands, Roman Catholics became a minority, on the fringes of the mainland Highlands, and in Barra, South Uist and the Small Isles. In Ireland, by contrast, the religious complexion was very different indeed, as it preserved a strongly Roman Catholic majority, with Protestantism strong only in parts of Ulster. The predominant Catholicism of Ireland, combined with the Home Rule movement, produced a heady brew which many Scottish Gaels preferred not to drink.

From a Scottish Gaelic religious perspective, therefore, Ireland was seen as a country which was infested with religious and political danger. It was a country too which lacked a proper spiritual – and Protestant – ministry in its own language. Among Scottish missionary leaders, it was perceived at best as an extension of the wider Gaelic mission field, but at worst as a benighted region which was very much darker and very much needier than the Highlands and Islands themselves. Ireland had to be changed and improved, and we find that some of the activists who sought to introduce Protestant schooling and literacy to the Scottish Gaels were active in Ireland also, though with much less success. Chief among these was the Rev. Christopher Anderson, the founder of a Baptist church in Edinburgh, and the main mover in the creation of the Edinburgh Society for the Support of Gaelic Schools in 1810-11.[30] Anderson's memorials on behalf of the 'native Irish', as he called them, influenced other Scottish ministers, and none more so than the Rev. Dr Norman MacLeod, 'Caraid nan Gaidheal', who was particularly active in Ireland in the 1830s, and produced an Irish version of the Metrical Psalms with the assistance of Thaddeus Connellan in 1835.[31]

It would take another paper to do justice to the perspectives of these reverend gentlemen from Scotland, and to deal with the prose as well as the poetry. Christopher Anderson is a figure of some significance who

---

[28] A useful general overview can be found in Ansdell, Douglas, *The people of the great faith: the Highland Church 1690-1900*, Stornoway 1998.

[29] Ansdell, *The people of the great faith*, 56-71.

[30] Meek, Donald E. (ed), *A mind for mission: essays in appreciation of the Rev. Christopher Anderson (1782-1852)*, Edinburgh 1992.

[31] Ó Baoill, Colm, 'Norman MacLeod, *Cara na nGael*', *Scottish Gaelic Studies* 23.2 (1981), 151-68.

deserves much fuller treatment than he has received to date. Suffice it to say at this stage that their desire to use Irish in ministry was motivated by missionary concern, rather than by any deep attachment to the Gaelic cultural continuities of the preceding centuries. At times it was an ambivalent view, which saw the use of Irish at worst as a stepping-stone to English, and at best as a medium for communicating the Protestant evangelical message. Good and bad came from this approach, and it is worth reflecting that the founding of the Chair of Irish at Trinity College in 1840 owed something to the support of Christopher Anderson.[32] This clerical perspective was also politically ambivalent, and less than positive. Anderson had no great interest in politics, but MacLeod was a potent advocate of British loyalty and adherence to the *status quo*. To that end he sometimes used the Gaelic dialogues which he published in his journals *An teachdaire Gaelach* and *Cuairtear nan gleann*. In one of these he cites the example of Ireland as an argument against the extension of the franchise in 1832, because he feared that the buying of votes would lead to abuse of the ordinary people by the landed class.[33] Ireland for him, and for others of the same mind, was an example of 'how not to', in political, religious and cultural matters. Rescuing the Irish from themselves was the overriding concern of missionary endeavour of this kind.

In this paper, I have drawn almost all my evidence from poetry, and much work remains to be done on Gaelic prose of the nineteenth century. Let me therefore conclude by quoting still another Gaelic poet, this time a lady, Màiri Mhòr nan Oran, 'Great Mary of the Songs' from the island of Skye. Mary MacPherson, as she was officially known, lived from 1821 to 1898, and advocated the crofters' cause in many of her best-known pieces. Yet, as far as I am aware, she makes only one reference to Ireland. It occurs in the context of sketching the panoramic view which could be obtained from the top of the hills of Skye:

Tha do lochan rìomhach
Sìnte staigh feadh d' eang,
Dealachadh ri chèile
Rèidhleanan is bheann;
'S ma tha neach le lèirsinn,
Chan i bhreug a th' ann,

---

[32] Meek, *A mind for mission*, 22-3.

[33] Mac Eachaidh, Tarlach, 'Caraid nan Gaidheal as discerned through the pages of *An Teachdaire Gaelach, 1829-'31*', in Ó Baoill, Colm, & Nancy R. McGuire (eds), *Rannsachadh na Gàidhlig 2000*, Aberdeen 2002, 141-7.

Chì iad bhàrr do shlèibhtean
Pàirt de dh'Eirinn thall.[34]

Your attractive lochs
stretch in among your points,
separating from each other
flat fields and bens;
and if one has the eyesight,
it is not at all a lie,
they will see from your hilltops
part of Ireland over there.

There is often a big-hearted innocence in Mary's verse, and it would be wrong to make too much of her symbolism. But she sometimes says much more than she intends, and this may be an excellent example of such accidental perspicacity. As far as nineteenth-century Scottish Gaels and Ireland were concerned, she spoke truly. It took an effort to see Ireland. One needed good eyesight, and a high vantage point, and even then one could see only certain parts of that distant island. The view, in short, was partial, in every sense.[35]

---

[34] Meek, Dòmhnall Eachann (deas.), *Màiri Mhòr nan Oran: taghadh de a h-òrain le eachdraidh a beatha agus notaichean*, Dùn Eideann 1998, 114.

[35] I am very grateful to Professor Colm Ó Baoill, Department of Celtic, University of Aberdeen, for his genial assistance with several points in this paper.